BLACK SCHOLARS MATTER

RESOURCES FOR BIBLICAL STUDY

Editor
Hyun Chul Paul Kim, Hebrew Bible/Old Testament
Davina C. Lopez, New Testament

Number 100

BLACK SCHOLARS MATTER

Visions, Struggles, and Hopes
in Africana Biblical Studies

Edited by
Gay L. Byron and Hugh R. Page Jr.

Atlanta

Copyright © 2022 by SBL Press

All rights reserved. No part of this work may be reproduced or transmitted in any form or by any means, electronic or mechanical, including photocopying and recording, or by means of any information storage or retrieval system, except as may be expressly permitted by the 1976 Copyright Act or in writing from the publisher. Requests for permission should be addressed in writing to the Rights and Permissions Office, SBL Press, 825 Houston Mill Road, Atlanta, GA 30329 USA.

Library of Congress Control Number: 2022947080

Contents

Acknowledgments ix

Foreword
    Adele Reinhartz xi

Abbreviations xiii

Introduction
    Gay L. Byron and Hugh R. Page Jr. 1

Part 1. #BlackScholarsMatter: Visions and Struggles

The Struggles: A Personal Reflection
    Cheryl B. Anderson 9

Lest We Forget: A Chronicling of the Early Years
    Randall C. Bailey 13

Navigating a Foreign Terrain? Ruminations on Old
Testament Studies from African-South Africa
    Madipoane Masenya (Ngwan'a Mphahlele) 27

Preliminary Thoughts: The Hermeneutical Dilemmas of the
Allies, Colleagues, and Guild of African American
Biblical Scholar-Teachers
    Shively T. J. Smith 39

On Leaving but Not Going Far
    Renita J. Weems 47

Tribunals of Jurists and Congresses of Gentlemen: Signifying (on) Biblical Studies as Colonial-Bureaucratic Masquerade
    Vincent L. Wimbush 53

Part 2. #BlackScholarsMatter: Lessons and Hopes

Moving in-between Places and Academic Disciplines
    Ronald Charles 75

Questions with No COVID-19 Answers
    Stephanie Buckhannon Crowder 93

Lessons and Hopes on How to Save a Life: The Life of the Black Biblical Scholar
    Steed Vernyl Davidson 103

What I've Learned
    Vanessa Lovelace 109

Mentoring Matters
    Kimberly Russaw...113

#StayWoke: The Next Generation of Black Biblical Scholars, the Society of Biblical Literature, and the Central Challenges of Ethical Leadership
    Abraham Smith 119

Part 3. #BlackScholarsMatter: Accountability and Next Steps

Latinidad in Dialogue with Africana Biblical Studies: A Perspective
    Efraín Agosto 129

Contemplative Collegiality: Caring for the Souls of Black Biblical Scholars
    Gay L. Byron 145

Black Bible Scholars Matter—Especially amid Perennial Crisis
    Hugh R. Page Jr...153

Contents vii

We Should Be There for Them: Creating Communities of
Support and Mentoring for Africana Biblical Scholars
 Sharon Watson Fluker 163

Come Join Us, Sweetheart!
 Mai-Anh Le Tran..177

A Call to Solidarity with Black Scholars
 Raj Nadella 187

A Duty to Act: Personal Reflections on #BlackScholarsMatter
 Adele Reinhartz..195

Afterword
 John F. Kutsko...207

Contributors...223

Acknowledgments

Editing this volume has been an opportunity to think critically about the lives and labor of Black biblical scholars; the various settings—academic, ecclesial, and public—in which their endeavors take place; their professional journeys; their life-stories; and the challenges they have confronted and continue to face today. We have been heartened and inspired by the remarkable achievements our colleagues have enjoyed. We have also been sobered by the difficulties they have encountered along the way. It is our hope that the critical discussions begun by this volume will continue in the future and pave the way for substantial and lasting change in our discipline, the guild that supports it, and the institutions where the work of Africana biblical scholarship unfolds.

We would like to thank everyone involved in the groundbreaking #BlackScholarsMatter Symposium on August 12–13, 2020 that led to the compilation of the essays in this volume—especially Tat-siong Benny Liew, Kimberly Russaw, and Raj Nadella, who were responsible for organizing it. We acknowledge the important role that the Society of Biblical Literature's Black Scholars Matter Task Force, Executive Director (John Kutsko), Consultant (Sharon Watson Fluker), and Council played in fostering discussions about issues impacting Africana scholars, especially during the difficult times following the murders of Ahmaud Arbery, Breonna Taylor, and George Floyd in spring 2020: Efraín Agosto, Christian Brady, Marc Brettler, Sidnie White Crawford, Tat-siong Benny Liew, Monica Jyotsna Melanchton, Laura Nasrallah, Judy Newman, Jorunn Økland, Hugh Page, Adele Reinhartz, Chris Rollston, Ehud Ben Zvi, and James C. VanderKam.

We owe special gratitude as well to those who assisted us in the preparation, design, securing cover art for, and production of this volume: Wil Gafney for providing the cover art image; Davina C. Lopez and Hyun Chul Paul Kim, editors of the Resources for Biblical Study series; and Bob Buller, Nicole L. Tilford, and Lindsay Lingo of SBL Press.

Finally, we are grateful for the contributors to each section of the volume, who have shared their stories and are opening the door for a new generation of biblical critics to gain a realistic perspective on some of the challenges and opportunities inherent in the guild and a dose of encouragement for navigating their own intellectual and professional journeys. In this spirit, we dedicate this volume to those who paved the way, those with whom we share this pilgrimage, and those yet to join us in generating transformative, visionary Africana biblical scholarship.

Gay L. Byron
Hugh R. Page Jr.
June 2022

Foreword

ADELE REINHARTZ

The #BlackScholarsMatter Symposium in August 2020, organized under the auspices of the Society of Biblical Literature, allowed viewers from around the world a glimpse into the professional worlds of twelve Africana biblical scholars. The experiences of these scholars varied, as did their thoughts about the changes needed in our institutions and ourselves to effect the transformation that is so sorely needed. Beneath and beyond these differences, however, these presenters shared the experience of being Black biblical scholars in a field predominated by white scholars and shaped by the ideologies of white supremacy.

I was riveted by the symposium. This is not to say that the existence of inequities and hierarchies within the field was news to me. As a Jewish New Testament scholar, I was used to feeling marginal in my subfield of Johannine studies, which remains a bastion of faith-based conservative Christian scholarship. As a woman who entered the field almost fifty years ago, I have often been the only woman in the room, though that has happened less and less as the years have gone on. And as a long-time participant in the Society of Biblical Literature, I was also conscious of the multiple ways in which Black scholars are marginalized at our meetings and in our guild more generally. But it is one thing to know that Africana scholars face challenges that I as a white person do not, and another to listen to them describe those experiences. I was deeply moved by the willingness of these colleagues to talk about such matters and also immediately convinced of the importance of making the symposium available in forms that could not only be heard but also read and cited by others, now and into the future.

For that reason, I am grateful to Hugh Page and Gay Byron for compiling and editing this volume and to the symposium participants for transforming their presentations into essay format.

Abbreviations

BIPOC	Black, Indigenous, and People of Color
BLM	Black Lives Matter
BSNA	Biblical Scholarship in North America
BTU	Bible Translation and Utilization Advisory Committee
CUREMP	Committee on Underrepresented Racial and Ethnic Minorities in the Profession
DEI	Diversity, Equity, and Inclusion
HBTIs	Historically Black Theological Institutions
JBL	*Journal of Biblical Literature*
JFSR	*Journal of Feminist Studies in Religion*
JITC	*Journal of the Interdenominational Theological Center*
JSOTSup	*Journal for the Study of the Old Testament Supplement Series*
NRSV	New Revised Standard Version
OBT	Overtures to Biblical Theology
OTE	*Old Testament Essays*
RBS	Resources for Biblical Study
SemeiaSt	Semeia Studies

Introduction

GAY L. BYRON AND HUGH R. PAGE JR.

The 2020 #BlackScholarsMatter Symposium

The image of police officer Derek Chauvin's knee on the neck of George Floyd, recorded by Darnella Frazier, a courageous seventeen-year-old on the scene at Cupp Foods in Minneapolis, Minnesota, was broadcast nationwide in May 2020. Although it was but one of many well-known and digitally recorded incidents of unwarranted violence against members of the Black (or more broadly known as Africana[1]) community in the United States, it helped galvanize public sentiment in support of movements to value and protect Black lives. The tragic deaths of Breonna Taylor and Ahmaud Arbery earlier that year, along with the devastating impact of COVID-19 on many in BIPOC (Black, Indigenous, and People of Color) communities, made all too clear the fraught circumstances under which minoritized and subaltern populations exist in our country. It was also an occasion for self-reflection within a broad cross-section of academic disciplines, not the least of which was biblical studies, where the legacy and lingering effects of European colonialism, anti-Semitism, and racism have increasingly been topics of discussion and the focus of scholarly investigation.

In the wake of Floyd's murder and in the midst of nationwide protests against police violence, the Society of Biblical Literature's Council,

---

1. The term *Africana* refers to the languages, cultures, and peoples of African descent in various locations throughout the world. Authors use terminology in various ways throughout this volume given their point of view and their social and geographical location(s) (African, Canadian, Caribbean, United States, etc.). We have honored their preferences throughout, with an eye toward acknowledging the fluidity that exists within scholarly and other communities in their discussions of the realities of life on the African continent and throughout the African diaspora.

the organization's governing board, constituted the Black Scholars Matter Task Force in spring of 2020, with then Society president Adele Reinhartz serving as chair. Once fully constituted in summer 2020, its membership included: Efraín Agosto, John Kutsko (ex officio), Tat-siong Benny Liew, Raj Nadella, Sharon Watson Fluker (consultant), James C. VanderKam, and the two of us. This group provided an open forum for the discussion of a wide range of issues impacting the lives and livelihoods of Africana scholars working in biblical studies and cognate fields. Of particular concern to those on the task force was the consideration of ways that the Society of Biblical Literature might be forthright in its condemnation of anti-Black racism and proactive in creating a positive environment in which Africana scholars and their intellectual labors may be nurtured, highlighted, and valued.

The major event sponsored by the Black Scholars Matter Task Force was the virtual two-part #BlackScholarsMatter Symposium, held on August 12th and 13th, 2020. This event, coordinated with the Society's Committee on Underrepresented Racial and Ethnic Minorities in the Profession (CUREMP), brought together twelve leading Africana scholars from various institutional settings—research universities, free-standing seminaries, Historically Black Theological Institutions (HBTIs), and so on—to share their perspectives on biblical studies and their experiences as scholars in the discipline. Participants in the first session were asked to align their comments with the overarching theme, "Visions and Struggles," while those in the second were asked to reflect on the topic, "Lessons and Hopes." These panels were unprecedented in their scope. Panelists shared memories, critical reflections, realizations, and future aspirations for the discipline. These sessions were occasions of evocative sharing and truth-telling. Each had several hundred live viewers. Recordings of both remain available on the Society of Biblical Literature website as resources for members and others interested in viewing them.[2] So distinctive, powerful, and potentially transformational were they that the task force commissioned an edited volume in which these presentations—in their extant or expanded form—could be featured, with the two of us taking on editorial responsibilities.

This volume documents that groundbreaking event. As coeditors, we realized that simply reproducing the remarks was not enough. We

---

2. https://www.sbl-site.org/meetings/blackscholarsmatter.aspx.

envisioned this volume as an opportunity to supplement the work of the panelists, which is contained in parts 1 and 2 of this volume, with a third section in which selected contributors would be asked to reflect on issues related to institutional and personal accountability and potential next steps in creating a more welcoming and inclusive environment in which Africana biblical scholars and scholarship might thrive. It is our hope that this volume on the whole will provide a point of reference for further thinking about the future of biblical studies, the Society of Biblical Literature, and the importance of Africana scholars to the future vitality of both.

Structure of the Volume

Part 1 includes essays by Cheryl Anderson, Randall Bailey, Madipoane Masenya, Shively Smith, Renita Weems, and Vincent Wimbush. These essays, on "Visions and Struggles," range in form and content from capturing blatant and subtle forms of bias and racism (Anderson and Bailey) to the need for solidarity among allies (S. Smith), to reflections about choices and options beyond the SBL (Weems), to the unique challenges of being a biblical scholar in South Africa (Masenya), to impactful forms of mentoring that open doors and pathways into various professions (Bailey), and to signifying on the very colonial, racializing orientations out of which the Society of Biblical Literature was formed (Wimbush). All of these panelists focused to some degree on visions and hopes but remained unequivocally clear that struggles abound and the aspirations of the guild have yet to be realized.

Part 2 includes essays by Ronald Charles, Stephanie Buckhanon Crowder, Steed Davidson, Vanessa Lovelace, Kimberly Russaw, and Abraham Smith. This panel was framed around "Lessons and Hopes," although a recurring theme of struggle, sacrifice, and lack of support continued to resonate in these essays, as well as particular challenges for colleagues who have overcome obstacles through various national tragedies, geographical locations, and academic disciplines (Charles). The lessons learned throughout the journey have been recounted (Lovelace) and questions have been raised about doing biblical studies during the COVID-19 pandemic (Crowder), which defy answers at this point. Mentoring continues to be a common theme among these panelists, with one colleague making a case for why it matters (Russaw). Another colleague names the challenges of "Staying Awake" as ethical leaders in creating a more welcoming environment for the next generation of Black biblical scholars (A. Smith). Finally, the real lesson and hope, for one colleague, revolves around "how to save the life of the Black biblical scholar" (Davidson).

As noted above, we chose to supplement the first two parts of this volume with a third, made up of essays by selected representatives of the Society of Biblical Literature and other stakeholders who have administrative and decision-making responsibilities in their respective schools or who have had long-standing involvement with the Society through partnerships and other acts of solidarity from different minoritized communities (Efraín Agosto, Raj Nadella, Mai-Anh Le Tran). Again, the necessity for mentoring continues to be a common theme in this section (Sharon Watson Fluker), as well as the importance of naming one's context and the many different settings that shape who we are as biblical scholars (Hugh Page). All the essays in this section, to some degree, highlight the need for institutional integrity, personal accountability (Nadella, Reinhartz, Tran), collegiality (Gay Byron), and unapologetic solidarity with Africana biblical scholars. It is our hope that these essays will offer a springboard for considering next steps that might lead to the creation of a welcoming and affirming ethos within the Society of Biblical Literature for Africana biblical scholars.

We are grateful for the vision and leadership of Adele Reinhartz and John Kutsko, whose foreword and afterword provide an overarching framework for this volume.

Rationale for Assembling Perspectives in a Single Volume

The panelists were invited to share their experiences of and aspirations for teaching, writing, and being Black biblical scholars in the academy. They were given a list of prompts to which they could respond, ranging from naming their biggest struggles and lessons learned and how they are making space for other Black biblical scholars up to sharing their vision for the future of biblical studies. They were invited to offer suggestions for ways the discipline might be reconceptualized to promote antiracism and to become more welcoming and inclusive of intersectional research, teaching, and service to the larger world. For some, this is the first opportunity to tell their stories of how they navigated the rough, often solitary, terrain of advancement through academic hurdles, systemic obstacles, and personal challenges. Having these stories in a single volume amplifies their voices and demonstrates that there is no one singular Black biblical scholar experience. Indeed, these essays demonstrate how institutional, geographical, political, and socioeconomic contexts vary among Africana scholars and influence their respective journeys. Furthermore, this volume serves as a resource for colleagues, administrators, and anyone concerned with the state of the field of biblical studies as well as some of the factors that continue to keep Africana biblical scholars *minoritized* within the guild.

Approach to Editing the Essays

Our goal as coeditors has been to honor the voices, experiences, and stylistic norms of the contributors; and to honor their stories, without imposing strict genre or word-count constrictions. There are so many instances in scholarly circles when editorial conventions and the norms of academic discourse suppress or silence the distinctive word choices and cadences of individual scholars. One example of this is in the terminology used when describing the histories, cultures, artifacts, and ideas belonging to peoples of African descent. Preferences and rationales among authors vary. Our goal has been to avoid such a heavy-handed approach in favor of a poetics that favors colloquial expression and stylistic freedom. We have, in sum, edited with a generous and light touch. We have done so recognizing the implicit value of the various approaches taken by contributors in the crafting of their essays. This is most evident in the capitalization of *black/Black* when describing the cultural experience of the authors and others in their communities. The issue of how the Africana community is described globally and in various locales has long been a topic of scholarly discussion and continues to be the subject of debate in academic and public discourse.[3] Readers can see this play out in the present volume, with some contributors using the lowercase and others capitalizing the term. Given the heterogeneity of opinions and practices in this area, we have allowed each contributor's preference to stand. In toto, these essays reflect the experiential breadth, depth, and richness of Africana biblical scholars and their lives within both their respective disciplines and in their involvement with the Society of Biblical Literature. As a result, we trust that readers will encounter the contributors to this volume not simply as scholars but also

---

3. See, for example, Appiah 2020 and Coleman 2020.

as multidimensional people whose intellectual endeavors and vocational lives unfold within a complex, heterogeneous, and global Africana milieu.

Future Hopes and Aspirations

We live in difficult circumstances. As we enter the final phase of editing in May 2022, two years after the murder of George Floyd, the city of Buffalo—and indeed the entire country—is reeling from the murder of ten Black shoppers and employees at a Tops grocery store in that city by Payton Gendron, an eighteen-year-old in the thrall of white supremacist thought. The dangers confronting people of African descent in the United States and around the world have not subsided. Much work remains to be done in dismantling ideologies of hate and structures that marginalize, oppress, and endanger Black lives, as well as in creating opportunities for the voices of Africana biblical scholars to be heard and their various labors—transparent and hidden—valued. Neither a single symposium nor an edited volume alone can accomplish this objective. They can, however, help leverage the remarkable efforts of those Africana intellectual giants and allies that have gone before us and hopefully mitigate the corrosive effects of the "stony road" and "chastening rod" we have collectively endured by keeping our hearts and minds attuned to the "steady beat" of freedom's song.

Works Cited

Appiah, Kwame Anthony. 2020. "The Case for Capitalizing the *B* in Black." *The Atlantic*. 18 June. https://tinyurl.com/SBL03112x.

Coleman, Nancy. 2020. "Why We're Capitalizing Black." *The New York Times*. 5 July. https://tinyurl.com/SBL03112y.

PART 1
#BlackScholarsMatter: Visions and Struggles

The Struggles: A Personal Reflection

CHERYL B. ANDERSON

When I was a doctoral student in the 1990s, I participated in two scholarship programs for African Americans. These programs offered financial support and, fortunately, also provided mentoring. For example, I remember Dr. James Cone telling us that our research should inform our teaching, and he said that mediocre research would result in mediocre teaching. Consequently, we learned that having an ongoing research agenda was a key feature of being a scholar. Since the mentoring meetings for both programs took place during the Annual Meetings of the American Academy of Religion and the Society of Biblical Literature, we learned by implication that attending the annual meetings was also an essential part of honing our research. Those annual meetings were where our ideas could be expressed, developed, and refined. It was (and still is) where our discipline takes shape, and I have regularly attended annual meetings for all of the more than twenty-five years since then.

In those days, I certainly knew that there were not many African Americans who were members of the Society of Biblical Literature. Even today, with just over 8,000 members, only about 4 percent of US-born members are of African descent ("2019 SBL Membership Data"). Yet, even at that time, there were clear signs that the field was opening up. There were already African American biblical scholars who held faculty positions. New approaches to biblical interpretation, including those reflecting the African American experience, were appearing, and *Stony the Road We Trod: African American Biblical Interpretation* (Felder 1991) had been published. Although I knew that my work would use womanist and liberationist hermeneutics, rather than the more traditional historical-critical methods, there was no reason to question if I had a place in the Society of Biblical Literature. However, one particular incident that happened about fifteen years ago challenged that assumption.

I had been invited to give a paper on a panel with two white men, and the respondent was also a white male. The two white men on the panel were not just ordinary Hebrew Bible scholars—they were very well-known senior scholars. As a result, they drew a crowd, and there was standing room only. I had been teaching only about six years then, so I was very much their junior in rank. Of course, I was nervous. After all, this was not a group I normally worked with at the Society of Biblical Literature, and I was in the presence of these two major scholars. We gave our papers, and things seemed to go well, until the respondent started to speak. He announced that he would not respond to our papers in the order in which they had been given, for reasons that would become obvious.

After responding to the other two papers with thoughtful consideration, his tone and demeanor changed when he got to me. His response became an attack. When I realized what was happening, I looked out at the audience, and I distinctly remember seeing for the first time that I was the only black person in the room. In fact, I was the only non-white person in the room. I felt a deep sense of isolation, and I knew that this same isolation had made me a very vulnerable target. It is important to note that his remarks cannot be explained as a heated debate or a vigorous discussion; they were qualitatively different. As he continued, I realized that he failed to engage what I had actually said. Actually, he mentioned points I had not made at all. Consequently, I knew that his attack had relatively little to do with the details of my paper.

It appeared to me that, somehow, something about who I was had triggered his diatribe, and, as a relatively junior scholar, I just had to sit there, and I could not and did not respond. Back then, I did not have the vocabulary to describe what I experienced that day, but I can now: it was a display of white rage. In her book, *White Rage*, Carol Anderson (2016, 3) finds "white rage" is "triggered inevitably by black advancement" and not "our mere presence." More specifically, she writes that the trigger "is blackness with ambition, drive, with purpose, with aspirations, and with demands for full and equal citizenship." Based on Anderson's analysis, I suspect that there were actually two triggers at work that day—my blackness as well as my womanist values of equality and justice that were presumed in my paper.

I felt brutalized by his response, and when he stopped speaking, I thought the worst was over—but I was wrong. It was worse to realize that the white people in the room were oblivious to the harm done to me. The respondent himself turned to me when the session was over, smiled, and said, "Cheryl, I was pretty rough on you." He was actually proud of what he had done! Then, the member of the steering committee who had invited me dismissed offhandedly his comments as simply being "part of a different discussion." But the members of the steering committee knew my work, so why had they invited me to speak before a respondent who was "part of a different discussion"? I thought that it was unfair to have put me in that situation.

After that session, I was acutely aware that the Society of Biblical Literature was white space—and that it could be a very hostile space for a black woman. In fact, I thought that, if white men would fight so hard to keep that space white and male, I would not fight to be there. Even though I had known since the early 1990s how important the Society and its annual meetings were to my life as a scholar, I was ready to stop participating—but I never walked away from the Society of Biblical Literature. In the years since that session, I have served on and chaired the Committee on Underrepresented Minorities in the Profession (CUREMP), I have served on and chaired the Nominating Committee, and I have served on the Council for two full terms. Given my deep disillusionment that day, the question has to be asked: What allowed me to remain? It was basically the support of primarily (but not exclusively) scholars of color—especially senior scholars of color who were well acquainted with the opportunities that the Society of Biblical Literature offers. On that very same day, when I told two of them what had happened, they immediately understood how I felt, and they assured me that I had a place in the academy and that my voice needed to be heard. However, those two scholars (as well as others like them) did more than just affirm me. They made sure that I volunteered for leadership positions in the Society over the years. Now, I have to admit that, at each level, I did not think I was up to the task. They trusted that I was ready, I trusted them, and I always served to the best of my ability.

I mentioned that these scholars who made the difference in my Society participation were primarily (but not exclusively) people of color. There are several key exceptions, and there is one white person in particular that I need to mention now. He happened to be one of the established scholars on that panel. I saw him later the same day, and he told me that he had been made very uncomfortable by the way the respondent had treated me. He then continued by saying that he had wanted to intervene, but, assuming that I was able to handle the situation, he did not. I assured him that I really had not handled it well and that I wished he *had* intervened! I have to admit, though, that I am not sure if he *should* have intervened, but I do know that I deeply appreciated what he said to me that day. First, he confirmed my experience. He acknowledged the harm, and he confirmed that what I had gone through was not normal, that it was unprofessional behavior. Second, he was a privileged white male who had been willing to use his privilege to help me. For both of these reasons, he models how white people who want to be allies could help black scholars in the academy today.

Looking back at that session after so many years, I realize that I learned several lessons from the incident. It is important to have mentors in academia, and it is even more important to have those who will support and affirm you when difficult situations arise. Finally, as Dr. Cone said, our research and our teaching are indeed intimately connected. Yet if our research and our teaching are to address the multifaceted challenges African Americans face, we must do the required contextual and interdisciplinary work, and we must remember that, by serving in leadership positions in the Society of Biblical Literature at any and all of its levels, we create the academic spaces we need for that work to flourish.

Works Cited

Anderson, Carol. 2016. *White Rage: The Unspoken Truth of Our Racial Divide*. New York: Bloomsbury.

Felder, Cain Hope, ed. 1991. *Stony the Road We Trod: African American Biblical Interpretation*. Minneapolis: Fortress.

Society of Biblical Literature. "2019 SBL Membership Data." https://www.sbl-site.org/assets/pdfs/sblMemberProfile2019.pdf.

Lest We Forget:
A Chronicling of the Early Years

RANDALL C. BAILEY

Let me begin by thanking Benny and Hugh for organizing this symposium and for engaging us constructively during the planning phases of this event. I also am thankful for the group of Black scholars on this panel. We have been on the stony road for a long time, walking with a steady beat, and I am not only thankful for the opportunity to share my story but also excited to listen to the stories of my fellow panelists as we've treaded paths with tears watered and most importantly with some victories won.

This essay is in many ways autobiographical in terms of my development as a Hebrew Bible scholar. My intention is to show how I developed into the scholar I have become, showing twists and turns along the way. My narrative is not to be viewed as normative or exceptional. I seek to show how race, gender, sexuality, and context impacted the development of myself and (most probably?) other Black biblical scholars. These stories of oppression and the new doors opening may remind readers of their own stories of development and growth and the stresses, which, managed successfully, have helped them overcome the forces of oppression and helped liberate our people from adherence to oppressive doctrines and religious stumbling blocks.

My intention is to also help younger scholars to see that many of us have made it through the maze, some scarred, some wounded, some still intact, but you can make it also. Some of us share our stories, while others find it better to keep them to themselves. I guess my earlier training in social group work pushes me to do the sharing, hoping that in retelling how I got over I can not only help others but also help my own healing.

My story of growing into and becoming a Black Hebrew Bible scholar began in my seminary journey. In a seminar on eighth-century prophets, we got to Amos 9:7:

> Are you not like the Ethiopians to me,
>   O people of Israel? says the Lord. (NRSV)

I asked if this was a positive or a negative statement. The professor had the PhD student (teaching assistant) give an impromptu lecture on Cush[1] and its location in the Sinai Peninsula instead of in Africa. The professor then said to me, "Now please stop asking questions irrelevant to the seminar." It took me ten years from then, in my article "Beyond Identification: The Use of Africans in Old Testament Poetry and Narratives" (Bailey 1991, 176), to finally be able to answer that question raised in that seminar. Amos 9:7 was a positive statement. As Gene Rice (1978, 38) noted, it was only Eurocentric negative views of Africans that led commentators to view this first person YHWH speech as negative. If only the guild could hear YHWH say:

> Aren't you like today's Black biblical scholars to me
>   O, members of this guild!

If only that instructor of the eighth-century BCE prophets seminar had viewed the importance of helping seminarians divest themselves from white supremacist constructs, I would not have had to ask the question. The instructor would have opened up the discussion in class that day to help the clergy in training to consider divesting themselves of racist views. One can rest assured that this was not the only time in my formation to be a Black biblical scholar that I was confronted with such racist comments from faculty members.

In my graduate school preliminary exegesis exam, I wrote an exegesis paper on the "she's my sister story" in Gen 26:6–11. In the redaction criticism section of the paper, I compared how both Abram in Gen 12, Abraham in Gen 20, and Isaac in Gen 26 sexually maligned the indigenous people, who turned out to be more honorable than the Israelite patriarchs. A professor noted how that part of the paper reminded him of the way that

---

1. The Hebrew text says "Cushites," which the NRSV translators render as "Ethiopians."

Israelis demonize the Palestinians and "how southern whites DID that to Negroes." I responded, "Really? Thank you for the observation." As I left his office, I wondered whether he was really saying that such innuendos against oppressed people in this country were no longer happening. I guess in his mind this was the case, since I would be the second Black student to graduate from that program, Stephen Breck Reid having been the first.

Many years later a faculty member of that school stopped me at an Annual Meeting of the Society of Biblical Literature and said, "You know, Randy, if at the gathering here there was a prize to the alum who was on the program reading the paper with the catchiest title, instead of honoring a distinguished alum, you would win most years." I responded, "You mean, I won't ever be honored as a distinguished alum? Actually, had you come to hear the paper I read today on sexualizing the Other in Hebrew Bible narratives, you would have heard how I used your concept of programmatic texts, taught in the seminar I took with you, to structure my argument." He looked shocked and walked away. I was never sure if the shock was my being surprised at never being considered as a distinguished alum or that I used his theory to construct my argument.

I would imagine all of us have comparable stories of how such supremacist ideas functioned throughout our careers, in formation and later, and how those who act this way have no idea of the problems of these behaviors. It becomes important that we share these stories with each other, as well as with students going through the graduate process, so they realize they are not the only ones experiencing these assaults on the psyche.

In fact, it was the experience of being in community with other Black biblical scholars, which resulted in the publication of *Stony the Road We Trod: African American Biblical Interpretation*, that provided the therapeutic salve to cover over these racialized attacks and grounded me as a scholar committed to addressing issues of concern to my community. In my generation of Black biblical scholars who had earned the PhD, most of us were one of two Black PhD students entering the Hebrew Bible program at our school the same year, and we were the one who graduated. The process was difficult to experience, since we knew the other student was done in, and we were never sure why it hadn't happened to us also. More than the elation after my dissertation defense was the sense of wholeness on a Friday evening at Saint John's University in Collegeville, Minnesota, where the group met for three years in preparation of the volume and when Tom Scott and I presented our dissertation scholarship to the group. In that moment I felt the power of the affirmation of the group. At the end of that evening, I told the group that it was their power and encouragement that gave me the strength to persevere in the last year of completing the project. There was power in their affirmation.²

I must be clear that this group was not monolithic. There were some who were Black biblical *scholars*. There were some who were Black *biblical* scholars. And there were some who were *Black* biblical scholars. What was germinating in the group was the loosening of the pains we had endured through our varied pilgrimages, which was soothed in those seven days of gatherings in the woods of Minnesota over three years. I was most proud when we agreed that all the royalties of the book, resulting from our work, would be donated to the Fund for Theological Education,³ for one male and one female student each year, so that our numbers would increase. It was clear to us that we had to do all we could to increase the numbers of Black biblical scholars, as well as having more female scholars, for the work was heavy, and there were many hands needed to pick that cotton in the hot sun.

Sadly, these colleagues never continued as a group after the project was completed. We must, however, call into our presence Charles B. Copher, Cain Hope Felder, Thomas Hoyt Jr., and David T. Shannon, who are seated at the ancestral table at this very moment encouraging us to continue on with the struggles and to share the joys of our successes.

Teaching in a Black seminary was also the right environment in which I could hone my skills and ground my understanding of texts. There were several times when administrators at white seminaries would contact me to encourage me to apply for a position at their schools, but the search committees did not see my work as worthy of consideration. Thus, I would never even be invited to the campus for an interview. I have seen

---

2. In my own academic journey through public schools in Massachusetts on through undergrad at Brandeis and the School of Social Service Administration (SSA) at the University of Chicago, it was only in my second year at SSA that I had my first course taught by a Black instructor. During my seminary experience, I had to go across town to the Interdenominational Theological Center to take a Bible course with Dr. Thomas Hoyt Jr. to have a Bible course with a Black professor. In fact, when I talked with Dr. Hoyt about pursuing the PhD in Bible, he told me that there were more Black PhD students in New Testament than in Old Testament, and given my background in that field I should consider doing the degree in Old Testament. In my mind, if this would help the group, I would do it. One shrink I had did not think this was a good reason to have made a professional choice.

3. Now known as the Fund for Theological Exploration.

this happen to other Black scholars who have promising careers but who have difficulty getting their foot in the door. In fact, many of the faculty at the Interdenominational Theological Center felt my work went overboard, calling it "too radical." Eventually I decided that it was best for me to stay at the Interdenominational Theological Center, for it gave me the chance to work with large numbers of Black students in formation and to identify more to continue the PhD trek.

Let me be clear, while teaching at the Interdenominational Theological Center, I was always under the scope of presidents and deans and bishops who felt I was heretical and needed to be put in check. It was my place in the guild, my national and international notoriety and publications, which held them at bay. In addition, it was my skill in mentoring students enabling thirty-six alums to be admitted to PhD and ThD programs over the years in a variety of fields, twenty-four of whom have their degrees and are teaching in seminaries and universities across the country, that helped protect me from the ecclesiastical foes. And God may have had a role in protecting me, also. Who knows for sure?

I got into structurally mentoring students in an interesting way. In reading Howard Thurman's (1979, 80–81) autobiography, I was struck when he mentioned that, while teaching in Atlanta, he would invite Morehouse students into his apartment for dinner and discussion on Saturday nights. Having been fortunate to have been in a cadre of Black theological students from around the country while I was in the graduate program who were invited to San Francisco for a weeklong dialogue with Dr. Thurman, I realized how powerful such encounters could be.

I began inviting eight students each year to join such a set of encounters. They would have had to have taken two courses with me and to be interested in exploring alternatives to church vocations that existed then. These were students who had been hurt by the church but were seeking new ways of experiencing church. I would prepare a four-course meal, with all of the silver and utensils, plates, and glasses on the table. One student would come early and serve as sous chef. That student would thereby also have private time for discussions with me. The dinner group discussion was student led and sometimes even embarrassed me. At the end of the evening, the student who had come early would leave, and the others would do *all* the cleanup. Part of my design was to make sure, were they to go on to graduate school and get invited to a student gathering at a faculty member's home for a group dinner, they would feel comfortable in a formal setting, should it be such, and be at ease in discussing theological matters.⁴ Given the above success numbers, the strategy may have contributed positively to their successes in graduate school.

Originally, I went to seminary to get an MDiv and DMin and work in an ecumenical agency. I had been representing my denominations, Progressive National Baptist Convention and American Baptist Churches, in several program ministries of the National Council of Churches of Christ in the USA.⁵ I was ready to stop teaching in the Atlanta University School of Social Work and felt I could do more work in such an ecumenical agency.

While in seminary my goals changed. I got into biblical studies to help further the Black theology movement, which was burgeoning in the 1970s. There were two schools of thought, one led by James Cone (1969) and the other led by J. Deotis Roberts (1971). I wanted to do the exegesis, which would assist these cadres of Black scholars to better do their work. At that time, on the faculty where I was studying there was no respect for Black biblical scholarship. There was, however, growing respect among some faculty members for feminist scholarship as being produced by Phyllis Trible (1984). This was as close as I could get to liberation exegesis, so I began studying and using these methods as tools for exegesis. I also understood that, as Afrocentric biblical exegesis would develop, these methods would in some ways be transferable. Along with Trible I later found guidance from the works of J. Cheryl Exum (1993) and Letty

---

4. Some might argue that I was employing my graduate education in social work and my years of teaching at Atlanta University School of social work for eight years prior to coming to the Interdenominational Theological Center in this endeavor, and they would be correct.

5. I am grateful for the trust placed in me by Dr. J. Alfred Smith Sr., then President of Progressive National Baptist Convention for appointing me first to the Commission on Faith and Order and then on to the Bible Translation and Utilization Committee of National Council of Churches. I am most proud of cosponsoring with Dr. Shannon Clarkson, representing the United Church of Christ on the Bible Translation and Utilization Advisory Committee (BTU), a policy that "in repentance for there having been no non-whites involved in the translation of the NRSV, $30,000 annually of the royalties of the NRSV shall be given to FTE earmarked for Asian, Black, Latinx, and First Nation Bible students, with equity of gender and Testament in the group, so that there would be a large enough number of biblical scholars from these groups to be involved in the future Revisions of the NRSV Bible." This motion was passed in the BTU and forwarded to the Council and passed in the Executive Committee. If one is to look at the composition of the current group of scholars involved in this endeavor, one can see the fruits of that policy.

Russell (1985),[6] as well as Patricia Hill Collins (1990) and Esther Fuchs (2000). By the same token Renita Weems's (1995) work in *Battered Love* forced me to confront my own misogynistic and patriarchal readings of texts and to address this in "The Danger of Ignoring One's Own Cultural Bias in Interpreting the Text" (Bailey 1998).

South African biblical critic Itumeleng Mosala (1989) was the most formative male scholar to impact my scholarship in the early years of my postgraduate studies. In reading his work and dialoguing with him over the years, I came to see how I could utilize my skills gained in previous degrees in sociology and social service administration. I began seeing that I had been doing this intuitively, as I was looking at the social organizations described in the biblical text (1995a) as well as identifying the systems embedded in narratives in terms of social stratification (1990). I just did not know there was a method that could guide my exegesis. Mosala and I would often argue with each other over the keys in the text we were utilizing. What was most helpful to me in this method were the attempts to argue against the text. I still recall the time he lectured in one of my seminary classes and then preached in our chapel. He utilized the parable of the talents in Matt 25. When he got to the end, with the slave who was thrown out for not doubling the talent, Mosala proclaimed, "And he was the only slave who was free!" The chapel fell out, and I learned one *can* preach against a text.[7]

During the 1990s, as I became an ideological critic engaging in postcolonial and queer studies, I was pushed aside by the Black theology movement, the group I most wanted to influence. When I read an unpublished paper at the International Meeting of the Society of Biblical Literature in Copenhagen on "The Anti-African Polemic of the Priestly

---

6. Letty and I had served on Faith and Order for the National Council of Churches, and for one term we were cochairs of the Unity and Renewal Study. She was a great teacher of how to get people to do things they swore never to do, as a tool of liberation. I am thankful for the times we had together. One of my most remembered learnings was when we were in disagreement on using a particular theory, I tried to push my point by saying, "But Jesus said we shouldn't put new wine into old wine skins, for they will burst." She quietly responded, "So maybe they should be burst."

7. Every time I preach at a church that follows the common lectionary and the gospel text is a parable involving a slave master and slaves, my sermon title is always, "I Sure Hope This Isn't the Kingdom into Which We Are Living?" I find that clergy are more upset with this than the congregation. This might also explain why I sometimes don't get invited back.

School in Exodus" (1989), I heard a major Euro-American senior scholar say, while leaving the session, "There is no room in SBL for such papers." The only other time I heard such a statement was at the Society for the Study of Black Religion, when I read a prepublication copy of my article, "They're Nothing but Incestuous Bastards: The Polemical Use of Sex and Sexuality in Old Testament Poetry and Narratives" (1995b). Leaving that session, I overheard one of the founders of the Society say, "There's no room for such work in the Society." What was disturbing to some in that presentation was my treatment of Ham and the so-called curse of Ham in Gen 9. On one level, I argued that Ham was described as participating in incestuous relations with either his father or his mother in the text saying "Ham saw the nakedness of his father," which was a euphemism for sexual intercourse according to Lev 20:17. This was problematic, since many Afrocentric scholars were holding on to Ham as the progenitor of the African nations (cf. Gen 10:6), as though Mr. and Mrs. Noah gave birth to three sons, each one of a different race.

On top of that, I called into question the traditional Black treatment of the so-called curse of Ham, which was utilized to support the African slave trade. The line of argument was that there was not a curse of Ham but rather a curse of Canaan, and by implication being good Judeo-Christians, we didn't like the Canaanites either.[8] My question was how could we, who have had chattel slavery in our background in this country, not be appalled that by virtue of birth a Canaanite should be a slave. So, I've been an equal opportunity disruptor.

In other words, within the complex of Black biblical scholars in the United States, there has been hesitancy in critiquing the text, beyond most proslavery passages, especially in exploring negative portrayals of God, Jesus,[9] the spirit,

---

8. At a National Council of Churches meeting, there was a special celebration hosted by the United Church of Christ. The banquet speaker was a noted Black preacher, who dealt with the spy story in Num 13 with Caleb and Joshua returning and pushing the upcoming invasion of the land. The preacher ended with, "Come on, Calebs and Joshuas, let's go get them!" The room was silent. When he returned to his seat, I passed him a note informing him that the United Church of Christ had many first nation members, and the denomination had been challenging the Hebrew Bible conquest narratives, and that is why they were quiet at the end of the sermon. He looked surprised.

9. I have been sent links to womanist scholars participating in the Seven Last Words services, preaching on "Woman Behold Your Son," who note that I have stated that Jesus was dissing his mother by referring to her as "woman" and then explain the

and definitely don't queer them? While several Black biblical scholars make reference to Thurman's grandmother throwing Paul out of the canon because of the Household Codes in Ephesians (see, for example, Weems 1991, 61–62), I haven't seen any of these writers follow his grandmother's actions.

I got into dealing with workshops in churches on sexuality and the Bible in an interesting way. I received a call from a friend who was pastoring and asked me how to answer a question of one of his members. It seems she was divorced and asked him if masturbating was a sin, based on the story of Onan in Gen 38, where Onan was killed for it. I told him to tell her that in that story Onan was not masturbating. He was practicing coitus interruptus, which medically doesn't work, and nothing happened to Tamar in the story, other than being sexually abused. So, tell her to get some good batteries and go for it. Also tell her, when the biblical story is patriarchal in intent, stop trying to fit into the narrative, which by social construction sees women as the property of men. He then brought me to do a series of workshops on the "Bible, Sex, and Sexuality" at the church. Some of my friends are courageous!

In line with teaching such a lesson with lay persons, I was doing a workshop for Lutheran laity on the Decalogue. Using ideological criticism, I pointed out that in the tenth commandment, dealing with coveting, the wife of the neighbor was on the level with other property of the neighbor, the house, the field, the oxen, donkey, and male and female slaves. In returning to the Sabbath law, I asked, who didn't get a Sabbath.

One of the men stated with confidence, "The wife!"

I said, "Correct."

He continued, "Someone has to do the cooking."

His wife jumped in and said, "Dr. Bailey, you are getting him in trouble!"

I responded, "No, ma'am. It is the Bible that is creating the problem. Your husband is just being in line with the Bible. But remember, the God giving these laws has already self-identified in the first commandment as being 'Jealous,' and we know what havoc jealous folks can create."

I later got into dealing with queer studies in response to a family crisis. My brother, Mark, was gay and accepted the idea that he got infected with

---

language as his not wanting to make her cry. I have asked some of them what they would do if their sons referred to them as "woman." They go on and say, "There goes Dr. Bailey!" This also reminds me of Musa Dube (1996, 117–19), showing how doing Bible study with women in Botswana on the Syro-Phoenician woman, whom Jesus likens to a dog, and they also give him a pass, saying, "If he said it, it must be true."

HIV/AIDS because God was punishing him for being gay. I never felt I could help him move beyond that teaching. Near the end of his life, while being close to comatose, the nurse who was providing hospice care said, "He kept saying, 'But God!' this afternoon." I responded, "Great, they are back on speaking terms!"

I realized there were other students in my classes, who were either dealing with this in their own families or in their congregations. I knew I had to do more dealing with sex and sexuality in the introductory courses. One summer, I was also teaching at the Institute for Black Catholic Studies at Xavier University in New Orleans. During noon Mass, one of the priests in my certificate course was the celebrant. In his homily he stated, "I used to think that what Dr. Bailey was saying in class was crazy, but then it hit me. In my parish there are two people who have HIV/AIDS, a twenty-three-year-old man and a nine-month-old baby. I realized I would go pray with that baby every week, but I had never visited and prayed with the man. When I get back home, the first thing I'm going to do is go pray with that man!" This is a testimony of how teaching that is helpful beats everything.

I would have hoped there would be more comradery among Black biblical scholars, especially in the mentoring of younger scholars. We have to be grooming master's level students for graduate school. This is also very important in being open with younger scholars in formation, especially in encouraging them as they go through formation in graduate school and early in their careers. This could be most helpful in brokering these scholars with publishers. This would also be helpful in citing each other's works, where appropriate, even in cases where there is disagreement. For example, it was Vincent Wimbush's critique of Copher and Felder's claims that "we were there," as to, "what were we doing there in the Bible," that got me to answer that question and propose a model for exploring the so-called, African presence in the Bible in "Beyond Identification" (Bailey 1991).

I have been disheartened to hear papers in the African American Biblical Hermeneutics group where people have not engaged the works of other Black scholars, even where there is agreement. In other words, as we develop canons, thinking one is the only scholar to have addressed a subject does not help in furthering the growth of oneself as a scholar. Some have responded to my critique on this issue that these students probably don't have any Black faculty to point them in that direction. I would respond that they ought to know how to do a bibliographic search and incorporate these works in their own papers.

I learned the politics of the guild while being on the Semeia Studies editorial board. At one time a volume was being proposed on third-world writers. It was going to be edited by Euro-American scholars. I raised the problem with such a construction, and the volume's editorial composition was reconstructed. At the same time, my next proposed Semeia Studies volume was held up for a year by one of the editors of the previous work, claiming that my proposal was not doing anything new in line with the series. In essence, I was proposing "old hat ideas." It's intriguing to learn the political nature of these interlocking systems.

Another time I had submitted an essay for the Festschrift dedicated to my dissertation adviser. My article was rejected by the editor of the volume. In conversation with the editor of the Festschrift, I noted that the theology espoused in the article was unconventional. The response was, "There are other essays in the collection that are outlandish." I responded that I had said my essay was unconventional, not outlandish.

I then emailed another Hebrew Bible scholar who was on a journal's editorial board and submitted the article. It got published. At the Annual Meeting of the Society of Biblical Literature that year, there was a breakfast celebrating my former advisor. I ran into him, and he told me he was being presented with a Festschrift. I congratulated him but told him I was rushing to get to a Semeia Studies editorial board meeting. A couple of months after that, once my article was published and I received offprints, I sent one to him, inscribing that it had originally been submitted for his Festschrift but was rejected. I realized that it probably got better readership in that journal than in the book. I also realized the Semeia Studies editorial board meeting was probably better than the Festschrift breakfast, since there were also Asian, Black, and Latino people there, and none at the breakfast.

I have just shared some of my experiences in the guild, which I have found to be characteristic of what happens to scholars writing while Black. One's work is challenged by antagonists on multiple levels. When we had a session at the Society of Biblical Literature where Mosala's book, *Biblical Hermeneutics and Black Theology in South Africa* (1989) was reviewed, one of the Black reviewers negatively critiqued Mosala by asking, "Is there any Black writer you like?" In another instance, a junior scholar presented a paper dealing with sexual violence against women in the text and was negatively critiqued by a senior Black scholar for reading such experiences as systemic, since that scholar saw them as episodic. Most distressing is seeing how some senior Black scholars respond to junior scholars, especially those who question established Black religious strands of giving passes to God, Jesus, or the Spirit when it comes to these biblical characters being presented engaging in misogyny, ethnocentrism, classism, and the like.

The joy of seeing former students present papers at the Society of Biblical Literature is really deep for me. This is especially the case when they take your concepts and employ them in new ways. I have often told them that a professor knows that one cannot complete all of her or his work. So, we pour ourselves into our students in the hopes that they can carry these teachings into new levels. When they do this, we fully realize that we have placed our work into the right hands.

Finally, mentoring younger scholars is most important. Being open to reading and reviewing their prepublication works, being open to dialogue with them on ways to navigate graduate school, and brokering them on Annual Meeting programs and on program committees are important strategies that established scholars should engage. Early in careers, one should seek out advice on how to negotiate promotions, working with publishers, and the like. By the same token, as one works through these spaces, one should realize there are those of our number who are not comfortable in assisting each other and do not take kindly to scholarly critique. Just ask Wimbush about being burned in effigy on an HBTI campus on the occasion of the publication of *African Americans and the Bible* (2001). Or ask Renita Weems about the reactions to her negatively critiquing the concept of chosen people. By the same token, I've been charged with not only looking white but writing white given my engagement with the writings of our colleagues. So don't take it all personally. It really is them.

In the final analysis, one must remember that not everyone wants to be free.

Works Cited

Bailey, Randall C. 1989. "The Anti-African Polemic of the Priestly School in Exodus." Paper presented at the International Meeting of the Society of Biblical Literature. Copenhagen.

———. 1990. "Reading the Book of Samuel as a Message to the Exiles: A Hermeneutical Shift." *JITC* 18:95–118.

———. 1991. "Beyond Identification: The Use of Africans in Old Testament and Poetry and Narratives." Pages 165–84 in *Stony the Road We*

Trod: African American Biblical Interpretation. Edited by Cain Hope Felder. Minneapolis: Fortress.

———. 1995a. "'Is That Any Name for a Nice Hebrew Boy?' Exodus 2:1–10: The De-Africanization of an Israelite Hero." Pages 25–36 in *The Recovery of Black Presence: An Interdisciplinary Exploration*. Edited by Randall C. Bailey and Jacquelyn Grant. Nashville: Abingdon.

———. 1995b. "They're Nothing but Incestuous Bastards: The Polemical Use of Sex and Sexuality in Hebrew Canon Narratives." Pages 121–38 in *Reading from this Place: Social Location and Biblical Interpretation in the United States*. Edited by Fernando F. Segovia and Mary Ann Tolbert. Vol. 1. Minneapolis: Fortress.

———. 1998. "The Danger of Ignoring One's Own Cultural Bias in Interpreting the Text." Pages 66–90 in *The Postcolonial Bible*. Edited by R. S. Sugirtharajah. Sheffield: Sheffield Academic.

———. 2009. "'That's Why They Didn't Call the Book Hadassah!' The Inter(sect)(x)ionality of Race/Ethnicity, Gender and Sexuality in the Book of Esther." Pages 227–50 in *They Were All Together in One Place? Toward Minority Biblical Criticism*. Edited by Randall C. Bailey, Tat-Siong Benny Liew, and Fernando F. Segovia. SemeiaSt 57. Atlanta: Society of Biblical Literature.

Collins, Patricia Hill. 1990. *Black Feminist Thought: Knowledge, Consciousness, and the Politics of Empowerment*. New York: Routledge.

Cone, James H. 1969. *Black Theology and Black Power*. New York: Seabury.

Copher, Charles B. 1993. *Black Biblical Studies: An Anthology of Charles B. Copher*. Chicago: Black Light Fellowship.

Dube, Musa. 1996. "Readings of *Semoya*: Batswana Women's Interpretations of Matt. 15:21–28." *Semeia* 73:118–28.

Exum, J. Cheryl. 1993. *Fragmented Women: Feminist (Sub)versions of Biblical Narratives*. Valley Forge: Trinity Press International.

Felder, Cain Hope. 1989. *Troubling Biblical Waters: Race, Class, and Family*. Maryknoll, NY: Orbis.

———, ed. 1991. *Stony the Road We Trod: African American Biblical Interpretation*. Minneapolis: Fortress.

Fuchs, Esther. 2000. *Sexual Politics in the Biblical Narrative: Reading the Hebrew Bible as a Woman*. JSOTSup 310. Sheffield: Sheffield Academic.

Mosala, Itumeleng J. 1989. *Biblical Hermeneutics and Black Theology in South Africa*. Grand Rapids: Eerdmans.

Rice, Gene. 1978. "Was Amos a Racist?" *The Journal of Religious Thought* 35:35–44.
Roberts, J. Deotis. 1971. *Liberation and Reconciliation: A Black Theology*. Maryknoll, NY: Orbis.
Russell, J. Letty, ed. 1985. *Feminist Interpretation of the Bible*. Philadelphia: Westminster.
Thurman, Howard. 1979. *With Head and Heart: The Autobiography of Howard Thurman*. New York: Hartcourt, Brace Jovanovich.
Tribble, Phyllis. 1984. *Texts of Terror: Literary-Feminist Readings of Biblical Narratives*. OBT 13. Philadelphia: Fortress.
Weems, Renita J. 1991. "Reading *Her Way* through the Struggle: African American Women and the Bible." Pages 57–77 in *Stony the Road We Trod: African American Biblical Interpretation*. Edited by Cain Hope Felder. Minneapolis: Fortress.
———. 1995. *Battered Love: Marriage, Sex, and Violence in the Hebrew Prophets*. Minneapolis: Fortress.
Wimbush, Vincent L., ed. 2001. *African Americans and the Bible*: Sacred Texts and Social Textures. New York: Continuum.

Navigating a Foreign Terrain? Ruminations on Old Testament Studies from African-South Africa

MADIPOANE MASENYA (NGWAN'A MPHAHLELE)

Social Location

The Afrikaans word *apartheid* is one of those words that not only sets South Africa apart from other countries on the African continent; through the years, the word has also come to form part of our identity as South Africans. The word apartheid entails separation. The apartheid policy's underlying purpose was to separate people according to their diverse races. In that toxic line of thinking, the then four main racial groups in the country—black, white, colored, and Indian—were supposed to develop separately and, even more importantly for the present essay, with unequal privilege based on one's racial identity. Hence, depending on one's skin pigmentation in relation to the normative white superior race, one's fate, including one's position on the country's socioeconomic ladder, would be sealed.

As could be expected in that repressive and alienating context, those of my own kind, that is, both African descendent and female, would be located right at the bottom of the country's racial and socioeconomic ladder since then and, dare one say, to date. Takatso Mofokeng, one of the former South African black theologians, reminds us that the arrival of armed colonial Europeans in the country determined how our ancestors would respond to such an incursion. He writes,

> Their act of forcing a foreign, capitalist economic system upon our forefathers as well as relegating them to a position of cheap labourers determined the nature of the social, political and economic history of South Africa. (Mofokeng 1986, 113)

The colonialists, and later on the apartheid masters, established a sociopolitical system in which a few white South Africans had tremendous power[1] over numerous blacks as well as over all the country's resources (economic, political, and social; see William 1990, 25).

For those of us who care to do biblical scholarship deliberately informed by our social location, the concepts of apartheid and/or post-apartheid thus become critical concepts in shaping the discourse at a specific point in time. The preceding interested stance is motivated by my persuasion that there is no value free interpretation of texts, be they legal, religious, economic, or political texts, among others. Our experiences form a critical part of the meaning-making processes of our disciplines.[2] Hence, the New Testament Catholic scholar, Teresa Okure is on target when she argues,

> Our contemporary life experiences are not only a valid standpoint for understanding the biblical text. They are the only standpoint we have. Experience is the primary context for doing theology and reading the Bible. Experience here is not feeling, but total emersion in life, being seasoned by life. (2000, 202)

I am a child of apartheid because I was born and bred during the apartheid period here in South Africa. At those rare moments when a rural/village child could find herself or himself in town, one would be stared in the eye by the following phrases: "Nie-Blankes" or "Blankes" (Afrikaans), that is, "Non-Whites" or "Whites Only" (English). The preceding phrases were dehumanizing and black-disaffirming phrases to one's black identity, to say the least. Noteworthy and disturbing though is that as a young African girl growing up in rural South Africa, I was not that conscious of how dehumanizing such phrases were to African people!

Elsewhere I have captured the preceding political naivety as follows:

> Looking back at myself at the time, I can see that although I was black and female, I was politically unconscious of the kind of life that my

---

1. In essence, they still wield such power since the economy of the country is still mainly in the hands of the historical winners.

2. Womanist Christian ethicist, Rev. Dr. Katie Geneva Cannon, reminds us of the need to think with our hearts and feel with our brains! Cannon (2017) recounts the painful experience of her white Hebrew Bible professor who became upset because the contents of her paper made him to "feel" with his brain!

blackness and female sex had plunged me into. I was politically and psychologically oppressed.... In my naivety and political slumber I negated philosophies and processes that were geared to enabling me to live a fully human life/ve in which my worth as a black person would be affirmed. (Masenya [ngwan'a Mphahlele] 2008, 115)

Despite the fact of my political naivety, the phrases "Nie-Blankes" or "Blankes" (Afrikaans)/"Non-Whites" or "Whites Only" still remain vivid in my memory[3] as I try to trace my first consciousness about race issues, possibly in the late 1960s. My African ancestry determined that my habitat would be a Bantustan.

A Bantustan was a deliberate creation by the South African apartheid government (with its horrendous policy of separate development of different races) to control the land and entrench white supremacy. As a matter of fact, I had all along been a resident alien in the land of my ancestors. I only became a South African citizen in 1994 after South Africa gained political independence.

With the preceding brief introductory background to the history of the place not only of my origins, but also the one from which I write, one in which I have lived the life of a foreigner (in what was supposed to be my home front) in many respects, I now give a brief sketch of efforts that were made to navigate the foreign terrain.

Foreign and Lonely but at Home?

My father was a teacher who was thoroughly colonized. His English accent was quite foreign to Africa. As children, we would be expected to prepare tea during certain slots (e.g., 10:00 am and 4:00 pm), and the instructions to prepare such would be made through English as medium of communication, in a village setting! As children, we had to attend a specific church.

---

3. In recent years (2004–2005 and in 2010), while visiting the Martin Luther King Center in Atlanta, Georgia, USA, I marveled at how the memory of such phrases was brought back by resonating phrases from the history of the enslavement of African people in the Americas. Also, Ellen Khuzwayo (1987, 104) gives us a glimpse of the effects of migrant labor on the black families then: "We know that the effects of migrant labour are seen on different levels. We experience separation from our menfolk, we have to survive on the low wages the men earn, and we have to endure starvation. We must help ourselves because we know that the South African government is unconcerned and without pity for the suffering and struggle of the black people."

The sermons imparted on our young minds were typical of the repressive apartheid status quo because they never enabled us to question the use of the Christian Bible for the oppression of blacks as the focus was on a believer's spiritual life alone. The teaching of biblical studies at universities was no different. All my professors (read: lecturers) were white and male. Hulisani Ramantswana (2020, 3) notes:

> The so-called "golden era" in Old Testament scholarship was an era of white dominance that thrived under the colonial-apartheid regime. For example, in 1983 at UNISA, the Department of Old Testament had fourteen lecturers, who were all white (Burden 1983, iv–vii). The number of lecturers in the Department continued to grow over time. Except for the respective size of the departments, the situation at other Afrikaans universities was no different-the Old Testament scholars were all white.

The historical-critical method that was and still remains the norm in American- and Euro-centered biblical scholarship was not helpful in opening black students' eyes to oppressive ideologies both in the biblical text and in our various contexts. I would later on in my scholarly journey capture the preceding alien context of an insider-outsider as follows:

> It is in this set-up, that I found myself totally lost. In my own "little" understanding, I thought I was "spiritually deprived" because of the critical approaches to Bible and Theology I consumed; "contextually empty" as the theology we were doing had basically nothing to do with my African context! It is in this context that we grappled with the biblical text—the emphasis was on the need for the knowledge of the original languages in order for one to be able to do 'proper' exegesis. We were expected to know the Sitz im Leben of a particular text in order to be able to understand it within its historical context. However, we did not attempt to move our fingers an inch regarding the text's relevance for the modern reader's context. If the latter was considered, it would be spiritualised and many injustices on the ground would thus be left intact. We seldom, or rather, never addressed theological questions on African-South African issues such as the land question, unjust political systems, patriarchy et cetera. Instead, we would be referred to the works of European theological giants such as Rudolph Bultmann, Karl Barth, Dietrich Bonhoeffer and so forth, works which had nothing to do with the African context. (Masenya [ngwan'a Mphahlele] 2004, 4)

Given the history of how the Bible was used to colonize and impoverish indigenous populations, how it was and still is used to perpetuate patriarchy and female subordination, one wonders why it did not dawn on the producers and teachers of the Bible and theology offerings to use the same, to transform the lives of the black masses. But could they? How could those who benefitted from the so-called objective stance of historical-critical research give up on their long held-traditions?[4]

Also, if the integration of the social concerns that affected many people on the ground was deemed as tampering with the hard-core content of Old Testament studies, could the teachers have dared to care to let such filter into the subject matter of Hebrew Bible? One of the fathers of the second generation of white South African Old Testament scholarship seemed concerned and anxious about what he viewed as the changing political landscape that was bound to have adverse effects on the quality of Old Testament scholarship in the country. Jurie le Roux cautioned:

> South Africa, is however, now standing on the verge of radical and far-reaching social and political change. These events will certainly cause dramatic changes to the university system and the nature of its staff. *The possible lowering of standards and the adaptation of courses in order to address the grave social and economic needs of Africa may endanger the good work of the past thirty years.* Radical changes may lead to the lack of a second and a third generation to continue the progress of the past three decades. (1993, 350–51, emphasis added)

But also, the professors could not have bothered about transforming the content of the offerings for the benefit of the black masses because *sešo se baba mongwai wa sona* ("a sore itches to the one who has it"). Bernadette Mosala's (1986, 132) exhortation is instructive in this regard: "liberation does not fall into one's lap. It must be claimed and protected.... Unless we are willing to exercise our right and to claim power and to do some-

---

4. Hans De Wit (2009, 9–10) could thus argue: "The fascination with history, the idea that texts are stable objects that can be controlled by means of proper instruments and the ultimate meaning of which can thus be discovered, historical distance not as a productive and fruitful given but as an obstacle to understanding, the imbalance between reason and spirituality, the history which develops from high to low, from primitive to erudite—all of this will be decisive for Western biblical studies for a long time."

thing about bringing about the challenges we believe are necessary we will remain the invisible creatures who are always in the inside looking in."

Given the pandemic of gender-based violence in South Africa, the growing gap between the rich and the poor, high levels of corruption, unemployment and poverty, as well as the current scourge of the global COVID-19 pandemic, why do biblical scholars in this country still choose to ignore present day contextual issues? Biblical scholarship continues to bear the mark of a detached scholarship whose products many of us are. Being the products of such a scholarship, we produce products who will equally take comfort in being academic pies in the sky. Amid the abstract theologizing that happened then (and even today), amid the foreign biblical studies subject matter that was consumed by African students then, even during the heydays of the apartheid era here in South Africa, there were dissenting voices that challenged the status quo. Such voices though were hardly allowed to enter the discourse of academic biblical studies and theology. As a matter of fact, holding on to such justice-seeking biblical and theological discourses could easily have landed one in prison. From such a repressive context, it thus makes sense that I could not be exposed to important works of theologians such as Mofokeng, Maimela, Boesak, Chikane, Beyers Naude, West, Tutu, and Mosala, among others. With hindsight though, I tend to be persuaded that exposure to such works could have contributed positively to the creation of balance between the theory and praxis of biblical scholarship.

The turning point in my academic life happened only in 1986 when I enrolled for a masters' degree at the University of South Africa (UNISA). My supervisor, a white man, interestingly, the late Professor Jasper J. Burden, impressed on me the need to integrate my African context with my research in Old Testament/Hebrew Bible studies. I was stunned! Apart from wondering about the possibility of such an endeavor and its rather strange mixture, I was probably also struggling with the idea that, once Africa is made an integral part of research in Old Testament studies, the end product could not have been worthwhile. With hindsight, it is easy to figure that already then, the repercussions of having consumed and become content with a foreign curriculum in my undergraduate/pregraduate work was evident. The idea of the lowering of the standards raised by le Roux earlier was probably haunting me, albeit unconsciously. Could this have been self-hate?

I ended up agreeing to embark on research that would investigate the theme of parent-child relationships in the Hebrew Bible book of Proverbs from an African Northern Sotho context (Masenya 1989).[5] A shift in my biblical scholarship then happened. Since then, I have always been fascinated by Old Testament research that has a bearing on the African continent in general and the African-South African context in particular. For example, in my doctoral research, I combined historical-critical approaches and sociohistorical approaches with literary criticism, ideology criticism, and reader-response criticism. I was persuaded specifically by my desire to use African women's experiences as a hermeneutical lens to engage the biblical text. At that point, I was deliberate in my wish to make Africa, her epistemologies, knowledges, and philosophies an integral part of my biblical scholarship. For example, in a deliberate effort to decolonize my research, I use African proverbs to unlock biblical texts and elevate some positive aspects of African cultures. In the process, I deconstruct the heavily Eurocentric slant that South African Old Testament studies continue to reveal. Also, my navigation from feminism through womanism to a gender-conscious approach closer to home led to my development of a *bosadi* (womanhood-redefined) approach (Masenya 2014).[6]

Some of my doctoral students (e.g., Mudimeli 2010) have used the *bosadi* concept in their different contexts, which, in my view, is a pointer to the impact of developing something new albeit at the cost of marginalization and/or being ignored. Worth noting is the keenness on the part of these emerging scholars for a gender-sensitive framework that speaks to the varying but also unique African women's contexts. My research has mainly focused on the Old Testament and Africa, foregrounding pertinent themes such as Africanness, patriarchy, gender, poverty, HIV and AIDS, and ecology. As could be expected, going against the grain of American-Eurocentric scholarship, as well as androcentric biblical scholarship, and

---

5. The title of the study was "In the School of Wisdom: An Interpretation of Some Old Testament Proverbs in a Northern Sotho Context."

6. The word *bosadi* (womanhood) comes from the root *-sadi*, which can be translated as "womanhood." The term *mosadi* ("woman") does not only occur in the Northern Sotho setting but also in other South African indigenous languages, for example, *wansati* (Xitsonga), *umfazi* (isiZulu), *musadzi* (Tshivenda), and *mosadi* (Setswana and Sesotho). As a matter of fact, the root –sadi occurs in other African languages outside of South Africa (e.g., *mwasi* in the Mongo of DRC; *-mkazi* in Chewa, Malawi; and *sadi* in the Tswana of Botswana, among others). The generic Northern Sotho word *mosadi* (cf. Hebrew *iššāh*) can be used to designate a woman irrespective of her marital status.

in the process also becoming the first[7] scholar in the field of African women's biblical hermeneutics in South Africa, I have felt like a foreigner and a loner on what was supposed to be my home front. Why so? In the following section, I respond to the question.

Struggles of Navigating a Foreign Terrain

First, having to navigate a white male field comes with a cost. What quickly comes to mind here are our engagements during a panel discussion on black theology at one of the sessions of the Annual Meetings of the American Academy of Religion and the Society of Biblical Literature in Atlanta, Georgia, in 2010. Womanist theologian Jacqueline Grant noted the high cost of scholarship that seeks to foreground the concerns of grassroots communities in their scholarship. Such a cost makes sense in contexts in which such context-oriented scholars have been, are, and remain a drop in the ocean compared to the Eurocentric scholarship in which they operate. Elsewhere I have argued: "Choosing not to mimic mainstream gender-sensitive frameworks, ones which would give first priority to the needs of local women, will naturally come with a price, a price so high that one might struggle to gain upward mobility" (Masenya [Ngwan'a Mphahlele] 2014, 189).

One would need to learn the skills and tactics of having to navigate the two worlds, to learn to satisfy the demands Katie Cannon (1995, 125) would regard one as world of the "canonical" boys and the other as of one's own context.[8] Going against the grain of white male scholarship would also entail that if one wished to climb the academic ladder, one would not always have the luxury of "writing what one likes" (see the title of Biko 2015). How one does research needed to necessarily tap into, if

---

7. When I received my PhD degree in September 1996, the citation written by my study leader read more or less as follows: "Madipoane Masenya (Ngwan'a Mphahlele) is indeed the *'eshet hayil* as she is the first black female to obtain a doctoral degree in Biblical Studies in South Africa and the first person to approach the Old Testament from a womanhood perspective at the University of South Africa."

8. A black womanist scholar, argues Cannon (1995), thus faces a dilemma of having to negotiate between two positions: traditional enquiry, i.e., possibilities in principle, and raising honest questions arising from the lived experiences of African American women, i.e., possibilities in fact. Cannon's lived reality of the intersection between race, sex, and class provided her with a different ethical orientation and a different ideological perspective.

not basically rely on, the American and Eurocentric epistemologies and philosophies for approval in scientific journals. One may thus struggle to get upward mobility, and push backs are certain to occur.[9] Second, in the global South (the African continent), calls for the Africanization of higher education offerings are now loud and clear. However, as long as the historical winners who are also the main gate keepers choose to be resistant to such calls, the status quo with its idolization of white supremacy will continue to remain with us for many years to come. Third, the repercussions of ignoring African biblical hermeneutics by many a white academic are mostly felt by black students. At times, I have had to recommend major revisions on the masters and doctoral works written by Black students who were supervised by white scholars. Why so? The probable reasons being the study leaders' lack of appreciation and/or knowledge about African philosophies and epistemologies and/or the tendency of many to ignore the invaluable insights from African biblical hermeneutics.

Conclusion: Visions about the Future

For black scholars to combat the apparent prevailing tendencies to disregard pertinent issues in the academy, low self-esteem, and self-hate, the following recommendations are in order:

- Being deliberately conscious to decolonize and Africanize courses/the teaching material in Bible/biblical studies. For those located especially in the Southern Hemisphere, these processes affirm that they have their own knowledges, epistemologies, philosophies, and civilizations. Reclaiming these and allowing them to shape the higher education sector's offerings and research ought to be prioritized. How the decolonization and Africanization of the teaching material shape our disciplines will differ from one context to the other.
- Choosing the discipline because of one's passion about it.
- Using one's discipline to plow back into one's community.

---

9. One of the peer reviewers of my essay remarked that, although my paper had a story to tell, it was not suited for an accredited journal but for a magazine! One scholar accused me of wanting to kill the historical-critical method.

- Refusing to let foreigners to oneself regarding race, class, gender, and geography, et cetera dictate how one should read the text.
- Facing the dilemma head on. In the African context an academic like myself faces a dilemma as a community/church member and an academic on two fronts: On the one hand, being expected to park one's brains/scholarship when entering a church's doorstep, shout the hallelujahs all the time, and pick them up on one's way out. On the other hand, being expected to park one's faith at the academy's doorstep, only to pick it up again on one's way out.
- As far as one can, the business of knowledge production is to be done in one's indigenous language. The Bible and theology course offerings at many a university continue to be conducted through the media of either English or Afrikaans or both and, yet as Ngũgĩ wa Thiong'o (2005, 164) reminds us, there is a need to retrieve our languages in order to use them in knowledge production and for the reclaiming and resuscitation of the African memory:

    > We cannot afford to be intellectual outsiders in our own land. We must reconnect with the buried alluvium of African memory and use it as a base for the further planting of African memory on the continent and in the world. This can only result in the empowerment of African languages and cultures and make them pillars of a more self-confident Africa ready to engage the world, through give and take, but from its base in African memory ... that African intellectuals must do for their languages and cultures what all other individuals in history have done for theirs. This is still the challenge of our history. Let's take up the challenge.

- Prioritizing those sources that address pertinent issues both in the biblical text and, in particular, those in one's specific context.

The impacts from the implementation of the content of these visions by the present generation of black scholars not only in South Africa, but also throughout the continent and her diasporas, will hopefully shed light on the fact that black scholars matter.

Works Cited

Biko, Steve. 2015. *I Write What I Like: Selected Writings.* University of Chicago Press.

Burden, Jasper J. 1983. "Foreword." *OTE* 1:iv–vii.

Cannon, Katie G. 1995. *Katie's Canon: Womanism and the Soul of the Black Community.* New York: Continuum.

———. 2017. "Thinking with Our Hearts, Feeling with our Brains." Ministry Conference. 24 October.

De Wit, Hans. 2009. "Exegesis and Contextuality: Happy Marriage, Divorce or Living (Apart) Together?" Pages 3–30 in *African and European Readers of the Bible in Dialogue: In Quest for a Shared Meaning.* Edited by Hans de Wit and Gerald O. West. Pietermaritzburg: Cluster.

Le Roux, Jurie Hendrik. 1993. *A Story of Two Ways: Thirty Years of Old Testament Scholarship in South Africa.* Verba Vitae.

Khuzwayo, Ellen. 1987. "Hungry in a Rich Land." Pages 99–100 in *Sometimes When It Rains: Writings by South African Women.* Edited by Ann Oosthuizen. London: Pandora.

Masenya, Madipoane. 1989. "In the School of Wisdom: An Interpretation of Some Old Testament Proverbs in a Northern Sotho Context." MA thesis, University of South Africa, Pretoria.

Masenya (Ngwan'a Mphahlele), Madipoane. 2004. "Teaching Western-Oriented Old Testament Studies to African Students: An Exercise in Wisdom or in Folly?" *OTE* 17: 455–69.

———. 2008. "An African-Conscious Female's Reading of Steve Biko." Pages 114–55 in *The Legacy of Stephen Bantu Biko: Theological Challenges.* Edited by Cornel du Toit. Pretoria: Research Institute for Religion and Theology, University of South Africa.

———. 2014. "For Ever Trapped? An African Voice on Insider/Outsider Dynamics within South African Old Testament Gender-Sensitive Frameworks." *OTE* 27:189–204.

Mofokeng, Takatso. 1986. "The Evolution of the Black Struggle and the Role of Black Theology." Pages 113–28 in *The Unquestionable Right to Be Free: Essays in Black Theology.* Edited by Itumeleng I. Mosala and Buti Tlhagale. Braamfontein: Skotaville.

Mosala, Bernadette I. 1986. "Black Theology and the Struggle of Women in South Africa." Pages 129–33 in *The Unquestionable Right to Be Free: Black Theology from South Africa.* Edited by Itumeleng I. Mosala and Buti Tlhagale. Braamfontein: Skotaville.

Mudimeli, Lufhuluvi M. 2010. "The Impact of Religious and Cultural Discourses on the Leadership Development of Women in the Ministry: A Vusadzi (Womanhood) Perspective." DTh thesis. University of South Africa, Pretoria.

Okure, Teresa. 2000. "First Was the Life, Not the Book." Pages 194–214 in *To Cast Fire Upon the Earth: Bible and Mission Collaborating in Today's Multicultural Global Context*. Edited by Teresa Okure. Pietermaritzburg: Cluster.

Ramantswana, Hulisani. 2020. "Past the Glorious Age: Old Testament Scholarship in South Africa: Are We Moving Anywhere Close to Blackening Old Testament Scholarship?" *Scriptura* 119.3:1–19.

Wa Thiong'o, Ngũgĩ. 2005. "Europhone or African Memory: The Challenge of the Pan-Africanist Intellectual in the Era of Globalization." Pages 155–64 in *African Intellectuals: Rethinking Politics, Language, Gender and Development*. London: Zed Books.

William, Jacquiline. 1990. "Towards a Womanist Theology of Liberation in South Africa: Black Domestic Workers as a Case Study." *Journal of Black Theology in South Africa* 4:24–35.

Preliminary Thoughts:
The Hermeneutical Dilemmas of the Allies, Colleagues, and Guild of African American Biblical Scholar-Teachers

Shively T. J. Smith

> It is within the context of an oppressive society—a society that in many ways diminishes the value of African Americans—that [biblical writings] the Scriptures have played an important role in helping African Americans to survive and maintain a healthy identity and hope. The African American biblical scholar has not been exempted from such oppressive treatment. As students, authors, teachers, most, if not all, of these scholars have shared a common history of overt and subtle forms of racism and rejection of the value of the African American believing community's contribution to the interpretative process.
> —William H. Myers, "The Hermeneutical Dilemma of the African American Biblical Student"

Like so many others since its 1991 publication, *Stony the Road We Trod: African American Biblical Interpretation* introduced me to scholarship at a time when I genuinely questioned whether viable pathways existed for African American women and other minoritized intellectuals. Can African American women earn a doctorate in biblical studies, gain stable employment, publish research acknowledged by the field, and earn tenure as respected biblical scholar-teachers? At first glance, it did not appear to be a viable path. My skepticism was informed by my observations of the cultural habits and institutional trends of theological studies in American and European institutions of higher learning in the first decade of the twenty-first century. Among my matriculating cohorts, African American and African diaspora students were small student populations (if they were present at all) at these institutions. In many cases, these low student populations drastically outpaced the ratio of African American faculty to graduate students in these same institutions. As an undergraduate student studying abroad in the United Kingdom and a graduate student studying in the US system, I did not need to look at the statistics produced by the Society of Biblical Literature or the Association of Theological Schools to recognize the reality. My eyes told me what I needed to know: people from my communities were not the scholars, teachers, or even the ideal target students and communities for academic study of biblical writings and histories.

William H. Myers's (1991) essay, "The Hermeneutical Dilemma of the African American Biblical Student," confirmed what my untrained undergraduate and graduate student eyes recognized. In his essay, Myers criticized the ethos of biblical scholarship in which the discipline's dominant methods during the twentieth century erased the embodied realities, sociolinguistic epistemologies, and cultural histories of its interpreters, especially people of African and non-European descent. It did so by projecting a false notion of neutrality, dismissing and denying the ways in which biblical writings were interpreted according to the standards of white Eurocentric orientations toward history and intellectualism, privilege and place, as well as ideologies and worldviews. After all, there were few faculty members and students from other social locations of the world among them, at the time Myers penned his essay. Few challenged conventional modes of interpretation and judgements about what constituted valid, plausible interpretation based on extant evidence from antiquity and present history.

Thirty years ago, within the academic environment of American biblical studies, Myers addressed this phenomenon by responding to what I call "the conundrum of omission." It is the historic double-edged phenomena within American and traditional Western biblical studies in which the interpretative histories of African Americans and others are disregarded. Related to this is the fact that many undergraduate and masters' level degree students of African descent are historically overlooked as prospective candidates for the future guild of intellectuals. Those who may most readily address historical gaps by carrying forward critical investigation and production with their own communities, values, and social locations as guiding resources in the enterprise are excluded from consideration and admittance.

Now, over thirty years later, Myers's essay is not yet out of date. It remains an affirmation and testament that *yes*, African American and African diaspora biblical scholars and students are thought-leaders and actors in critical biblical studies. Their work continues to recover histories of interpretation absent from the scholastic record produced by previous generations. They unveil the prejudices of former historical-critical endeavors, particularly text-based historical work. Interpreters deploying historical critical methods traditionally ignored the socially conditioned cultural and theological perspectives guiding their foci and assessments (Smith forthcoming, 37–54). Driven by the Enlightenment's impulse to emphasize reason to the exclusion of social, religious, and personal markers and concerns, critical biblical studies disembodied and dislodged biblical writings from the interpersonal interactions between texts and contemporary interpreters (as if one can ever escape herself as "interpreter, the person"). The challenge African American and African diaspora biblical scholars have laid against traditional biblical scholarship, as represented in Myers comments in the opening epigraph of this essay, resonates with Hans-Georg Gadamer's 1960 critique of the Enlightenment's hermeneutical endeavor in *Truth and Method*: "The overcoming of all prejudices, this global demand of the Enlightenment, will itself prove to be a prejudice.... If this is true, the idea of an absolute reason is not a possibility for historical humanity" (Gadamer 2004, 277–78). In a word, the work of African American and African diaspora biblical scholars over the past three decades pulled the veil back on the bigotry infecting historical endeavors within biblical studies.

More importantly, for the current moment, Myers's essay is *also* a clarion call about the work ahead for the Society of Biblical Literature and its membership. We are a learned society composed of international intellectual communities. Our global collective employs diverse approaches to researching and teaching the histories of biblical literature and its related contextual and extracanonical writings and materials. Yet, there is something instructive about the cognitive dissonance and the common problem many African diaspora biblical students and scholars faced over thirty years ago, which lingers, to varying degrees, in our scholarship, institutions, and teaching today.

While Myers is clear that the work of retrieval and inclusion is a task of the African American biblical scholar, he does not dismiss the possibility that others should do this work as well. Where he is subtly suggestive, my position thirty-years later is stronger: It *is* the work of our guild—as arbiters and interpreters of not just ancient texts and histories but arbiters and interpreters of knowledge—to articulate the contextual dimensions and biases of our traditional hermeneutical approaches and contemporary hermeneutical developments. Moreover, *it is our collective responsibility to work at interpreting from new centers of biblical history and literature.* We have the tools to recover overlooked sites of contextual meaning and the theoretical apparatuses to distill more inclusive modes of epistemological inquiry and reason. It is no longer merely the task of African diaspora scholars to resource and center our cultural stories, sources, and epistemologies. Rather it is a shared dilemma and responsibility that should be taken up by the *entire* field. Our intellectual community can reframe hierarchies of knowledge in biblical exegesis, history, theology, and hermeneutics to not only include but launch critical inquiries from neglected sites of interpretation.

The journey toward reframing, to put it succinctly, begins with no less than four endeavors. First, critical biblical history must widen its gaze to include formerly omitted interpreters of the Jewish and Christian bibles in its histories of American biblical interpretation. The aim is to highlight previously elided models of critical hermeneutics and exegesis extant in American and Western-controlled societies—such as nineteenth century African American women writers like Anna Julia Cooper. Second, underrecognized models can supply new resources for theory in the study of religion and hermeneutics which transgress divisions in time and space. Such studies might more readily explore the correlations and dissimilarities between ancient and modern contexts. We can trace and examine different genealogical trends in interpretation and, thereby, shift understandings about the significance of biblical literature for contemporary discourses. Such an endeavor helps interpreters avoid reinscribing into present social constructs, ancient sensibilities that proved prejudicial, narrow, and violent. Third, other strategies for interpreting biblical writings and history that operate outside Western epistemological schemas requires resourcing. To this end, the field should not only reach for nontraditional Jewish and Christian interpretive configurations but also more readily engage the interpretive practices of other religions. Last, reframing only occurs if the field disrupts the echo chambers of its traditional Eurocentric scholarly circles through the compositions of its faculties, doctoral cohorts, and other graduate and undergraduate students. Radical inclusion of those historically denied access to the conversation requires more than tokenism. It requires reallocating the benefits of security, honor, resources, and time for those communities that do not have long-standing histories of presence, power, and place in the halls of academia.

With these four endeavors in mind, my scholarly response to Myers now also necessitates a reframing. Whereas he titled his essay, "The Hermeneutical Dilemma of the African American Biblical Student," in today's current moment, my titled response shifts the challenge of the hermeneutical dilemma to a different audience. The populations among the Society of Biblical Literature's membership facing the hermeneutical dilemma today are the allies, colleagues, and guild of African diaspora biblical scholar-teachers. Keeping my four propositions for reframing critical studies of the bible in mind, I offer preliminary remarks to those populations of the Society of Biblical Literature seeking to identify as coworkers and partners in the task of expanding and reorienting the very modes out of which critical biblical studies has traditionally produced scholarship and operated as a guild.

In an 1886 address about the purpose of education and the right for African Americans to have equal access to quality educational opportunities, Anna Julia Cooper, the fourth African American woman *in the world* to receive a doctorate made a provocative assertion. Cooper said it is the work of education and the collaboration of intellectuals to tend to the greater good, equity, and inclusion of earth's peoples, especially those with histories of historical exploitation, omission, and disinheritance. Here is Cooper's statement:

> As interested in the education of a neglected people, and as educators in a circumscribed field of work, we are confronted by a peculiar danger.... Whether from force of circumstance or from choice and loving consecration, we are ministers [servants] of the Gospel of intelligence, of moral and material uplift to ... a people who are habitually reasoned about en masse as separate, distinct, and peculiar; a people who must be fitted to make headway in the face of prejudice and proscription the most bitter, the most intense and the most unrelenting the world has ever seen.[1]

According to Cooper, the task of intellectual communities is to create opportunities of scholasticism and its accompanying doors of prospect and possibility for those who have historically been silenced and excluded. Regarding our discipline, that means expanding our accounting of the histories of interpretation and hermeneutical developments not only as a historical corrective but as a pedagogical strategy, epistemological dis-

---

1. See her 1886 essay, "On Education," in Lemert and Bhan 1998, 250.

cipline, and moral duty. For example, our traditional study of the history of biblical interpretation acknowledges the interpretative methodologies and significance of figures like Origen and Philo in matters of allegorical interpretation. But Cooper supplies another model of allegorical interpretation that exists beyond an ancient, foreign context. Her reading strategy interprets the gospel of Jesus as illustrative of the work of intellectuals on behalf of the historically disenfranchised, marginalized, and disinherited of the world. This is in keeping with Myers's assertion that sources of African American biblical history must be retrieved and centered as sources of biblical interpretative practice and knowledge. Yet I am not convinced that thirty years later, the task of retrieving and centering sources of biblical knowledge heretofore undervalued and discarded as resources for the interpretative task is solely the work of African diaspora scholars and other scholars of colors.

To do this work as a guild of allied intellectuals, faculty colleagues, and international communities necessitates confronting the availability and esteem we assign to *diverse and intersectional* primary source material, especially sources reflecting biblical interpretive practices and histories our field has historically overlooked and, even less frequently, centered as starting points for critical interpretative investigation, reconstruction, and comprehension. At times, we will have to act and read against the grain of our intellectual formations and training. Consequently, in those moments, we will have to do the fundamental work, as intellectuals, we were trained to do as those conversant in what Cooper refers to as, the "Gospel of intelligence." That fundamental work is, namely, to educate ourselves about new subject matters and knowledge and to muster the courageous humility and intellectual will to become informed about other peoples, histories, and locations about which we are uninformed.

In conclusion, let me say: as an African American woman biblical exegete and historian, a researcher and teacher, a writer and editor, an advisor and mentor, a faculty member and colleague, and a public intellectual and religious leader, I am forced to prepare myself for Myers's descriptions about the politics of omission and Cooper's caution about the peculiar dangers facing African Americans and other minoritized scholars. Yet, I and others like me, living embodied intersectional histories, persist in the scholarly endeavor with rigor and integrity because we are committed to our scholarship, our classrooms, our communities, our institutions, and our guild. We do our work with an incessant hope that others in our guild—among the societies and cultures represented by our global membership—will realize that *they too* are accosted by this dilemma of omission and its peculiar dangers. As I said at the beginning, if I were to respond to Myers's essay thirty years later, my topic would be: "The Hermeneutical *Dilemmas* of the Allies, Colleagues, and Guild of African American Biblical Scholar-Teachers." I would invite allies and colleagues of our learned society and beyond to join us in the work publicly, no longer under the cover of darkness as Nicodemus in John 3. But out in the open in our guild and faculty meetings, classroom sessions and syllabi design, scholarly books and refereed articles, collegial evaluations, and public lectures. And this is how we *might* reconceptualize the discipline to promote antiracism and to be more welcoming and inclusive of intersectional research, teaching, and service to the larger world in the Society of Biblical Literature.

Works Cited

Gadamer, Hans-Georg. 2004. *Truth and Method*. Translated by Joel Weinsheimer and Donald G. Marshall. 2nd ed. New York: Continuum.
Lemert, Charles, and Esme Bhan, eds. 1998. *The Voice of Anna Julia Cooper*. Lanham: Rowman & Littlefield.
Myers, William H. 1991. "The Hermeneutical Dilemma of the African American Biblical Student." Pages 45–56 in *Stony the Road We Trod: African American Biblical Interpretation*. Edited by Cain Hope Felder. Minneapolis: Fortress.
Smith, Shively T. J. Forthcoming. "Historical Criticism: Methods." Pages 37–54 in *The New Cambridge Companion to Biblical Interpretation*. Edited by Ian Boxall and Bradley C. Gregory. Cambridge: Cambridge University Press.

On Leaving but Not Going Far

RENITA J. WEEMS

In academia there is an assumption that faculty don't walk away from the professoriate once they earn tenure. For reasons that made sense to no one other than myself back then, I walked away in 2005 from a tenured position at a Research 1 (R1) university. I left because I ran out of reasons why I should continue to work in a profession and at an institution where I was treated like a permanent interloper. I left convinced there were other ways to do scholarship and safer places in which to do it. I thank the organizers of this two-part #BlackScholarsMatter symposium for making space for racial-ethnic minority scholars to talk openly about our experiences in a predominantly white guild. As I listened to younger scholars in the field share their experiences in the academy in the sixteen years since I walked off the job, I felt like I was listening to talk about a long lost lover. I couldn't help feeling that I was given a chance to listen in as his current wife describes all the ways that the former lover has and has not changed in the ensuing years.

Systematic theologian Willie Jennings writing on the presence of people of color in predominantly white theological institutions captures the matter succinctly.

> One of the untold stories of theological education in the last 60 years has been the painful struggle of scholars of color to thrive in these institutions. There is a trail of tears of minority faculty members that match a trail of missteps and backwards steps by institutions. At issue has been the willingness of institutions to receive fully the changes that minority faculty members bring to the articulation of their disciplines, to the teaching of their subject matter, and to administrative leadership. (2014, 38)

Nothing prepares you for what it means to be the first, the only, one of a handful in your profession. The first Black. The first female. The first anything. To be a Black female academic, navigating the double jeopardy of race and gender, means, for one thing, to think, write, and teach under a cloud of suspicion that says you're not good enough, not serious enough, not smart enough. You are forever the outsider, the interloper, the Other in a world that centers whiteness and maleness as the abiding images of inquiry. To participate in the world of the mind as a Black woman scholar means you will likely wind up working in institutional spaces where you are constantly required to justify the knowledge you produce, the sources you cite, the publications you publish, the course work you assign. Having to constantly justify yourself is one kind of hostility one faces in one's field. Invisibility is the other form of hostility you're likely to face. Invisibility that is liable to leave you feeling lonely, marginalized, isolated, and constantly questioning your choice of profession. Jennings's "trail of tears" refers to the trail of tears that extends from your classroom to your office as you make your way back to your office after repeated challenges and threats of uprisings by students with questions about your competence; the trail of tears from your office to the chair or dean's office where you are summoned to explain something on your syllabus or to be told that students find you intimidating; a trail of tears from the faculty meeting to your office where you retreat to keep from coming apart after being constantly overtalked or dismissed by one particular toxic faculty colleague. A trail of tears visible and known only to you. No matter how accustomed you are to being alone, you never get over the loneliness.

It is an unresolved wound, this work of being a Black woman intellectual especially if you're a Black female intellectual, especially one whose research interest involves centering Black women's voices in order to theorize Black women's lived experiences (Weems 1991). It's not the feeling alone, marginalized, invisible that gets you. It's feeling like you've been betrayed by something or someone you once loved. For most of us who choose scholarship as our profession, school was the place that once brought joy into our lives. It was where we felt safe. Scholars tend to be people who loved school when they were younger. School was the only place that made you feel alive. School gave you identity. You loved school because you loved books, you loved reading, you loved figuring out the answers, you loved the attention of your teachers, you loved being known as an academic achiever. But for racial ethnic minorities things change in graduate school. School was no longer where I felt welcomed. My experience as a Black woman graduate student in Old Testament during the 1980s can best be described as one of genteel benign neglect. I was allowed to study and progress through the program as long as I didn't disturb things, break anything, demand much, or create a fuss. The unspoken expectation was this: keep your head down, your nose clean, do your work, speak when spoken to, and, for the Goddess' sake, pretend not to be bothered by the white, Eurocentric colonialist preoccupations of the field. And for the most part that's what I did. The betrayal continues the further up the rungs of the ladder you go. Becoming a Black female professor only made school that much more difficult to relax and to be myself. School, which was once an affirming place for a smart Black girl, soon becomes a very hostile place when the smart Black girl presumes to occupy the space as a Black female intellectual. Even long after you should have become accustomed to the challenges, you catch yourself still being caught off guard by some hostility, the ad hominem attacks, the raised eyebrows, the subtle and not so subtle comments made about your personal style, about your scholarship, about your very presence (Cooper 2017).

I tell myself that had I possessed an arsenal of powerful multivalent terms such as microaggression, implicit bias, white fragility, whiteness, antiblackness, intersectional invisibility at my disposal like younger scholars today have to classify, analyze, deconstruct, and describe the "stubborn invisibility of whiteness" (Tupamahu 2020) they encounter in their dealings with guild politics, I may have remained—a little longer. By the middle of the 2000s when I left white academia, the field had begun patting itself on its back for the genteel reforms happening in its ranks. The field had come a long way since the 1970s when Katie Cannon, the first Black woman admitted to a PhD program in Hebrew Bible (Union Seminary, New York), was dismissed by her adviser after completing all her coursework with the spurious charge that she was not a serious enough student (Weems forthcoming). By the middle of the 2000s with almost a dozen racial ethnic women in the pipelines for terminal degrees in Bible, the field turned a deaf ear to charges of racism and sexism within its ranks.

Thirty years after the landmark publication of *Stony The Road We Trod* (1991), the field of biblical studies continues to have a race (and sex) problem. The changes that the biblical studies field continues to need won't be made until it faces its racist past. Biblical studies is at its core a racialized enterprise that was founded to shore up empires while simultaneously subjugating the Other. As one Indonesian New Testament colleague baldly puts it, "To be a biblical scholar is to be white. Biblical scholarship training is a whitewashing machine" (Tupamahu 2020).

I left the guild, but I never stopped being a scholar. I left the professoriate, but I remain a teacher at heart. I left the academy, but I did not cease being an academic. I left the professoriate, but I found ways to continue writing, teaching, and making use of all the skills I learned as a scholar (researching, organizing, problem solving, and tinkering). Plans shift. Circumstances change. Life values evolve. As the academic job market continues to shrink and full-time, tenure track jobs becoming fewer and fewer, PhD graduates are being forced to pivot and discover for themselves how to translate their skills in nonacademic careers. It makes sense that graduate theological education, including biblical studies, would take their heads out of the sand, look out over the horizon, help their graduates imagine new vocational possibilities, and take the lead in preparing their students for more than just teaching. Churches may be dying, but religion is not going away. The world of diplomacy, commerce, technology, and medicine can do with more experts in religion. I stopped being a professor because I wanted to take advantage of new opportunities. I trusted the skills I had as an intellectual, a scholar, a critical thinker, an interrogator, a writer, a teacher would open other doors for me. And they did just that.

The field and its guild have come a long way as seen in the very fact that twenty, thirty, forty, fifty years ago the Society of Biblical Studies Literature would never have lent its name and platform to a conversation like the one we are having here in this symposium. The discipline was too devoted to notions of objectivity and relegating the Bible's meaning to its past meanings to take its head out of the sands to acknowledge that modern day atrocities like the murders of black and brown bodies by police (e.g., Breonna Taylor, George Floyd, Tamir Rice, Michael Brown) are legitimate objects of scholarly inquiry for biblical studies specialists. The field would never have been willing to entertain any notion of its complicity in maintaining whiteness, and the status quo thereby makes these murders and the disinformation surrounding the global pandemic possible. For a long time the biblical field prided itself on the slow glacial pace in which change took place in the field. It was an academy that prided itself on its traditions, its whiteness, and its European origins. That we're even having this conversation about race and scholarship, power and domination, identity and pedagogy—all under the hashtag #blackscholarsmatter—says that change is happening, cultural studies is making its mark, the field is stirring, and that finally the presence of several generations of Black biblical scholars within its ranks is causing the field to rethink some of its core assumptions about its past, its identity, its values, and its responsibility to train scholars who can make an impact beyond the classroom.

Works Cited

Cooper, Brittany. 2017. *Beyond Respectability Politics: The Intellectual Thought of Race Women*. Champaign, IL: University of Illinois Press.

Felder, Cain Hope, ed. 1991. *Stony the Road We Trod: African American Biblical Interpretation*. Minneapolis: Fortress.

Jennings, Willie James. 2014. "The Change We Need: Race and Ethnicity in Theological Education." *Theological Education* 49:35–42.

Tupamahu, Ekaputra. 2020. "The Stubborn Invisibility of Whiteness in Biblical Scholarship." Political Theology. https://tinyurl.com/SBL03112a.

Weems, Renita. 1991. "Reading Her Way through the Struggle: African American Women and the Bible." Pages 57–79 in *Stony The Road We Trod: African American Biblical Interpretation*. Edited by Cain Hope Felder. Minneapolis: Fortress.

———. Forthcoming. "The Biblical Field's Loss Was Womanist Ethics' Gain: Katie Cannon and the Dilemma of the Womanist Intellectual." In *Walking through Valleys: Womanist Explorations in Justice, Leadership, Embodied Ethics and Sacred Texts*. Louisville: Westminster John Knox.

Tribunals of Jurists and Congresses of Gentlemen: Signifying (on) Biblical Studies as Colonial-Bureaucratic Masquerade

Vincent L. Wimbush

Pregnant with the world, the poet speaks. "In the beginning was the word..." Never did [anyone] believe it more powerfully than the poet.
    And it is on the word, a chip off the world, secret and chaste slice of the world, that [the poet] gambles all our possibilities.... Our first and last chance.
    More and more the word promises to be an algebraic equation that makes the world intelligible. Just as the new Cartesian algebra permitted the construction of theoretical physics, so too an original handling of the word can make possible at any moment a new theoretical and heedless science that poetry could already give an approximate notion of. Then the time will come again when the study of the word will condition the study of nature. But at this juncture we are still in the shadows.
    —Aimé Césaire, *Lyric and Dramatic Poetry, 1946–82*

Founded in the late nineteenth century, the Society of Biblical Literature was founded in an era that ushered in the rise of hyper-nationalizations and nationalisms, including the end of US-style slavocracy and the reactionary Jim-Crowism. Now, nearly a century and a half later, it is time to more broadly and deeply analyze and critique and reform this institution. Such analysis and critique and reform ought to be pursued in the spirit of ongoing (self-)criticism by all members of the Society since, for my argument in this essay, all have been and can hardly avoid continuing to be overdetermined by the refractions of modern racialization. But it would in my view be very disappointing if not scandalous were Black-fleshed/-identified members to avoid participating in—even loudly blowing the horns for—this hard and necessary work I would term *excavation* (not exegesis). The *critical* history and ongoing presence of Black-fleshed peoples as members of the Society of Biblical Literature simply must not be ignored. We must also not reduce the analysis to the challenges of some or many or the successes of the few. Although personal travails are never to be rendered unimportant, much more is at stake and at issue. This essay cannot function as anything near to what is demanded; what I provide here is only a baseline or springboard for consideration of such analysis. I frame the essay in terms of historical phases—of Black presence and participation in the Society of Biblical Literature—that can in turn provoke thinking not only about what has transpired, but also what remains to be considered, what ought to be raised as a set of questions and issues, what ought to be challenged, what ought to be stressed, what ought to provoke reorientation and practices different from those still so common in connection with the Society.[1]

We are in this moment, at the beginning of the third decade of the twenty-first century, well beyond the first phase—which lasted from about 1880 to the 1940s (as still-not-collected and scattered archived records seem to show)—with the few persons of color, scattered here and there, as is usually the case in persistently highly racialized groups, allowed membership, presence, and limited participation in what was then called the "Society of Biblical Literature and Exegesis" (with *exegesis* emphasized). These few were no doubt exceptional in training and bearing, temperament and discipline. They had to be. Although it is unlikely that there were avowed segregationists guarding the doors at Union Seminary in New York City—the venue for meetings until the 1960s—to prevent Black persons from entry and participation in the Society's meetings, there were nonetheless issues and challenges aplenty that determined who could even get to and present themselves to the company gathered in those faux-Gothic

---

1. I am aware of the fairly recent critiques provided by others, including the book by Stephen Moore and Yvonne Sherwood (2011) and the extended essay by Jacques Berlinerblau (2006). I share many positions with them, but I differ from them in their lack of emphasis on racialization and their too easy emphasis on (the critical—philosophical and literary—orientation to) religion as solution of a sort (Moore and Sherwood) or the suggestion that the Society of Biblical Literature simply try to be more secular. As the reader will see, I do not think scriptures should be left to the domain of religion. And I am convinced that inattention to or denial of racialist ideology in the invention and management of scriptures explains much about serious lack of change in the practice of scholarship on the Bible and other scriptures and the scriptural.

buildings way uptown. It is much more likely that it hardly occurred to the all-white-fleshed nearly all-male, earnest, and sternly Protestant persons in these gatherings that Black persons even wanted or could ever muster interest, expectations, or assumed requirements for participation in such high-minded gatherings. Much like those who constituted the first US department of comparative literature established in 1891 at Columbia University—whom the first chair is recorded to have described as "tribunals of jurists and congresses of gentlemen" (Said 1993, 47)—the crowd at the Society of Biblical Literature and Exegesis probably did not think Black-fleshed peoples mattered to their interests. Like the gentlemen at Columbia, the small group of (likely reverends all or at least broadly churchly) gentlemen that first met in the Union Seminary office of church historian, philologist, theological encyclopedist, and ecumenist Phillip Schaff (1819–1893) and laid the foundations in 1880 for what has become the Society of Biblical Literature[2] did little or nothing to encourage Black persons to participate (or even to be thought about, much less addressed).

---

2. Schaff was also the founding figure of what became in 1888 the American Society of Church History. This organization-building work, along with other activities, reflects even more clearly Schaff's strong orientation to what he understood to be modernist historical and philological work, even as the latter was motored by religious interests and convictions. There was no doubt that the Society of Biblical Literature, more than other related guilds, would register more loudly in presence and influence, a function of the Bible as cultural including religious touchstone. The western Protestant, if not the whole of the western theological curriculum, with its changes notwithstanding, is pretty much an extension of focus on and approaches to the study of the Bible. This is the case with almost all early guilds having to do with religion: the American Academy of Religion (originally National Association of Biblical Instructors!) grew out of the Society of Biblical Literature and its "foster[ing]" of biblical interpretation. I have heard from some that this organization was for decades viewed by the Society's revered gentlemen scholars as the junior league, involved in the teaching of texts to undergraduates. Herein is another part of the fault line begging to be addressed. Records show that there had been efforts before what became the Society of Biblical Literature to organize scholars of the Bible, but these efforts were conceptualized and strictly drawn along confessional/denominational lines. I maintain that it is this sort of fault line—if not about denominationalism exactly, about the problem of the unanalyzed confusion of orientation to broad religious interests and textual study—has always haunted the Society of Biblical Literature. Is it about religious interest? Or about some other interests? My long-held stance is that only when this problem is addressed with honesty and courage will a (likely smaller) but more sharply defined and oriented Society be formed. Consider this essay more challenge and provocation in this direction.

Those Black-fleshed persons simply did not psychologically register—or matter. Every bit of evidence regarding the founders (as types of figures in religion-inflected polite if not high society) would seem to indicate that their discourses and their associated practices and orientation, including their congresses (about the Bible! no less), did not inspire or provoke much if any consideration for the Black-fleshed. Except in terms or within the bounds of textual exegesis.

An example is breathtaking: Schaff's earlier extended essay (1861!), *Slavery and the Bible: A Tract for the Times*, sadly indicates the extent that Black-fleshed peoples—most of whom within his lifetime, including the time of the founding of the Society, had actually been enslaved and/or were formerly enslaved—might be thought about at all as real persons. Schaff's book reflects the sad truth that among scholars of his ilk slavery might be addressed in writing only and insofar as it could be in some way interpellated into a (colonialist-)textualist ideology, weirdly (over)determined by "the text." There was reference aplenty to slavery in or limned by the text. Written as the winds of civil war were felt, this orientation seems rather horrifying and sad. With Schaff as any sort of reasonable measure or example, the new professionalized biblical scholars followed (in their mind) the (ancient-cum-modern colonial-settler-imperial) *text*—the text, the text, always the text. What goes begging from this unsettling, but still not fully critically analyzed observation, is the question about whether—and if so—when, why, and how the Society came to be different from the several white gentlemen's clubs or tribunals of self-authorized jurists, about whom the aforementioned first chair of comparative literature spoke, who masqueraded their status in annual ongoing congresses and through related obsessive academic guild practices and initiatives. More research on this matter is also in order.

Not much seemed to change until the 1960s, a time in which peripherals or marginals began to find and raise their collective voices and place their bodies in the way of the standing order. In these politically charged times, with the differently named "Society of Biblical Literature" (such a radical gesture!), along with some ongoing changes in rules and protocols, a few more persons of color here and there were recorded as being in attendance. That some among us can name and count them is commentary enough on the situation. Perhaps all the white gentlemen were respectful, even welcoming of and courteous to these new (types of) individuals. But there is no record of any special organizational gestures made during the time. Perhaps, the change in venue during the 1960s was a signal of the need for change in definition and orientation. I remain doubtful that this change in venue was strong enough signal for radical changes needed.

We are also now beyond what I consider to be the second phase of Black presence in the Society of Biblical Literature—which lasted from the 1940s to the late 1970s and 1980s. This was the period in which persons of color—first, Black-fleshed persons; then other self-identified individuals/groups of color—began to claim the right and the opportunity to constitute formal and informal circles of conversation and programming both within and alongside (and at times even outside) the formal programming of the Society. A cursory look at other learned societies would likely establish that this phase among the Society's membership was somewhat belated if not also timid. (This matter also begs more study.) At any rate, the still-not-totally and systematically collected records show efforts to establish programming that reflected a certain heightened political intentionality, including gaining safe and free gathering space and time for conversation about matters having to do with—for lack even today of a more precise and analytically and sociopolitically functional rubric—Black peoples and the Bible, for example. The Society-sponsored recruitment conference initiatives of the 1990s (the first one in 1996, interestingly or poignantly enough, also took place at Union in New York City) were conceptualized and organized and directed by the awkwardly named Committee on Underrepresented Racial and Ethnic Minorities in the Profession (CUREMP). And the related national and a few (later) regional program units connected to the Annual Meetings were around the same time established and by their very presence made statements of and about difference within the largest academic professional guild of biblical scholars.

In the latest third, now contemporary twenty-first century moment or phase of Black-fleshed presence and participation in the Society of Biblical Literature, we somewhat lazily follow the language of the Black Lives Matter movement (as though the powerful sentiment behind the movement had never been thought about or brought to expression!). We must take steps beyond this movement's language, which is provocative but vague as framing and agenda-setting language, even as we draw upon it for perspective and orientation. We must, as I indicated already, go beyond (the imposed from without) racial essentialism, the dreamy racialist nostalgia, beyond stories about individual experiences that include, without doubt, true stories about the struggles, challenges, setbacks, and even successes that mark Black-fleshed peoples' relationship to the Society of Biblical Literature. This sort of storytelling, which this volume (following an earlier Society initiative) aims to capture is, I want to make clear, justified and is needed. But I should like also to argue that for this phase—the third for my historical-analytical purposes—which finds me and finds readers of this essay positioned well into the twenty-first century, what Black-fleshed presence and participation might or should mean for the discourse and programmatic orientation of the congress that is the Society of Biblical Literature has not yet been made clear. Whatever else this argument or drawing of the strings might entail, it must include but frankly go far beyond storytelling for its own sake or for the sake of translating tales of individual challenges and/or heroism. That the latter is part of the truth to be told, again, I do not here gainsay, but I maintain that the telling of stories of challenges overcome or gains won by individuals is simply not enough. Left at this level the status quo is upheld. Required now and going forward is thick and deep/radical critique and rewriting/reorientation of the Society—away from being identified as congresses of (white) gentlemen to critical discourse(s) and practices that signify in powerful terms that Black scholars do matter. (Also, of course, all those other Others who elect to be in solidarity with what such metonymic tagging may represent.) Black scholars must matter now not as accomplished or honored individuals but as fulcrum of a sort for reforging or recasting discourse and for getting at structure—what Edward Said (1993, 52), inspired by Raymond Williams, termed "structures of attitude of reference." What apt language for gentlemen who play exegetical games.

Some exploratory ideas about how to help make this reforging/reorientation happen through thick and deep critique and rewriting is the modest contribution of this essay. But the contribution must be understood to claim no more than making the argument and at least suggesting a defensible approach. Beyond being a collective effort, such an approach must be risk-taking, ex-centric, a going far beyond the entrenched framework that the Society still represents (along with all other learned societies by definition). This means assuming a position that is beyond, even disruptive of, whatever rewards assumption of the (Society-specific) center (with its vexed gestures toward confessional communities) represents. The approach should be disciplinarily transgressive—a mix of practices that in the end represents ex-centricity and a rather undisciplinary posture and orientation. This is in my view the sort of difference that Black scholars can and should challenge others to address. The very history of Black nonpresence, nonparticipation, forced silence, and (in the view of some) their loud-talking—all should force consideration of some of the issues needing to be addressed in our times, even if not exactly on terms that I propose here.

I should like to begin here with more focus on what the figure of the scholar in association or collaboration represents in the modern world and use such to relate what more precisely the Black scholar associated with the likes of the Society of Biblical Literature might contribute. This figure, the scholar—called "biblical" (this adjective has never made sense to me)—until recently mostly white male and mostly clerical high Protestant, was assumed to be in solidarity with whatever type of Europeanist colonial imperial regime was most relevant. There is no long list of social-political and ideological mavericks on the rolls. Too many were for too long well-behaved. But it is very important not to be misled by the practices and orientations and sensibilities that have historically defined this figure. Gentility of bearing and obsessive focus on canonical/classical texts do not translate into benignity or innocence. Complicity of participation is often expertly masked—as passionate advocacy for investigation of Moses or Jesus or Paul or ... as Black guys.

I return here to Said's rendering of Columbia's gentlemen professor George E. Woodberry. A look at the extended remarks of the latter in celebration of the establishment of the first comparative literature department in the United States reveals much that is pertinent to the argument made in this essay. I have in mind the barely masked giddiness around academic participation and investment in the study of what had already been named and engaged in academic circles in Europe as *Weltliteratur*. The latter was understood to be helpful in the advancement and management of European colonial empires-cum-nations and their nationalisms and the homiletical rhetorics and faux principles and hopes around unification of nation/empire:

> The parts of the world draw together, and with them the parts of knowledge, slowly knitting into that one intellectual state which, above the sphere of politics and with no more institutional machinery than tribunals of jurists and congresses of gentlemen will be at last the true bond of all the world. The modern scholar shares more than other citizens in the benefits of this enlargement and intercommunication, this age equally of expansion and concentration on the vast space, this infinitely extended and intimate commingling of nations with one another and with the past.... He lives in a larger world—is, in fact, born ... to that new citizenship in the rising state which ... is without frontiers or race or force, but there is a reason supreme. The emergence and growth of the new study

> known as Comparative Literature are incidental to the coming of this larger world.... The study will run its course, and together with other converging elements goes to its goal in the unity of mankind found in the spiritual unities of science, art and love the art and love. (Said 1993, 46)[3]

So many issues are packed into and are provoked by these soaring remarks. It is enough for me here to take the opportunity to focus on only one set of issues having to do with the too easily made connection between scholars of comparative literature, *Weltliteratur*, and something approaching the pacification/unification of the world. I am aware of the rather eerie resonance the terms here have with Chinua Achebe's message to readers in his provocative novel *Things Fall Apart* (1958). I took note of Achebe's understanding of the colonial empire's understanding and use of the British colonial empire's notion of pacification as a kind of violence done to subject peoples in *Scripturalectics* (2017). That such pacification/unification can be realized only through vigilance in governance of the empire (that it paradoxically refuses to acknowledge) is made clear. The extent to which Woodberry speaks for many about what and for whom his university department stands for is stated clearly and strongly enough. And it should be noted this matter is registered without extended exegesis on the content of a particular text! It is as though access to and engagement of the literatures of the world on the part of gentlemen scholars portends, if it does not already in the strongest possible way signify, world unification. The unification can be imagined, is potentially realizable, if not guaranteed, and is assumed to be ordered and managed by that world in which Columbia University gentlemen in and through their tribunals and congresses play jurists. And if nothing else comes through in Woodberry's remarks, it is most evident that those referenced stand in solidarity with and in support of the order of things. After all, who but the elite gentlemen in collusion with empire can access and conceptualize and make defensible (the study of) the spoils—in this case the literatures—of the world as sign of domination and then make use of the spoils as reflectors of world unity? A most tidy and mostly unsubtle collusion should be evident to all but those suffering from the most severe bouts of denial and occlusion.

This focus on literature should be deemed relevant to those interested in the doings and issues related to the Society for Biblical Literature. No matter whether and what the Columbia professor Woodberry thought of

---

3. Also see text in Woodberry 1973, 211.

the Society's doings—there likely was some degree of personal collaboration in those days—the development of the latter took a course similar to that of the dynamics of the circles of those who advanced the cult of *Weltliteratur*, with similar ramifications for ideological orientation or captivity. The Society of Biblical Literature can be argued to have been a subset of comparative literature, a forerunner of it, a belated development or a contemporary development running on a different track or in a different context or domain. Perhaps, there is a degree of reality around all possibilities. The historical and philological interests of Schaff and his colleagues cannot and must not be ignored. That there were also longer standing and current theological-confessional interests among some that were quite separate from if not hostile to philology and that represented a different interest and set of practices should not flummox the observer or threaten the argument. It was also the case that some if not most also made these interests overlap in complex ways. This confusion of the philological and theological-religious interests seems from the beginning to the present day to haunt the Society of Biblical Literature.[4]

At any rate, this matter leads to consideration of at least one other contemporary development. It is required for the sake of coming to terms with what the Society represents or how it should be framed in critical analysis. I have in mind the prior and concurrent development of another field or discourse that might also be analyzed as another example not only of the incubation of what becomes the Society—with more albeit complicated affinity in terms of academic setting—but also how the scholar becomes a type of colonial bureaucratic functionary. The field of discourse is *Weltreligionen* (science of religion/comparative religions, with Germany as the undisputed epicenter of this development). It is in the discourse that has to do with *Weltreligionenen* that the development of the Society can be seen to be most embedded and invested—at least in the early period, among the founding gentlemen. The discourse and related social-cultural dynamics and movements grew out of and converged with impetuses having to

---

4. Are we/they funny kinds of theologians or weird historians/philologists? Clearly, readers must agree with me that more serious analysis of this issue is in order. But beyond the tepid arguments and vague hesitant nonconclusions drawn by Tomoko Masuzawa in her otherwise insightful book *Invention of World Religions: Or, How European Universalism was Preserved in the Language of Pluralism* (2005), 309–28, note her throwing up of the hands—with her use of the term *bewitched*—to summarize what she thinks of the confusion of theology and history of religions discourses.

do with *Weltliteratur*. This was the case even as different types of politics and other challenges—within and beyond the academy—obtained in the development of and the dynamics between the two fields.

The bridging relationship is seen clearly in the career of F. Max Mueller (1823–1900), one of the most famous and influential Sanskritists of the nineteenth century. He is also credited with being one of the architects of the modern study of comparative religion. His massive and controversial multivolume project *Sacred Books of the East* (1879) is itself enough to establish him as a major factor in the construction of the discourse. The project claimed to contain most of the texts of the religions of the world (thereby formally and lastingly classifying them as world religions). But the exception of Christianity and Judaism, reportedly against Mueller's position, revealed too much about what was really going on with this so-called scientific project. It could not really pass the test of comparative critical scrutiny. This library of volumes—overdetermining the shaping of departments and academic programs in religion for decades—chocked full of sacred books, was then and can still be seen now as a consistent and expected project reflecting a particular set of intellectual and ideological assumptions.

Even as questions and criticisms persist, Mueller's lectures, his academic guild organizational work, and his research and the arguments of his scholarship must be reckoned with. More important, what cannot be ignored in any consideration of the beginnings or theoretical groundwork for the development of comparative religion/history of religions is his hugely influential lectures (among many others) that are collected in his *Introduction to the Science of Religion* (Mueller 1873). In these lectures he earnestly and passionately advances a specific monogenetic theory of the development and classification of languages/religions turning around a strange tripartite division: "Aryan, Semitic, and Turanian." All the categories are fraught. The last one was a rather weird reference to the developments and dynamics associated with the Asiatic continent, mostly China. The Aryan and Semitic were argued—mostly assumed, with little real evidence—to be superior traditions. They happen to represent developments closer to Jewish and Christian traditions as they unfurled in history. A modern-world irony of ironies, Mueller found he had at every turn to convince others not to draw negative—including narrow racialized—inferences from the conclusions regarding theories of superiority associated with these developments that he shared with so many others. And deserving of even bigger exclamation of surprise—"Aryan" became a sign for overly romanticized connections between an imagined India and Europe. "Semitic" came to represent in narrow terms only Jewish and Islamic traditions. (A monster had been created for moderns, if not resuscitated/reanimated.) From this larger theoretical schema six relatively superior religions were listed by Mueller: "Brahmanism"; "Zoroastrianism"; "Buddhism"; "Mosaism"; "Christianity"; and "Mohammedanism." And then there were the offshoots. Beyond them was darkness, primitives.[5]

Mueller also argued in a larger framing theoretical key the nexus of language and religion, more specifically, the development of a "science of religion" out of the "science of language." Mueller and other scholars insisted on seeing inflection as the most important index of the complexity of the development of language and argued for a "genealogical relation" between language and religion as the basis for the classification of religion. From this, Mueller was led directly to the conceptualization and hierarchicalization of religion, which placed "book religion" as the "aristocracy" of religions.

> The truly genetic classification of religions is the same as the classification of languages, and ... there exists the most intimate relationship between language, religion, and nationality. (Mueller 1873, 143)[6]

In these words and in others, Mueller declares himself to be a believer in the invention of religions of the world and "world religions"—and the respective societies and cultures they reflect and refract—through certain uses of language. Again, with such views he also found himself at times fighting with and disturbed by scholars and others who through his views and long before and aside from his view had already conflated his language and religion with racialization or the hierarchicalization of race (see Masuzawa 2005, 237–38). Mueller protested and sighed often and loudly, but the ideological die had, long before his era and his work, been cast: there was then and there is now no honest way to deny what was at stake in the roiling throughout the nineteenth century (if not in different degrees and different tones before) around the establishment of the discourse we now refer to as world religions (as complementary and adjunctive parallel to if not subset of the one larger set of social-cultural cum academic dynamics that led to the discourses of comparative literature). Among the conclud-

---

5. See discussion in Masuzawa 2005, 210–11.
6. See the discussion in Masuzawa 2005, 217.

ing arguments the religious studies-trained now self-described scholar of "European intellectual history and literature" Tomoko Masuzawa (2005) makes in her provocative and already much-referenced book, *The Invention of World Religions*, is that the giving birth to and the roiling over the construals of world literature and world religion discourses is (nothing other than?) a window onto the making—I might add the solid construction—of the modern European. The fights and discourse-construction work amounted in Masuzawa's view to a

> complex bundle of concerns and contestations over the spiritual legacy of Europe ... a series of attempts at theorizing and historicizing Europe, no longer as a geographical location but as an identity ... that is distinct, in principle from Christendom. (256)

In the twentieth century, Masuzawa goes on to argue, the theories and arguments of the previous century were "co-opted and converted to placid facts." Put another way, the turn taken from the nineteenth century in the twentieth century had deleterious effects that observers and critics, academic and journalistic, can recognize and detail. The academic fights about what religion is, how it evolved, and how religions should be classified and researched and taught (in university settings, in specific fields/departments) and debated—all such sadly resulted in the twentieth century and into our own century with the same recognized European colonial empire assumptions and schemas. So, according to Masuzawa,

> There is indeed little difference between the nineteenth-century characterization of various religions and the general description of the same religions under the new discursive regime of the twentieth century.... Buddhism generally appears to be benignly compassionate, contemplative, and metaphysical to the core, if also tending toward effete quietism; Islam, on the other hand, is considered fastidiously elemental and constant, tending toward fanatic militancy.... What has thus become invisible under the new discursive regime, then, is the very speculative logic that rationalized and legitimized these commonplace characterizations in the first place. (256)

Judaism, Christianity, anyone? Where are they in this schema? For whom are they signs of identity? It does not take years of study of the inflections of Sanskrit to see what has developed here: like Mueller's *Sacred Book of the East* collection, like his arguments in his collected lectures, religion—as

Masuzawa and others have noted that J. Z. Smith (1982) brilliantly recognized—was constructed (and ideologized and classified) at the scholar's desk. Whose empire, whose nation, is being scored/legitimized by such scholars at their desks? Despite his denials of the racialization and racisms inherent in and solidified by the theoretics that were *Weltliteratur* and *Weltreligionen*, Mueller's work—carried out at his desk!—contributed much to the invention and development and mimetic-obsessive practices associated with religion, including guild and other representations of exegesis.

I must make another pivot here—back to the Society of Biblical Literature. The latter might be considered in relationship to Mueller and company and Woodberry and company to be in a smaller context or of lesser import. Maybe. This depends on who is counting and sizing up things. I return to that possibly smaller, seemingly odd, but no less psycho-socially-politically influential discursive circle that is biblical studies. I shall do this by drawing attention first to Chicago, 1893, to what was billed as the World's Fair and as, a significant part of it, the first Parliament of World Religions. After the height of nation-building or consolidation, this event, staged in the middle of the nation emerging as the last and mightiest empire, were representatives of all the players of concern in this essay. The fair showcased much of what the relatively new nation-empire had to offer. Of course, this included not a little of what many would call the bizarre and the lowbrow. But it also included some things among the highbrow who, interestingly enough, seemed to want to be represented and translated at the event. That religion was at all a feature was astounding enough. This meant the scholars of the sort we associated with Mueller had already accomplished much—religion could be isolated and discussed among peoples around the world as phenomenon in the world. It crossed national boundaries as well as boundaries within societies. It could be isolated and examined, talked about, paraded outside religious camps. What captured the attention of many was the reality of religions that were other than *Landesreligionen*, beyond modern national and tribal boundaries.

Scholars who had for decades been in the academic-scholarly trenches with Mueller were invited to the parliament. That such invitations were extended was most interesting: this was acknowledgment that religion could and should be examined by those thought to be the high-minded outside religious domains. Mueller wrote a paper to be read, but he was not in attendance. This was the case with most other scholars of his stature and orientation. There is speculation that it was advanced age that explained his absence, but there is reason to believe he was not a little anxious over what was being made of his work: religions around the world, including world religions, were being showcased as developments or phenomena for proselytizing or other similar purposes (Masuzawa 2005, 265–74). Might this interest also have been the flip side of the politics of governance among nations or empires?

A generally available photo of the gathering shows (the person I take to be) Schaff in attendance and slated to read a paper. He appears gaunt. Records indicate he was indeed ill, even near death but wanted to attend. He was unable to read his paper.[7] The image I include with this essay is striking: it shows the coming together of all the interests addressed here in this essay. There it stands, as though on museum-, if not circus-, like display for the public—religion (or the male human stand-in for such). Here is religion to be considered outside of religious contexts. Religion to be talked about, made real through performance of discourse, mainly about texts, some coopted, embraced, stolen. All made to be venerable, canonical. Here literature/discourse and religion are tellingly confused. All delegates—including representatives of jurists and tribunals—and visitors are unified in a sense under the umbrella(s), the protection(s), of the empire(s) of the day.

How were delegates presumed or understood to relate to nations and empires that define themselves in relation to this or that religion? How could they be understood as other than officers or bureaucrats of a sort for nation/empire? What or whom did Schaff represent? I argue that he represents in one simple sense a particular type of religious movement (European-rooted Protestant evangelical), but at another level, perhaps, he represents what he and others at the time thought of as right-thinking ecumenism. But in a sense more poignant and to the point of this essay, he represented—through his religious affiliation, his teaching and scholarship, and through his guild-construction work, shaped by his Americanist orientation—what I prefer to call scripturalization, the modern regime of psycho-social-cultural and political-economic governance control. The different levels and types of affiliations and identities fold into and are best interpreted as this one phenomenon and dynamic. It is akin to what (as referenced already) Said (1993, 52) referred to as "structures of attitude and reference." This was what was in common, what was being staged or

---

7. See D. Schaff 1897, 469–510, especially 486–87. Interestingly, the son as author does not mention founding of the Society of Biblical Literature!

1893 Parliament of World Religions. Source: Wikimedia.

museumized at the Parliament. It is also what was at issue and the point of the academic-intellectual roiling during much of the nineteenth century. It can easily be argued to have been a major part of the impetus behind the founding and growth of the Society of Biblical Literature. The latter I take to be best understood as reflection of the interest in participating in the larger western psycho-politics of classification. Getting to the roots— the origins—of the movement, the religion that led to the formation of the modern and contemporary dominant empires—this is what mattered, even if empire did not always take note of the inside operations. For the most part policing the operations was not required. This is because, as Michel Foucault (1985) has taught us, all operations in the various domains learned how to participate in the regime of scripturalization as the genuine police.

Scripturalization became the common religion, the ideological formation around which the world—the civilized world, the discourse-cum-text-writing, text-manipulating, world—turned. All those peoples who were without religion, that is, without texts made (up to be) sacred, were deemed to be of a different order. They could and should be governed—*divide et impera* (Masuzawa 2005, 216). Relations with such peoples would be based less on the content of textual traditions about any group—although there were earnest and passionate exegetical gymnastics aplenty—than on the perception that peoples who possessed no texts might and should be judged and governed by the practices and politics of scripturalization. Scriptural play and politics could be extended to the point of ideologizing and fixing through discourse/writing the relative worth of the world of the nonscriptural readers/users. Here classification meant more than placement on a rung of the civilized; it was license to write on the bodies of the outsiders, to define, to fix identities and social position. The play of the scriptural within the regime of scripturalization was made broader, wider than the religious domain. It determined the orientation of all driving sectors and domains of society. Writing, as Levi-Strauss (2012, 299) and others have made clear, was invented to facilitate violence, slavery.

What was involved was more than exegesis. The latter was a sideshow, a masking of the driving dynamics. Exegesis represented obsessional mimetics—and silence, distraction, regarding the ongoing agenda of the politics of the regimes of scripturalization. Although play it was, exegesis was nonetheless deadly serious: it could be made to facilitate the fabrication and fixing of identity; it was the facilitator of psycho-social death.

How and why does Black flesh enter and help define (or disrupt) the situation? After first contacts—with the Others, with peoples of color—defining the modern order, a way and a reason needed to be found to fix the discovered peoples within the classification schema or hierarchy. As with the serious excavation of and play with language, especially the discovery of the function of inflection of language, so with the Black-fleshed, it was hard to resist ideologization of the inflection of bodies in the new schema of hierarchy. Black flesh from the perspective of white-fleshed men represented so much and too much in terms of difference. So Black flesh (later made body) was looked upon as if a text to be analyzed, manipulated, and written on. It was in fact too richly different, too layered, too haunting in the wake of all the violence done to it, not to be made into text" that is, made meaningful, scripturalized, hyper-signified (Long 1999; Miller 1986).[8] That is what Sojourner Truth, despite her incapacitation in terms of negotiation of western letters or texts, figured out about the reality of the violence of scripturalization, when she, in response to a journalist who asked if she would permit the writing of her life story, reportedly responded that she was not "ready" (ever?) to be "writ up" (Gilbert and Titus 1991, 234, 253). She knew the drill, the operations, and the stakes. That is why she preferred her own honest and self-elevating brand of masquerade, embodied performance, if not exactly in the poetics that Aimé Césaire called for, which she called "Sell[ing] the Shadows to Sup-

---

8. Provocative discussions about all such can be found in Long 1999 and Miller 1986.

port the Substance." (See her image of famous *carte de visite* below.) She refused to sell herself for or to others. A story with her antiscripturalism and persistent critique of scripturalization as focus in historical perspective also begs to be told.

The history of writing is filled with the history of violence, either of obsessive mimetic masking silence/denial/refusal/erasure or of obsessive mimetic playing of academic games. Whether under the auspices of churchly or academic guild or other types of organizations or institutions—political, social-cultural, and so forth—the violence that is scripturalization persists and must be addressed. That Black flesh has, since the development of modern-world regimes, been the special focus of, the social hermeneutical palimpsest for, scripturalization should give us—especially those of us defining ourselves as scholars of scriptures and carriers of Black flesh—deep

Sojourner Truth, "I Sell the Shadow to Support the Substance," 1864. Source: Metropolitan Museum of Art.

pause. Why would those of us who are carriers of Black flesh—finding ourselves within a professional society, a strange hyper-obsessive tribunal of jurists that is a blurry reflection and refraction, mostly silent and obsequious to be sure, of the regime that is scripturalization, with little or no history of self-reflexivity regarding such matters—why should we continue mimetic participation in, work to extend and legitimize, such a thing? Nothing short of a radical reorientation to the scriptural, inspired and provoked by the inflections that are Black-fleshed bodies, should justify continued guild participation.

Works Cited

Achebe, Chinua. 1958. *Things Fall Apart*. London. Heinemann.
Berlinerblau, Jacques. 2006. "What's Wrong with the Society of Biblical Literature?" *The Chronicle of Higher Education*. November 10. https://www.chronicle.com/article/whats-wrong-with-the-society-of-biblical-literature/
Foucault, Michel. 1985. *History of Sexuality*. New York: Vintage Books.
Gilbert, Olive, and Frances W. Titus, eds. 1991. *Narrative of Sojourner Truth; A Bondswoman of Olden Time, Emancipated by the New York Legislature in the Early Part of the Present Century; With a History of Her Labors and Correspondence Drawn from Her "Book of Life."* New York: Oxford University Press.
Lévi-Strauss, Claude. 2012. *Tristes Tropiques*. Translated by John Weightman and Doreen Weightman. New York: Penguin.
Long, Charles H. 1999. *Significations: Signs, Symbols and Images in the Interpretation of Religion*. 2nd ed. Aurora, CO: Davies Group.
Masuzawa, Tomoko. 2005. *Invention of World Religions: Or, How European Universalism was Preserved in the Language of Pluralism*. Chicago: University of Chicago Press.
Miller, Christopher L. 1986. *Blank Darkness: Africanist Discourse in French*. Chicago: University of Chicago Press.
Moore, Stephen, Yvonne Sherwood. 2011. *The Invention of the Biblical Scholar: A Critical Manifesto*. Minneapolis: Fortress.
Mueller, F. Max. 1873. *Science of Religion: Four Lectures Delivered at the Royal Institution; With Two Essays, on False Analogies, and the Philosophy of Mythology*. London: Longmans, Green.
———. 1879. *Sacred Books of the East*. Oxford: Oxford University Press.

Said, Edward W. 1993. *Culture and Imperialism*. New York: Vintage Books.
Schaff, David S. 1897. *Life of Phillip Schaff: In Part Autobiographical*. New York: Scribner's Sons.
Smith, J. Z. 1982. *Imagining Religion: From Babylon to Jonestown*. Chicago: University of Chicago Press.
Wimbush, Vincent. 2017. *Scripturalectics: The Management of Meaning*. Oxford: Oxford University Press.
Woodberry, George E. 1973. "Editorial." Pages 207–14 in *Comparative Literature: The Early Years, An Anthology of Essays*. Edited by Hans Joachim Schulz and Phillip K. Rein. Chapel Hill: University of North Carolina Press.

Part 2
#BlackScholarsMatter: Lessons and Hopes

Moving in-between Places and Academic Disciplines

RONALD CHARLES

Places are important. We are all from one particular place or from several places. I am from a place of laughter, of dance, of crying, of horrors, of dreams, and of nightmares. I am from Port-au-Prince, Haiti. It is a place that has formed who I am in great measure. From this place, I have learned to love, to play, to cherish life's blessings, to struggle against all kinds of obstacles, and to never take anything for granted.

My Childhood

I had a relatively peaceful and enjoyable childhood. Although my parents were not rich, my father had a small business that helped us to live in a decent home with a nice enough yard where I used to play soccer with my friends. I loved the outdoors, the plains, the rivers, and the outings I had with the scout group I joined when I was about nine years old.

I enjoyed going to church as well. Although my father was not a Christian as I was growing up, he took me to church with him sometimes. I still remember going to a Baptist church with him when I was about seven. The pleasant atmosphere of the church fascinated me. I even liked the shuffling sound of the Bible when the members were turning the pages to look for a passage. My dad's brother was a preacher at a different, smaller, Baptist church nearby. I was fascinated with the number of people cramped in that little congregation. The *leçons dominicales* (Sunday school) and the *moisson* (the harvest), when folks brought all kinds of provisions to the church, were all fascinating to my child's mind and imagination. I continued to frequent a Baptist church until I was thirteen.

I stopped going as a form of protest against the way the pastor of that church dealt with a child in the middle of a church service. The restless child was being noisy, so the pastor stopped his sermon in the middle of the service, took out his belt, and beat the child to submission and silence so that he could continue his preaching. I was disgusted. I stopped going to church for about a year.

I came back to church a year or so after that incident. I had then, not a conversion experience, but a sense of a needed response to God. I was baptized that year in a Pentecostal congregation.

Political Turmoil and Books as Safe Havens

The first event that pushed me to be aware of social injustice was when the so-called *Tontons Macoutes* (the bandits working to support the dictator Jean-Claude Duvalier, Baby Doc, son of the former dictator Francois Duvalier, Papa Doc) came to evict a poor family from their shack. These poor people were hopeless. I was angered by what happened to them, but I could not do anything. In early 1986, the Haitian population rose in thunderous fury against the regime, and Baby Doc had no choice but to leave. The US and French governments secured a nice and safe departure for the dictator. The major Western powers were simply interested in defending their own economic and political interests in Haiti, maintaining the status quo, and keeping at bay the specter of a second communist like Castro in Haiti.

Prior to the dictator's departure, many Haitians had been killed. Anyone could be eliminated, as long as they were suspected or perceived to be standing somehow against the dictator. I realized later on that my name was on a list of people to be killed. I was labeled a communist because I was a reader. Since I always carried a book with me wherever I went, that identified me at the young age of fifteen as a person to be eliminated. When I later learned that I was targeted, I became more careful about how I would carry my book, either in my pocket or hidden somewhere under my shirt so that I would not draw attention to myself in any way. Carrying a book in a neighborhood composed of mostly poor and illiterate folks came with its risks. Thus, I tried to protect myself by hiding my book.

Saved by Books

I love to read. I started to read seriously when I was thirteen years old. The first book I remember reading, and a book that had touched me profoundly, was a book by an Italian writer called Dino Buzzati (1967). The title of the book is *Le K*, taken from one of the stories from the collection. The K is a sea-monster that is capable of killing anyone who actually sees it. A young boy visiting his father, a sailor, sees the sea-monster following them. However, no one else does. He is cursed. His father lets him know that anyone who can have a glimpse of the sea-monster is cursed and will be certainly be killed by it. To protect his son, the father ensures that his son never comes back near the ship or near the ocean. Later on, the father dies, and the son becomes an adult. He never ventures near the sea. After a life fleeing from the sea-monster, the son now old, resigns himself to confront the sea-monster in mortal combat. Armed with his harpoon, he goes on the attack. The sea-monster appears to him sometime in the middle of the night. "I have been looking for you for so long," says the sea-monster. "I am tired and old from tracking you down. I have been looking for you all over the earth but not to devour you, as you thought. The ruler of the sea simply charged me to give you this." It was a magnificent pearl of great value. Two months later the man was found dead in his little boat with something in his hand that resembled a rounded stone.

I was stunned by this story. Here I was in Port-au-Prince, in my city full of dust and of noise, reading such a magnificent story. I vowed then never to run away from any monsters. I accepted the gift of reading.

Undergraduate Years

I was twenty years old when I finished high school. Because I wanted to continue helping my local church, I went to a Bible school in the morning. The goal was to attend for only two years until I could travel to the United States and be with my father. As the oldest in a family of five, I could help him to support the rest of the family. In the afternoon, I went to study for a degree in applied linguistics at the State University of Haiti. I loved languages and literature, and I wanted to teach high school. Instead of me emigrating to the United States, it was my father who came back to Haiti to die of a brain tumor. He was only forty-nine. I became extremely depressed and wanted to abandon everything. But for some reason, I did not. I persevered and graduated with a diploma in theology after four years, and I obtained a position as a translator working for the office of literacy in Port-au-Prince because of my training in linguistics.

Moving to Canada

Shortly after my graduation from the Bible school, I was asked by the leadership of that school to come and teach a class or two. In the course of that gig, the missionaries supporting that school approached me and asked me whether I would be interested in going to Canada to study at a seminary for a two-year master's program. Then I would return to Haiti and be part of the leadership of the school. Without hesitation, I accepted the offer. I said goodbye to my family and to my fiancée, promising her I would come back to marry her. I went to Toronto in August of 1997 to study at the Toronto Baptist Seminary and Bible College.

Toronto is the second place that has molded me. Toronto is a city of immigrants, with more than 50 percent of the residents born outside of Canada. I loved Toronto. It is extremely vibrant, unapologetically multi-ethnic, multicultural, and truly a cultural feast. I knew no one there. In fact, before going to Toronto, I knew nothing about it. When I landed in Montreal, I called the seminary's registrar to come and get me since I had arrived in Canada. He laughed on the phone and told me that yes, I was in Canada, but no, he could not come to get me since Toronto is about seven hours away from Montreal.

Seminary Years in Toronto

I felt truly blessed and privileged to study in Toronto. I also felt very lonely. I did not know anyone. I did not really speak English that well, having only learned it in my early twenties. I did not know anything about Canadian culture, the history of the place, the people, or the food. It was a real culture shock. I did not let any of that discourage me. I had to survive and to excel in a different world. I made very good progress in speaking English. I also managed to study Greek and Hebrew in that third language.

At the seminary, in my eagerness to learn, I took too many courses a semester. As a sponge, I wanted to absorb everything I could. I was so thankful for all I was learning in seminary. I was also discovering Canada as a great place to live, although a place with its problems as well, which I did not grasp at all during these times.

I did not understand the subtle and not so subtle anti-Black racism of Canada. One night, as I was walking to go buy some pizzas, a police car stopped by me. One of the officers said to me that they were looking for someone who looked like me. They wanted to see an ID. I gave them my seminary student card. They looked at it and said I was probably not the person they were looking for. I made nothing of the incident. I simply did not understand what was happening.

My seminary training was good, insofar as it allowed me to immerse myself more in Protestant and evangelical theological works. However, this kind of training did not help me to understand the nuances related to other belief systems. The seminary granted me a third year scholarship so that I could do an MDiv and write a thesis. I wrote my thesis under the supervision of Don Garlington, and soon after I went back home.

Back to Haiti

I went back to a Port-au-Prince in shambles, to a place where journalists were being killed, where those who could leave the country were departing en masse. I went back to a church that did not want a preacher who was deemed too political and too oriented to social justice in his preaching. I went to a position that was about to be terminated just about one year after my return.

After about two years back in Haiti, I was without a job and with a second baby. Shortly after, a Christian college located outside of Port-au-Prince invited me to teach and to reside on their beautiful and green campus. I loved it. My students loved me, and they thought I was so good at what I was doing that I should think of pursuing a doctorate in theology or New Testament. I agreed. I applied to Durham in order to do a PhD in New Testament and study with John Barclay. I was accepted, but because of lack of funding and with no support (none of my contacts in North America responded to any of my requests for help), I could not go to the United Kingdom.

Back to Toronto

I returned to Toronto after three and half years serving in Haiti. I could no longer tolerate the suffocating atmosphere of Haiti. The very oppressive climate of political unrest made it impossible for me to thrive. I felt hopeless and traumatized. I did not see any future for my kids. I returned to Toronto, now no longer a student but an immigrant. I continued to dream I could one day continue to study, but I had to pay the bills. Dreaming about doing a PhD was not realistic. I was then in my mid-thirties, with a wife and two kids in a foreign land.

After several failures at applying to various schools to continue with my studies, I was admitted by Wycliffe College, an Anglican seminary within the Toronto School of Theology located on the University of Toronto campus, to do an MTS. I finished my MTS at Wycliffe College, where I wrote a thesis under the supervision of Terry Donaldson.

I never enjoyed the luxury of simply focusing on my studies. I always did some kind of work to support my family. During my time as a graduate student in Toronto, I was also blessed to go on various tours with a Christian orchestra and choir for many summers, for about three weeks each time. These tours allowed me to visit many countries (New Zealand, Hungary, Serbia, Ukraine, Germany, France, Switzerland, Sweden, Argentina, Costa Rica, Puerto Rico, and the Dominican Republic). In my own professional travels, I have done research in Tübingen and in Israel-Palestine. Places are fascinating. No wonder I minored in diaspora studies and that I did my PhD thesis at the Department for the Study of Religion at the University of Toronto on Paul as a diasporic figure enmeshed in the highly complex and contested, ever-in-flux, and crisscrossing ways of the diaspora (published as Charles 2014).

Lessons Learned

My life has been rich in a variety of ways. Many places have shaped who I have become today. I have started my life with not very much, in terms of cultural and intellectual capital. One thing led to the next. The good hand of God has always guided me. I have opened myself to learn and to appreciate my blessings. I will briefly ponder on the lessons learned along the way.

1. Learning to do what is of interest to me, to continue to be myself, to accept my marginality

"Exile means that you are always going to be marginal, and that what you do as an intellectual has to be made up because you cannot follow a prescribed path" (Said 1994, 62). I have always accepted the fact that I was out of place. Career or fame have never been part of my mentality. Working hard, asking questions, and trying to understand various issues have propelled me forward. When I went to Toronto, I continued with my normal demeanor. I studied, I read voraciously, and I observed. In the course of my encounters with some colleagues, I realized that often career is at the forefront of their preoccupations. What they read, who they meet, where they go to school, everything is well orchestrated to guarantee academic success. Life has never given me, and so many others, the luxury of planning. We had to move; we had to leave home sometimes to escape from death, to flee from starvation, from persecution, from a life without any future, from the horrors that drove us away from our homelands to become misfits, out of place. In my case, I had a good family, a few good friends, some natural talents, but nothing else. I did not strive to study something with the prospect of elevating me up in the social ladder. My interests have always been to serve. Going to Bible school was so that I could serve my local church. Studying linguistics was to serve my people and understand them profoundly. To understand the language(s) of a people deeply allows one to understand the culture, the mores of these communities, and to continue to serve them better. I became interested in adult literacy, in translation, in teaching in general so that I could serve.

However, in my exile here in Canada, every so often I feel that I have failed. I have not been serving my people. I am wondering whether it has occurred to some academic colleagues that filing for promotion may be antithetical to the worldview of someone coming from noncompetitive cultures. I know I have worked hard and the evidence speaks for itself. However, in having to display my work and myself (this sounds even pornographic: hey, look at me!), I somewhat felt, especially in the process of applying for rank and tenure, that I was doing something I did not quite want to do. I felt I was asked to boast; I felt I was asked to show my individuality. Never in the process did I feel that my collective self was something important to ponder. I feel I need to acknowledge my ancestors, God, my family, my friends, and my colleagues in helping to shape who I am today. I did not do it on my own. I did not feel, or to be more precise, I *do* not feel I have accomplished much. I teach at a Canadian University, but what does that really signify? What does that mean to the countless brothers and sisters, many of them brilliant, with practically nothing? In a way, I feel guilty. I feel that I am maybe part of a larger problem, that of the successful postcolonial academic making it in the West.

How does one live with the sense of purpose and drive to explore academic matters while accepting one's marginality and sense of failure for not having been there with others from one's homeland? I cannot return home. One never goes home again. But then, what is home? Home is not static; home can be plural, and home may also be what Avtar Brah (1996, 16) calls "a homing desire."

While I was a graduate student at the University of Toronto, I was also fortunate to work as a volunteer coordinator with at-risk youths in very ethnically diverse schools in the Greater Toronto Area. I was also very present in the Haitian diasporic community in Toronto, serving as translator, speaker, and musician. I became very interested in trying to understand what it meant to be part of the Haitian diaspora, by critically thinking about structural and sociocultural factors that operate to reproduce powerlessness among Haitians in the diaspora. I came to understand that serious attention must be given to the culture, experience, and contributions of Haitians in the diasporic world. Attention must also be given to the intersection of religion and cultural expressions in the Haitian diaspora by understanding the importance of religion in the Haitian diaspora's experience of both oppression and liberation.

Haitians may be unaware of the experience of the Jewish diaspora, usually considered a prototype of diaspora, but they have learned and lived with the notion that home is more than a geographical entity. We create home by walking, by living, by dancing, by eating, and by making love and giving birth in new lands. We make home by dying here and accepting that it is impossible to go back. We cannot just go back home. I cannot plan to retire in Haiti. This thought alone is devastating, but that is the reality. Other immigrants can plan to buy a piece of property back home and dream of days when they are ready to depart to be among loved ones, at peace on their ancestral land to return to their ancestors. I cannot have such a dream. The North American soil, the cold Canadian land, will receive my bones. Many of us have to accept the reality that we will never be at home. Not in this life, nor in the next. We are forever scattered. We will never rest.

2. Reading broadly

I learned to read broadly, contrapuntally. My reading taste has always been very eclectic. The great collections of French literature in Lagarde and Michard introduced me to various periods of French literature from the sixteenth to the nineteenth century. I was an excellent high school student in French and Haitian literature. The Haitian authors of the nineteenth century did not divorce literature from political and social commentaries. When I went to university, I delved seriously into twentieth century Haitian authors. Haitian literature is extremely rich and versatile. I became a high school teacher to teach French and literature because of my love of reading. I shared my passion with my students by having them read and comment on these important and beautiful texts. Most of my books on Haitian literature are lost, or they are somewhere in a box at the family home in Haiti. This, too, adds to my sense of loss and of disconnect. Early in my twenties I was reading Fanon, Camus, Chomsky, Plato, Eduardo Galeano, Gabriel Garcia Marquez, Alejo Carpentier, Regis Debray, Karl Jaspers, Roland Barthes, and Paulo Freire. I contributed to writing opinion pieces on education, music, and philosophy for the main newspaper in Haiti (*Le Nouvelliste*) during this period in my life (1991–1996). It never occurred to me that students would later tell me when I started to teach at the university level in Canada that they are not readers. What a contradiction!

Naturally, when I started to do my scholarly work I integrated various authors into my thinking. I did not know the word *interdisciplinary* before coming to North America, but I guess that is what I have always been doing. My work is interdisciplinary in nature because I do not have the privilege of simply being a scholar of religions in the ancient Mediterranean worlds. The rigorous training in biblical languages, ancient history, and the patient learning of how to read ancient texts very closely has been extremely valuable in my scholarly work. However, as one from an impoverished Caribbean island, I always had to read a variety of critical texts (history, politics, linguistics, philosophy) in order to help me understand my own social location and the politics that have affected me and others like me. Thus, in graduate school, I was all the more eager to learn a lot from my seminar on method and theory in the study of religion and to take a year of directed study in sociology, coupled with a very important class on diaspora studies. These forays into various areas of enquiry enabled me to understand not only my field better, but also to understand my own place in the world in new and more sophisticated ways. In a sense, I feel I had no choice but to branch out of some of the narrower ways that sometimes characterize the field of New Testament studies. I had to continue exploring issues of identity, of identity formation, of silences, of gaps, of exploitation, and of power control. My research has been informed by diaspora studies, subaltern analysis, and postcolonial readings of cultural/religious texts.

As I look back at the books and articles I have been able to work on, there is a common thread that appears, namely, that of translation (see Charles 2015). Translation is about trying to bridge gaps between cultures, establishing intercultural dialogue and exchange. I see my interdisciplinary research as the labor of a cultural translator who is engaged in making connections between traditions and history. Doing history means continually questioning and reviewing some crucial moments in order to go beyond any unsophisticated understanding of the past. The past is not self-evident; it is always given through certain lenses that highlight and obscure certain perspectives. The researcher is necessarily engaged in a type of reflexive mode by moving between theory and evidence, by reflecting on his/her social positioning in doing certain work, and by exploring critically and reflexively what one's assumptions are in asking (and not asking) certain scholarly questions. This is why I did my book on *The Silencing of Slaves in Early Jewish and Christian Texts* (2019).

I want to continue to explore the religious and social contexts of migration and translation with an interest in understanding how religious texts continue to fascinate and direct the lives of many in the modern world. I feel I do not have the privilege to be lost in the ancient world and not be able to think critically about some of the complex issues facing the contemporary world.

I do not have the privilege of not having to worry about police violence against Black bodies. I live in that body. I have no choice but to try to find a sense of home. Where is home? What is home? The university is far from being the beacon of social justice. I need to know how to survive and how to thrive without losing my soul in this space that does not see me as one who deserves to be here. I cannot ignore that my ancestors were slaves, that many Black bodies like mine are enslaved today. I need to find a way to comprehend the genealogy of modern slavery by going back to some foundational myths.

All of these interests and difficult terrains means reading more (I try to read a book a week), studying to the point of exhaustion, questioning everything, and being overwhelmed by various realities. This kind of life is, of course, one that is extremely stressful but, to me, it is also an exhilarating one. I enjoy studying and sharing with others. I find pleasure in laughing at the structures of racism that impede me and others from moving forward. I don't get bitter; I get better. I do not have the privilege of being at home in one discipline. Not having that privilege allows me to understand the bewildering complexities of what interdisciplinary thinking entails. Not having the privilege of devoting myself solely to one discipline pushed me to be a better scholar of the humanities.

3. Imposter syndrome

I learned that the imposter syndrome, the nagging feeling that I am not good enough, may never go away, even after publishing three books in the span of five years.

Before writing these lines, I never mentioned my life in Haiti before in the context of my academic work in North America. I always felt that it was of no interest to others, either to fellow students, professors, or colleagues. My CV gives small hints of a life before here. However, "here" never seems to be too interested about "there," except to conceive it as caricature. Life's complexities in a country seen as a failed state is of no interest to many here in the beautiful and polite Canadian landscape. Sometimes I wonder whether it is not safer to be open about our frustrations in the context of the United States than in the Canadian context here. I frankly do not see how we could have a session on some of the issues raised during this Society of Biblical Literature #BlackScholarsMatter Symposium during a Canadian Society of Biblical Studies meeting. It is all about serious scholarship and not about issues of power, violence, and so on and so forth.

There are structural/systemic barriers that are in place in Canada (yes, here as well) that prevent racialized groups from advancing in many ways. These structures have affected the professional and personal lives of the very scholars we should be supporting for a healthier guild in biblical and theological studies. Too often diversity becomes a buzzword bereft of action.

However, any time I have felt discouraged I have reached out to scholars mainly in the United States, who are like me and who had to develop various ways to succeed. I know we deal with a lot, and I know people are busy and are very much focused or interested in their particular areas of expertise. I, too, have been busy developing as a scholar. However, I do not have the choice, or even the luxury, not to develop other areas of expertise (race critical theory, postcolonial studies, etc.) to understand the discursive landscapes, to navigate the systemic barriers, and to continue to grow as a person and as a scholar. The pains, the tiredness, the frustrations, and the invisibility are real.

My humanity matters. My stories matter. I certainly want to be respected for my excellence, but please understand what I had to go through to be where I am today. Do not brandish a supposedly objective criterion and pretend we all come from the same social, structural, and economic platform. I still have my self-doubt; my professional demons keep whispering into my ears that I am not good enough and that I will be exposed as a fraud. I do not want to be treated as a special case or as someone to be handled like a delicate glass. However, I sure need help; we all do. Helping means guiding; it means sharing. Helping a Black student or a Black colleague means sharing opportunities, sharing power, and making room for others who are unlike you. It means understanding the multiple hurdles a person of color had to go through to be where he or she is and offering words of wisdom, jobs, and opportunities.

It has been six years since I defended my doctoral dissertation. That same day in 2014 (February 7) my eldest son was celebrating his fourteenth birthday. I was forty-three. Today, my son is twenty. I am thinking of how time goes fast and what I have been able to do since my dissertation defense. I have now published three books, edited one volume, had several articles accepted in reputable journals, done countless book reviews, been accepted as a member of the *Studiorum Novi Testamenti Societas*, taught various classes in the discipline of biblical studies as well as classes in sociology, served on various committees (and continue to do so), and finally landed a tenure-track position in religious studies in a small undergraduate university.

I look like a success story, but somehow I do not feel happy. I am always struggling to find a bit of time to think, to write, and to find colleagues with whom I can discuss scholarship. I find the field of biblical studies to be somewhat limited in what it offers me. I keep wondering how one may make serious contributions in it and be engaged in conversations that do not necessarily care about the theological or church affiliations. I am not happy because of the direction of postsecondary education in general, with the university following more and more the corporate model, almost at the expense of quality education. I am not happy that I do not seem to have any time to grow as a scholar, to know my Greek better, to study more German, and maybe try Coptic. I am not happy that I have become a bit pessimistic about life and do not have more time to enjoy nature, to play my violin more, to have a life.

I guess there comes a point in every scholar's life when she or he realizes that she or he will never accomplish all that she or he had in mind.

There comes the realization that there is too much to be done and too little time to do it. When that scholar faces undue external pressures, that realization hits even harder. Not only do I deal at all times, consciously and unconsciously, with the destruction and abandonment of my own country of birth, now ten years after the massive earthquake that destroyed Port-au-Prince, I also have to deal as an early mid-career scholar with a world in utter and increasing disarray. Such consciousness of events outside our lives make our own sense of limitation as scholars, as immigrant scholars, even sharper. On the one hand, Haiti lies in ruins and utter dejection; on the other hand, the world is beset by a radical crisis in the world-system, one that encompasses any number of quite severe crises in their own right. Any individual with a sense of dignity and justice is bound to register such situations and developments at the core of their minds and bodies. Bodily health is affected, as is mental health. Illness and depression follow.

I hope I will be able to center myself in isolating that which keeps me going, making it the heart of life, and letting it encompass all else. It is no panacea, but it is a strategy, and one that has to be reinforced repeatedly. At the heart of it, there must be an option for life, for dignity and justice, for contentment and wellbeing. In my case, Haiti and social justice must be at the very center of such a heart.

4. Saying yes

I learned to say yes, but I need to learn how to say no. But how do you say no to a student who sees you as a role model and a voice for change? How do you say no to:

- speaking at a session on anti-Black racism at an orientation for new faculty
- serving on a Racial Justice Leadership Grant Adjudication Committee (2020)
- being part of a committee on the Status of Women and Equity (2016–2019)
- serving as campus representative on a committee on Aboriginal and Black Students Success

How do you say no to struggle and to joining in the struggles of others, while you try to be an active researcher? A senior scholar advised me to say yes to every invitation at the beginning of my career. I have followed this well-intended recommendation, almost to my own peril. I have tried to do well in everything that I promised I would do, but one can only do so much. I did not think of the physical toll such an attitude would foster.

I need to learn to say no, but how do you say no to students who see you as a role model? How do you say no when the university asks you to be part of conversations around race and equity? How do you say no to talking with a female and racialized colleague who is suffering from anxieties from being bullied by students, especially white male and very privileged students?

Recently, I have served as a panelist at two sessions for the Maple League Universities, answering questions from professors and colleagues working in the four Atlantic provinces about how to engage in decolonized pedagogy. I was also one of the speakers to offer a session to new professors at the university in 2020 on anti-Black racism, which focused on ways to teach that respect the humanity and the culture(s) of all students. My service extends to my profession at large by serving on steering committees and saying yes to being a voice for the Society of Biblical Literature: #BlackScholarsMatter (August 13, 2020). This reflection comes from that context.

I certainly need to learn how to say no. Recently a senior colleague sent a very wise unpublished reflection on "Making Choices—When to Say Yes" to me. I will need to continue learning and find a balance. Minoritized faculty members have the extra work of serving as a mentor, as a confidant who understands the loneliness and the extra burdens linked to systemic racism and oppression BIPOC students and colleagues need to navigate, and as a role model for minoritized students. This kind of service needs to be acknowledged because it is one that may not be noticed or described in any quantifiable way. I am happy to serve, even though in doing so I expend considerable time, effort, and mental energy. It is important that such ways of serving are clearly recognized and put within a larger framework of a system that almost requires minoritized faculty members to be stretched to the limits some time.

Hopes for the Future

1. I hope to see more people like me in a position to shape the field.

My first Annual Meeting of the Society of Biblical Literature was in 2007, while I was still a graduate student. That year, I barely had enough funds to go. I slept basically on a hotel room floor that two former professors of mine occupied. I felt totally lost. It was when I went to a session organized by the Fund for Theological Education that I felt part of a group that seemed to get what I was going through (the loneliness, the bewilderment, the lack of funding to move further in my studies).

2. I hope to see more people like me supervising graduate students at research universities.

I work in a religious studies context. I am one of two Black professors working in a public institution and being in a religious studies department in Canada. I am the only Black scholar teaching biblical studies in a public university in Canada. I was hoping the situation might be slightly different in the United States, but I am learning there are very few Black scholars in New Testament studies teaching at research institutions in the United States. This is what I have gathered thus far:

>   Richard Newton, University of Alabama
>   Demetrius Williams, University of Milwaukee
>   Musa Dube, Emory University

I would be happy to learn that there are in fact more. So, in the whole of North America, there might only be four of us teaching New Testament at a public (research-oriented) university. This is really stunning. The question to ask is why?

3. I hope New Testament scholars would read a little bit more about ancient history and about modern theories, especially postcolonial studies.

In graduate school, I was even more eager to learn a lot from my seminar of method and theory in the study of religion and to take a year of directed study in sociology, coupled with a very important class on diaspora studies. These forays into various areas of enquiry enabled me to understand not only my field better, but also to understand my own "being-in-the-world" (a good Sartrian concept) in new and more sophisticated ways. In the religious studies field, for example, there is a lack of sustained exploration of Paul's texts as ideological tools. The apostle's writings are hardly ever studied from a comparative standpoint and by using the tools of other disciplines such as comparative religion, sociology, historiography, anthropology, or cultural studies. Moreover, there is a lack of theory, or theoretical sophistication, that would inform the field. Also missing is a lack of reflexive historiography related to Pauline studies.

A comparative approach would make it possible to explore the conditions of knowledge by interrogating data shown as evidence of certain theories and by probing the categories of thought, methods, and instruments of analysis that enter into practice in the analysis of a given problem. I am here, of course, influenced by the French sociologist Pierre Bourdieu. New Testament scholars would learn much from reading theoretical works that have guided many disciplines in the humanities in the last fifty years or so. I really wish that scholars working in the biblical field would try to understand it through a wider enquiry of religious studies. We simply cannot isolate the biblical field from other related fields of academic enquiry or even other religious traditions.

4. I hope New Testament scholars would read beyond their safe academic borders.

Finally, I hope New Testament scholars would take some time to read poetry and great novels, to read and to listen to voices from the margins. Scholars from the margins of what is considered serious/proper scholarship have a way to show what has been missing and to interrogate some taken-for-granted readings or conclusions. I have been much impressed and influenced in my thinking by reading Fernando Segovia, Musa Dube, R. S. Sugirtharajah, and others. I would like to conclude with these words from Sugirtharajah:

> The question is: do we want to replicate the colonial game of occupation and capture the center in the name of the oppressed, or do we want to demolish the center itself and redraw its parameters? The next set of questions will be: How many centers should we have? Who will provide the parameters? And whose resources will we draw upon to redesign them? These questions should keep biblical interpreters busy for a foreseeable future. (2006, 9)

Works Cited

Brah, Avtar. 1996. *Cartographies of Diaspora: Contesting Identities*. London: Routledge.

Buzzati, Dino. 1967. *Le K*. Paris: Presses Pocket.

Charles, Ronald. 2014. *Paul and the Politics of Diaspora*. Minneapolis: Fortress.

———. 2015. *Traductions Bibliques Créoles et Préjugés Linguistiques*. Paris: L'Harmattan.

———. 2019. *The Silencing of Slaves in Early Jewish and Christian Texts*. Routledge Studies in the Early Christian World. New York: Routledge.

Said, Edward. 1994. *Representations of the Intellectual: The 1993 Reith Lectures*. New York: Pantheon.

Sugirtharajah, R. S. 2006. *Voices from the Margin: Interpreting the Bible in the Third World*. 3rd ed. Maryknoll, NY: Orbis Books.

Questions with No COVID-19 Answers

STEPHANIE BUCKHANON CROWDER

Our profession as biblical scholars pivots around questions. Inquiry drives research. Research leads to more questions, queries, and quizzing. Questions conscript us. Yet, answers deem us scholarly worthy. Essays and articles uniquely resolve inquiry. Monographs and volumes in response to academic interrogatives place us on the lecture circuit and position us on esteemed panels. It is scholarship that nuances the answers. Such is the production that makes Luce pay attention, the Louisville Institute call, and Lilly affirm.

Answers are low-hanging fruit. Questions make us pause and savor the moment.

The first Black biblical scholar I encountered as an undergraduate student at Howard University was the late Dr. Cain Hope Felder. Although he was a profound staple in the Howard University Divinity School, it was not there where I first met Dr. Felder. Our paths crossed when he preached at Metropolitan Baptist Church in Washington, DC. His identity as a New Testament scholar and preacher intrigued me. As a child I was precociously fascinated with the who, what, when, and where of the Bible. Dr. Felder's sermon and presence further ignited that fire.

Not long after hearing Dr. Felder preach and while reading his *Troubling Biblical Waters: Race Class and Family* (1990), I became curious about Black women New Testament scholars. I wanted to know if there were persons who looked like me doing what I thought I wanted to do.

Where were the women? Answers are low-hanging fruit. Questions alter the trajectory.

All roads led to Dr. Clarice J. Martin. I met her during the inaugural "What Does It Mean to be Black and Christian?" conference at Vanderbilt University. Dr. Martin led a workshop on biblical studies and women as interpreters. Afterward I nervously introduced myself and told her what

I was contemplating for my professional future. It feels peculiar telling someone you want to "grow up and be like her," yet it was the truth. Now I had a visual to coincide with my vision.

I would connect with Dr. Martin again upon my acceptance to Vanderbilt's doctoral program years later. I phoned her, and much to my surprise, she returned my call. I inquired of what was then a *Stony the Road We Trod* scholarship fund. *Stony the Road We Trod: African American Biblical Interpretation* (Felder 1991) is the seminal volume featuring African American biblical scholarship. I had heard a certain amount of royalties from the book were set aside to provide financial support for African American students pursuing theological education. There were no more funds, but I had a fruitful conversation with Dr. Martin.

Where were the women? Questions alter the trajectory and shift a room.

In considering the ways in which #BlackScholarsMatter, I begin with a question Dr. Martin posits in her article entitled, "Womanist Interpretations of the New Testament: The Quest for Holistic and Inclusive Translation and Interpretation" (1990). Martin queries: "What concerns do womanist biblical interpreters bring to the translation and interpretation of the Bible?" (41).

What of questions? Questions shift a room and change one's course.

As Martin astutely answers this and many other poignant questions in her article, the interrogatives themselves remain just as contextually relevant now as they were thirty years ago. Therefore, for the sake of this exercise allow me to recontextualize past inquiries in this present setting using this tag: "Questions with No COVID-19 Answers."

What of questions? Questions make us pause and center ourselves.

The world is now more than a year and half into a COVID-19 context. Millions across the globe and hundreds of thousands in the United States have succumbed to a microscopic virus. Education shifted and is recalibrating its modalities. Theological institutions have not gone unscathed. What was once the bread and butter of in-person pedagogy is now the meal of online positioning and virtual instruction reality. The accelerated shift to remote work and teaching in the pandemic did yield moments of tedious rumination. Questions that captured my scholarly attention include:

- Who would have imagined efforts to expound on biblical contexts in a coronavirus context?

- Did anyone dare to surmise teaching exegesis, reading out, leading out of the Bible while trying to see one's way through a COVID-19 conundrum?
- When did the hallowed halls of academia instruct its subscribers on the tools of interpretation in the midst of stentorian social, emotional, and physical isolation?
- Where was the model for getting students to focus on methodologies while wearing a mask?
- Why is it no one told aspiring professors that someday lectures on soteriology, sanctification, *Sitz im Leben* would be filtered through hand sanitizer, bleach, Pine-sol, and Lysol?
- How are instructors supposed to stay calm, stay the course, stay connected, and perform biblical scholar due diligence when every day is "WTH," when there is always a "WTF" moment?
- When the name Fauci is just as pronounced as Foucault, Felder, and Fiorenza, what of this current situation?
- Where was the pedagogical path, the educational model for this watershed moment?
- To pivot from Martin's query, what concerns do womanist (*and all Black biblical*) interpreters bring to the translation and interpretation of the Bible in a context where, according to the *New York Times*, "Black people are three times more likely to contract the coronavirus, six times more likely to be hospitalized as a result, and twice as likely to die of COVID-19" (Wezerek 2020).

What of questions? Questions compel us to pause and ponder, particularly in a pandemic.

These are indeed COVID-19 questions for which our scholarly labs did not prepare answers. Such are the queries that render historical, form, and source criticism moot while leaving structuralism and deconstruction theories just as impotent and irrelevant. Nonetheless, as the theme of "Lessons and Hope" guides this #BlackScholarsMatter project, I posit one lesson for consideration: *sans* minimizing the context, there are moments that conscript us to magnify the question and let it carry the day.

What of questions? Questions conscript us to ponder and pensive posture in a pandemic.

Our profession pivots on questions. Yet, we cut our scholarly teeth on providing answers. We know how to deliver content within context. We are skilled at recreating settings. Our acumen is exhibited through decontextualization. Thus, although the past year or more has posed more than an ample share of dissonance, dis-ease, and discomfort, our discipline as biblical scholars offers some tools to recontextualize this time. Ours is the call to build biblical studies houses in a milieu that in many locales still mandates sheltering in place. Ours is the vocation to erect Hebrew Bible, First Testament, Old Testament, New Testament, and Second Testament edifices when places of shelter are unsteady and insecure at best, when a home is not home (Crowder 2020). To quote the late theosocio-musicologist, Luther Vandross (1981), such are the times when a "house is not a home" because home is now the faculty office, gym, preschool, and classroom.

The task is to revamp and reconstitute the skills mastered to unravel sacred texts and employ them for meaning's sake today. This is what methods do. Methodology is a path to meaning, a road to understanding, and a guide for getting to clarity. Of choice is cultural studies as an umbrella for placing social location in conversation with a given text. Identity shaped by geography, gender, economics, education, family, financial status, able bodiedness, religion, and race enter into spaces where reader and any work converge. A reader's who-ness is a guidepost on a road to sense making and stands center as interpretation shifts to practice. Thus, my existential reality as a Black woman is how and where and when I enter to engage questions.

Returning to Martin (1990, 41), "What concerns do womanist interpreters bring to the translation and interpretation of the Bible?" Through a womanist biblical interpretive lens, more succinctly, I strive to make meaning and find answers in this COVID-19 context. Some aver that with three vaccine options, these are post-COVID days mandating appropriate overtures. However, as not all have hopped on the vaccination train, may we proceed with cautious optimism. Thus, the present pandemic situation still looms large. It is in this virus-laden backdrop with womanist eyes that I attempt to comprehend the complexities of the global condition.

Womanism is a triangulation of race, gender, and class. Etymologically speaking womanism finds its roots in Alice Walker's (1979, 15) "womanist" while branching into theological spheres.[1] For Black women

---

1. Walker coined the word *womanist*. She chose the term over *Black feminist* because she deemed it more reflective of Black women's culture, especially Southern culture. Walker employs color play to define womanist as different from feminist. She maintains that womanist is a deeper shade of feminist just as purple is a deeper shade of lavender. See Walker 1997, 80; 1983, xi–xii. Delores Williams (1993, 34) asserts

dissenting with feminist agendas, Walker's womanist phrasing and framing were the catalysts to do a new thing. Since its inception and into current praxis, it is a means by which Black women could be both Black and female and work for the liberation of all Black people, especially the poor. According to Raquel St. Clair (2007, 56): "Walker's nomenclature furnished them [African American women] with the language and framework to be who they are and pursue liberation from sexist, racist, classist and heterosexist oppression."

Thus, what concerns do womanists and all Black biblical interpreters bring? Questions coerce us to ponder the present pandemic.

We bring ourselves, our whole selves, known, unknown, areas hidden, and those yet to be formed. To mine deeper this path, road, hermeneutical guide moves from cultural studies to womanist molding and rests at womanist maternal thought. Womanist maternal thinking is the gaze from which I, as a mother, wrestle with racism, sexism, classism, and the sundry of -isms and -phobias that were the prevailing pandemic before this pandemic. COVID-19 exacerbated these systematically oppressive measures.

A womanist maternal hermeneutic brings to the forefront voices of Black mothers within this racial, ethnic, spiritual and sociological context, whether the mothers are biological or women who for one reason or another took responsibility for another's child (Crowder 2016, 22). Womanist maternal thought addresses the specific racial context of Black women and the mothering challenges connected to it. It purports vicissitudes that are unique to mothers in this social and racial context, and therefore it is not universal.

Examining motherhood through the lens of Black women maintains circumstances that would seem to be general in nature become compounded due to race factors. Just as issues of racial identification shroud the actions by and perceptions of Black people, so do such elements touch the existence of Black mothers. Akin to the manner in which society attempts to demean women's existence and constrict their opportunities,

---

that a womanist theology challenges all oppressive forces impeding Black women's struggle for survival and for the development of a positive, productive quality of life conducive to the women's and the family's freedom and well-being. As a means of differentiating itself from other approaches to feminist hermeneutics, womanist theology branches off in its own direction, introducing new issues and constructing new analytical categories needed to interpret simultaneously Black women's and the Black community's experience in the context of theology or *God-talk*.

such efforts are more stacked against Black women. I purport Black mothers not only have to filter through sexist measures and racial roadblocks, but they, we, must also find ways to maneuver systemic blockades and speed bumps that devalue familial status. Thus, there is a triplicate hardship through which Black women who are mothers have to pummel. A womanist maternal thought is a triple-layered approach to understanding the nature of what it means to be Black, a Black woman, and a Black mother. It desires to reveal the organic complexities of women who live, move, and have their being in this ontological, racial, sexual and familial existence (Crowder 2016, 22).

There is a fourth dimension that perhaps yields a womanist maternal quadrilateral. This method not only scrutinizes the intersection of race, family, and gender constructions related to Black mothers, but this interpretive method also holds class dynamics to the light. Womanist maternal thought underscores economic status and its connection to Black mothers who work. The framework examines how categorical employment defines and is a determining factor in a Black mother's fiscal standing. Womanist maternal thinking undergirds that a core component of the role of Black mothers is their work or activity contributing to their children's wholeness and well-being. As corporate arenas and academic institutions erect monuments of career immobility for women, and Black women especially, the same obstacles present themselves to Black mothers forced often to choose between career and family.

Why mention womanist maternal thought in a COVID-19 context? Questions compel us to pause.

Estimates of over three million women left the workforce during the COVID crisis (Cerullo 2021). In many families, Black women are the primary child caregivers and have had to juggle working at home with children also at home. The jobs of mom, manager, teacher, counselor, cafeteria worker, and CEO all morphed into one online profession with little to no Zoom relief and at the same pay and exponential stress. The Brookings Institute contends that most Black mothers tend to be single, some by choice (Smith and Reeves 2021). Where family support is limited or nonexistent, mothers are the be all, end all in a pandemic or not. In addition any number of Black mothers work low wage jobs where paid time off is a premium. COVID-19 hit sectors such as retail, hospitality, and dining the hardest, and these industries tend to employ any number of Black women (Smart 2021). Furthermore, there is a dearth of scaffolding around race and childcare. The privilege of taking leave with pay to take care of child or self does not come so easily. Are there exceptions? Absolutely. The academy affords any quantity of such luxuries for so many of us #MotherScholars. Our gaze must also be on the working mothers who clean our academic offices. What of their COVID-19 lot?

Why mention womanist maternal thought in a COVID-19 context? Questions compel us to pause.

Black maternal health was compromised prepandemic. Black women were four to five times more likely to die in childbirth before COVID-19 (Adams 2021). The well-being of expecting Black women remains just as precarious. While it will be sometime before substantial COVID-impact data is ascertained, the stress from the pandemic, economic fallout for families, and that Black people in general have been three to four times more likely to die from the virus offer a dim glimpse of what could be the effects on Black expecting mothers. From a different maternal angle, a June 2020 report from the Guttmacher Institute—a research organization dedicated to advancing sexual and reproductive health and rights—discovered that more than 40 percent of women had changed their plans for motherhood because of COVID-19 (Young 2021, 79). Of the 2,009 cisgender women age eighteen to forty-nine surveyed, 44 percent of Black women said they now want fewer kids or have decided to have them later (Young 201, 79). Testing positive for COVID-19 and uncertainty around sound prenatal treatment during the pandemic are among the factors.

Why mention womanist maternal thought in a COVID-19 context? Questions call us to pensive positioning.

On May 25, 2020 a fake twenty dollar bill cost George Floyd his life. For over nine minutes, a now convicted Minneapolis police officer felt it not inhumane to kill Floyd. This man in blue drove his knee into Floyd's neck. During what seemed like hours, Floyd voiced not being able to breathe. He pleaded and cried for his life. Before he died, George Floyd called for his deceased momma. He is now buried near her.

Questions shove us to pause, pray, and protest.

As a biblical scholar, administrator, author, minister, and, more importantly, mother of two sons, I have been asking, How did COVID-19 happen? When will it end? How many contracted the virus today? How many died? What does all of this mean? Since March 2020 when my home became a college dorm, I have been wondering what my dearly departed grandmother would have done to traverse this coronavirus world? I have ruminated day in and day out on my mother who took her own life. What would she have done in the midst of these unsettling times? Live the questions now.

I have been leaning on the womanist maternal shield because from birthing centers to daycare facilities to the sanctuaries of churches, mosques, temples, and synagogues to the corridors of colleges, universities, seminaries, and divinity schools, the coronavirus has left nothing unsullied or unscathed. Homes were and some still are community centers, recreation centers, cafeterias, playgrounds, homerooms, first through sixth periods, and summer camps. Parents were teachers. Big Momma was the tutor. Nana was IT director. MaDear was the principal. Papa was guidance counselor. A womanist maternal lens in these COVID times illumines community mothers, other mothers, AuntieSisterMoms, UncleMomma, church mothers, and all maternal figures in whatever gender manifestation and identification and whether biological or not. This has been and remains an all maternal hands on deck state of emergency. The vacillation between past and present is noteworthy as there are now three vaccine options. Conditions have ameliorated, but are not completely resolved.

What concerns do womanist biblical interpreters bring to the translation and interpretation of the Bible?

This exercise has in a circuitous way addressed what womanist biblical interpreters bring to the translation and interpretation of the Bible. I am clear its scaffolding has centered on what womanist biblical interpreters bring to any context, particularly a coronavirus context. Because before we engage texts removed thousands of years from the present, womanist biblical interpreters interrogate by reading the here and now.

This work has asked innumerable questions. The #BlackScholarsMatter symposium also posed a question, "What are your hopes for biblical studies?" My answer resides in womanist maternal thought and rests with my mother and, more specifically, my grandmother.

When I was a child, I recall hearing my grandmother say of a friend, "I appreciate Ms. Peterson. She really came through for me. She hoped me." I responded, "What do you mean she hoped you?" My grandmother chuckled. "When I say she 'hoped' me, that means she helped me."

What might have been a homonymic error or mistake in semantics to me, for my grandmother was an existential reality and proleptic positioning, for to help her was a way of giving her hope. The help she received rendered her hope for a better today and, perchance, a brighter tomorrow. Her hope grew deeper, because the source, the community, of her help grew wider.

Romans 8:24–25 says, "For in this hope we were saved. But hope that is seen is no hope at all. Who hopes for what they already have? But if we hope for what we do not yet have, we wait for it patiently" (NRSV).

What concerns do womanist biblical interpreters, do Black biblical scholars, bring to the translation and interpretation of the Bible in this coronavirus context? Here is an answer to another question posed in this exercise: we bring hope. We render hope that our identity must feed interpretation; our who-ness sojourns with hermeneutics. We offer hope that our guild will never force anyone to sacrifice the sanctity of their sociological status for the sake of sound biblical exegesis. *But if we hope for what we do not yet have, we wait for it patiently.*

Our profession pivots around inquiry. Interrogatives drive research. Queries conscript us. We wrestle with, and wait in, the questions despite the absence of COVID-19 answers.

Works Cited

Adams, Char. 2021. "In Pandemic Times, Black Maternal Health Is More Important than Ever." *NBC News*. April 14. https://tinyurl.com/SBL03112b.

Cerullo, Megan. 2021. "Nearly 3 Million U.S. Women Have Dropped out of the Labor Force in the Past Year." *CBS News* February 5. https://tinyurl.com/SBL03112c.

Crowder, Stephanie Buckhanon. 2016. *When Momma Speaks: The Bible and Motherhood from a Womanist Perspective*. Louisville: Westminster John Knox.

———. 2020. "When Home Is Not Home." *Church Anew*. 14 July. https://tinyurl.com/SBL03112d.

Felder, Cain Hope. 1990. *Troubling Biblical Waters: Race, Class, and Family*. New York: Orbis.

———, ed. 1991. *Stony the Road We Trod: African American Biblical Interpretation*. Minneapolis: Fortress.

Martin, Clarice. 1990. "Womanist Interpretations of the New Testament: The Quest for Holistic and Inclusive Translation and Interpretation." *JFSR* 6.2:41–61.

St. Clair, Raquel. 2007. "Womanist Biblical Interpretation." Pages 54–62 in *True to Our Native Land: An African American New Testament*

Commentary. Edited by Brian Blount, Cain Hope Felder, Clarice Jannette Martin, and Emerson B Powery. Minneapolis: Fortress.

Smart, Tim. 2021. "COVID-19 Job Market Wreaks Havoc on Black Women." *U.S. News and World Report*. 15 April. https://tinyurl.com/SBL03112e.

Smith, Ember, and Richard V. Reeves. 2021. "Black Moms Facing the Toughest Childcare Crunch: How Policy Can Help." *Brookings Institute*. 24 February. https://tinyurl.com/SBL03112f.

Vandross, Luther. 1981. "A House Is Not a Home." Track 7. *Never Too Much*. Epic Records.

Walker, Alice. 1979. "Audre's Voice." Pages 79–82 in *Anything We Love Can Be Saved: A Writers' Activism*. New York: Random House.

———. 1983. *In Search of Our Mother's Garden*. Orlando: Harcourt.

Wezerek, Gus. 2020. "Racism's Hidden Toll." *New York Times*. 11 August. https://www.nytimes.com/interactive/2020/08/11/opinion/us-coronavirus-black-mortality.html.

Williams, Delores. 1993. *Sisters in the Wilderness: The Challenge of Womanist God-Talk*. New York: Orbis Books.

Young, Taiia Smart. 2021. "An Unexpected Change of Plans: Black Women, Motherhood, and the Pandemic." *Essence Magazine*. May/June.

Lessons and Hopes on How to Save a Life: The Life of the Black Biblical Scholar

STEED VERNYL DAVIDSON

A sincere word of appreciation is due to the organizers of the #BlackScholarsMatter Symposium. You have offered me an exciting opportunity in a year when excitement is all too uncommon. This event helps to fill the deep gap created by a virtual annual meeting and the absence of the opportunity to take advantage of what the Society of Biblical Literature and its Annual Meeting has meant for me: the place for networking with the scholarly community that I have created over the years. Make no doubt about it, the Society is an intensively white space. However, with enough social capital, curiosity, collaborative work, and charm, the Annual Meeting has become host to a set of shared parasitic tendencies necessary for the intellectual and scholarly survival of those in my community.

I have found myself in organic communities at the Society of Biblical Literature that I may or may not have formed, may or may not have been invited into. As things happen, these fluid groups, if they should be called that, gather around the rejection of the presuppositions that form the Society as an arm of the university and by extension the knowledge/power component needed to sustain the colonialist structures of western modernity. Over the years, we have had various versions of these current conversations, raised our voices in strategic places in the guild, as well created alternative spaces to pursue the sort of work that could sustain our lives. By lives here, I do not mean the way words and goals like diversity take on "institutionalized lives" as Sara Ahmed (2012, 60) sees it. Ahmed speaks not only of the "tiredness" (61) of the word diversity but the way it "sticks to certain bodies, such that bodies in turn can become stuck" (62). In the end, we live these lives trying to speak to institutions whose ears are blocked with buzz words and actions that might get a paternalistic response. We keep up these vain actions in order to maintain our place in the university. What I mean instead is life. And I mean work that fills life out. In these reflections, therefore, I carve out a space described as revolutionary and fugitive, informed in part by the work of Stephano Harney and Fred Moten (2013, 26) who propose postures such as the "refugee colony," the "gypsy encampment, to be in but not of" as "the path of the subversive intellectual in the modern university."

The legacies of my Caribbean identity as placed within the contours of the Haitian Revolution, maroons in Jamaica and St. Vincent, or the numerous rebellions and acts of sedition staged by enslaved Africans in the archipelago also inform this revolutionary and fugitive posture. I invoke these formations here because I have become all too aware that securing and sustaining a place within the academy means constantly responding to the academic interpellation of Black scholarly life. Edgy enough to be seen as cool. Rigorous enough to be taken seriously. Afrocentric to the extent that it does not displace Eurocentric ways of being and ways of knowing. In other words, don't protest, don't oppose, and don't be revolutionary; be content with having a place on the inside. Growing up with racism without racists made it possible for me to respond to the siren calls of the academy. The slow recognition that I could not attune my voice to the academic accents or twist my writing to the acceptable styles without a great deal of agonizing effort has made me more despondent but also more defiant.

When I wrote my dissertation, I included a quotation from African biblical scholar Musa Dube that describes the legacies of the Bible in Africa and the experience of Africans engaging the Bible. Dube (1997, 13) describes the experience of reading the Bible as "dangerous memories of slavery, colonialism, apartheid, and neo-colonialism. To read the Bible as an African is to relieve the painful equation of Christianity with civilization, paganism and savagery." This quotation stuck with me for several reasons. For one, I thought it was a harsh assessment. Second, I thought that this was the terrible African reality that didn't apply to my experience in the Caribbean. Despite my easy dismissal of her view at that time, fifteen years later the insight remains with me to the point that I can embrace it as my experience. Settler Christianity convinced me that, within the Bible it promoted as divine word, I had a copy of the sweet loving Jesus. Instead, this Bible is more the product of the cultural, political, and religious movements within European empires that shape our modern world.

As I am writing a book on postcolonial biblical criticism within the excesses of neoliberalism, I come to realize how racial capitalism has shaped a world with the complicity of biblical texts. When I wrote my dissertation at the time of the US invasion of Iraq and the counterinsurgency, I was living out in real time ancient imperial aggressions and imperialist logics that I was reading in the Bible that were also emerging from the country where I lived. These are deeply searing experiences that by rigorous academic standards should be editorialized out of my writing. And should I include them, the resultant work will be assessed as less than scholarly. Systems like these persist because the daily work of reforming them by people like me sustains them in their missions. Admittedly, I name my complicity in the reforming and therefore the perpetuation of the systems: professor of Hebrew Bible, academic dean, general editor of an SBL Press book series. These are comfortable titles, prestigious if the aim of my life is to build these credits. Instead, I aim for the revolutionary place where I use positions like these to undo the systems that do not support real life.

The fuller life I want for myself and for others beset by the colonialist project is the revolutionary life, the life of protest, escape, and destruction of systems that never were designed for us or our full thriving. Not yet sufficiently courageous, I take small steps with the hope to join the work of others in dismantling the minions of racial capitalism with agents such as settler Christianity and the university. I embrace acts of sedition: slow writing and rejection of a value system that wishes to evaluate me based upon my production of writing for the increasingly narrow and limited audience of scholarly biblical work. My revolution consists of sleeping at night in order to preserve my body rather than surrender it to the tiresome demands of the celebrity adjacent status I could achieve if only I perform the mimesis that at best gets me to the point of "almost the same but not white" or "not quite/not white" (Bhabha 2004, 128, 131). I advocate for the type of scholarly writing that enables the use of what Edward Kamau Brathwaite (1984, 5) regards as "nation language" defined as the English of "the people who were brought to the Caribbean, not the official English now, but the language of slaves and labourers, the servants who were brought in by the conquistadores." This expressive form of English disrupts the assumptions and "language of the conquistador, the language of the planter, the language of the official, the language of the anglican preacher" (8). I do so, knowing that the issue is more than simply words but the interruption of systems that have forced people to learn and reproduce knowledge that has no relevance to their lives.

This opportunity can be a moment where we tinker around the edges to pursue the path of diversity, equity, and inclusion within a system designed to exact value from Black bodies. Managing diversity has always been an imperial preoccupation. Instead, this opportunity can be one where we rethink the systems of scholarly engagement and knowledge production around the Bible. In doing so, we come to terms with the fact that our work is about deconstructing the great "English book" (Bhabha 2004, 146) and its related book culture that emerged out of colonialist western modernity. The ancient text is largely lost to us. In this revolutionary and fugitive work, we value various ways of knowing, various tongues, and importantly invest in life giving work. My reflections here may be short on specifics and long on zeal and enthusiasm to burn something. Including an affective touch to my reflections serves part of my point of how academic life requires us to sunder aspects of our selves. Because Black lives are already seen as not *quite*, to bring our Black selves into academic spaces with the colonialist assumptions of the university means we enter as less than whole beings. The Society of Biblical Literature, if it is to truly value Black life in all of its fullness, needs to attend to the structures that implicitly and explicitly truncate the Black scholar at the point of formation with a misshapen existence as the best possible future of scholarly existence. At its best the Black scholar's life exists within the nuances of the community, attentive to the searing questions and felt needs of people whose lives continue to be distorted by a colonialist system that thinks that it is good and doing good in the world. Black scholarly life interprets, translates, and communicates the murmurs, groans, and celebrations of Black people, indigenous people, queer folk, disabled folk, and on and on, the aspirations of those made of no account who indeed matter. That's the life that I am willing to invest in and join the revolution to see it happen or head to the hills to build it if it cannot be built in existing spaces.

Works Cited

Ahmed, Sara. 2012. *On Being Included: Racism and Diversity in Institutional Life*. Durham, NC: Duke University Press.
Bhabha, Homi. 2004. *The Location of Culture*. New York: Routledge.
Brathwaite, Edward Kamau. 1984. *History of the Voice: The Development of Nation Language in Anglophone Caribbean Poetry*. London: New Beacon.

Dube, Musa W. 1997. "Towards a Postcolonial Feminist Interpretation of the Bible." *Semeia* 78:11–26.
Harney, Stefano, and Fred Moten. 2013. *The Undercommons: Fugitive Planning and Black Study.* Brooklyn, NY: Minor Compositions.

What I've Learned

Vanessa Lovelace

I want to focus on what I've learned as a Black woman scholar in the Society of Biblical Literature, and what I've learned first is to give honor to whom honor is due. So, I begin by acknowledging those Black biblical scholars who preceded me in the academy and continue to be major influences on my scholarship today: mentor and former colleague Randall C. Bailey, Renita J. Weems, Charles B. Copher, Cain Hope Felder, Clarice J. Martin, and Vincent L. Wimbush.

I learned from them that, instead of waiting for someone to acknowledge your research as a scholar and finally publish your work, to invite Black and other scholars of color to publish their own edited volumes so that their scholarship is accessible in the classroom. *Stony the Road We Trod: African American Biblical Interpretation*, edited by Cain Hope Felder (1991), remains a classic text used in introductory biblical studies and African American hermeneutics courses. There is also the *Africana Bible: Reading Israel's Scriptures from Africa and the African Diaspora*, edited by Hugh Page, Randall C. Bailey, Valerie Bridgeman, Stacy Davis, Cheryl Kirk-Duggan, Madipoane Masenya, Samuel Murrell, and Rodney Sadler (2009); *African Americans and the Bible: Sacred Texts and Social Textures* edited by Vincent Wimbush (2000); and *They Were All Together in One Place? Toward Minority Biblical Criticism* edited by Randall C. Bailey, Tat-siong Benny Liew, and Fernando F. Segovia (2009).

Their example of collaborative work and cooperation was the model for *Womanist Interpretations of the Bible: Expanding the Discourse*, a volume Gay L. Byron and I edited in 2016. I don't know if it is true for them, but I can say that *Womanist Interpretations of the Bible* grew out of a series of ongoing conversations at the Annual Meetings of the Society of Biblical Literature, specifically the Annual Meeting in San Francisco in 2011.

I also learned from them the importance of citing Black and other minoritized scholars, especially Black and brown women scholars in all my work. I have cited every one of these scholars at some point in my teaching and writing. If we do not promote and share one another's work, who else will? And not just in print but also on social media. I love the hashtag #CiteBlackWomen. Every chance I get I "like," tweet, or retweet the work of Black and other minoritized scholars that I see mentioned on social media. This is how we extend the important work that we are doing to a wider audience.

I learned the importance of paying it forward. My teaching and research have advanced over the years because someone—and not just Black scholars —invited me to serve on a committee or to contribute to a writing project, passed along my name to write a book review or article or chapter, wrote a reference letter on my behalf to apply for a grant or workshop or job, read or edited a writing assignment or proposal or just offered their support. A number of these encounters or opportunities occurred at the Annual Meetings. I would like to pause to acknowledge some of these people—Nyasha Junior, A. J. Levine, Claudia Camp, Cheryl Kirk-Duggan, Gale Yee, Ahida Pilarski, Julia O'Brien, Susanne Scholz, and Ken Stone, among other biblical scholars who offered their support and extended publishing opportunities early in my career.

I have paid this forward by identifying and encouraging new and potential scholars to investigate and apply for the Forum for Theological Exploration fellowships. I have submitted names of new faculty members to attend the Wabash Center for Teaching and Learning in Theology and Religion new faculty dinner held at the Annual Meetings of the Society of Biblical Literature. I encourage students to attend the Society of Biblical Literature and American Academy of Religion annual or regional meetings. I invite doctoral students and junior scholars to serve on the Society's Women in the Biblical World unit, which I cochair, or as session moderators and panelists at the Annual Meetings. I read papers, write reference letters, and offer whatever assistance I can to help advance them in their career. One of the things I am most proud of is the decision by Gay and I to include an independent scholar, junior scholars, and a PhD candidate to contribute to *Womanist Interpretations of the Bible*. This is not about me but about the importance of the obligation to pass along what I was given to early career faculty and graduate students.

I am encouraged by the young scholars of color that are celebrated each year at the Forum for Theological Exploration reception at the Annual

Meeting, those rising scholars that I have been privileged to collaborate with—Ericka Dunbar, M. Tong, Justin Reed, and Febbie Dickerson—and those doctoral students who are in the pipeline. As hopeful as I am by their potential, I am yet dismayed that over thirty years after the first US-born Black women earned terminal degrees in Hebrew Bible/Old Testament and New Testament/early Christianity, in 2020 Black women with terminal degrees in biblical studies number just under forty. Of those, two are deceased, and at least five are no longer working in the academy at a seminary, divinity school, or religion or philosophy department at a college or university.[1] Indicative of this observation is the fact that the overall reported number of members in the Society of Biblical Literature of African descent in 2018 is just above 5 percent ("2019 SBL Membership Data").

Given the recent purging of faculty at US colleges and universities during the coronavirus pandemic, I wonder whether there will be a job for those doctoral students and graduates upon the completion of their degree program.[2] Black scholars matter. The loss of these brilliant Black and other scholars of color in the academy will be woefully felt for a generation. The damage to our intellectual enterprise, not experienced since the attacks on Black educational achievement, recounted by Carol Anderson in *White Rage: The Unspoken Truth of Our Racial Divide* (2016) that documents the dismantling of Brown v. Topeka Board of Education decision by white supremacists will be immense. #CiteBlackWomen. Some may say given the isolation and discrimination against Black scholars that they are better off without the academy. That may be true, but the academy would not be better off without Black scholars.

Black scholars matter. I bring my embodied Black woman self and womanist scholarship to my classroom. My students and colleagues benefit from my teaching and my research matters. I have unapologetically written as a womanist scholar on the intersection of the Hebrew Bible, race, gender, sexuality, and class and have taken every opportunity given to share biblical scholarship from the context of Black women and other women of color's experiences despite the resistance and challenges to me

---

1. African and Caribbean women who earned terminal degrees in biblical studies in the United States bring the list to just over forty.

2. The Department of Labor reported that in 2020 US colleges and universities cut 650,000 jobs due to the impact of the coronavirus pandemic. While these numbers represent 13 percent of higher education workers, nontenure track faculty, adjunct, and contingent faculty took a big hit from the layoffs (Bauman 2021).

as a teacher and scholar. I am nonetheless grateful that I have been privileged to enjoy the vocation of academic ministry that has allowed me to learn along with students on this theological educational journey as I hone my teaching and research skills in the classroom. Black and Black women scholars matter. Lastly, I am excited that, since the Black Scholars Matter Symposium took place, we can celebrate the election of South African biblical scholar Musa Dube as the first Black woman president of the Society of Biblical Literature after more than thirty years of Black women members in the guild.

Works Cited

Anderson, Carol. 2016. *White Rage: The Unspoken Truth of Our Racial Divide*. New York: Bloomsbury.

Bailey, Randall C., Tat-siong Benny Liew, and Fernando Segovia, eds. 2009. *They Were All Together in One Place? Toward Minority Biblical Criticism*. SemeiaSt 57. Atlanta: Society of Biblical Literature.

Bauman, Dan. 2021. "A Brutal Tally: Higher Ed Lost 650,000 Jobs Last Year." *The Chronicle of Higher Education*. February 2021. https://www.chronicle.com/article/a-brutal-tally-higher-ed-lost-650-000-jobs-last-year.

Byron, Gay L., and Vanessa Lovelace, eds. 2016. *Womanist Interpretations of the Bible: Expanding the Discourse*. SemeiaSt 85. Atlanta: SBL Press.

Felder, Cain Hope, ed. 1991. *Stony the Road We Trod: African American Biblical Interpretation*. Minneapolis: Fortress.

Page, Hugh, et al., eds. 2009. *Africana Bible: Reading Israel's Scriptures from Africa and the African Diaspora*. Minneapolis: Fortress.

Society of Biblical Literature. "2019 SBL Membership Data." https://www.sbl-site.org/assets/pdfs/sblMemberProfile2019.pdf.

Wimbush, Vincent L., ed. 2000. *African Americans and the Bible: Sacred Texts and Social Textures*. London: Continuum.

Mentoring Matters

Kimberly Russaw

The title and purpose of the two-day #BlackScholarsMatter Symposium lends itself to considering not only what it means to be a Black scholar of the Bible but what it means to support both Black biblical scholars *and*, more to my point, Black graduate students in the area of biblical studies. For the time that is mine, I invite us to focus our attention on *targeted mentoring* and *instructional ethos* as critical components of the larger enterprise of our guild transforming our academic spaces so that these spaces become more welcoming and supportive of black, brown, and beige bodies.

I am particularly invested in the work of mentoring and helping to prepare emerging scholars of color in theological and religious studies education, especially Black biblical studies students. For the last several years, I have coordinated the doctoral mentoring efforts of the Forum for Theological Exploration. The Forum for Theological Exploration is a leadership incubator dedicated to cultivating diverse young adults to be faithful, wise, and courageous leaders for the church and the academy. Important for this evening's conversation is the Forum's long-standing commitment to supporting doctoral students of color *through* graduate school and *into* vocations of teaching and scholarship in theological education and religious studies. The Forum includes a mentoring component in its doctoral fellowship program. This mentoring component partners scholars in the Forum's network—many of whom were fellows themselves—with current doctoral fellows. This mentor-mentee program is designed to journey with doctoral fellows as they matriculate during their fellowship year, through scheduled check-ins with the fellows *and* their academic advisors. This mentoring approach responds to research, which demonstrates that when our fellows connect with mentors and receive support, they simply fare better in their programs.

Recently, the Forum's data reveal three challenges for students of color in theological and religious studies programs from which our guild can learn. These challenges are: ways of being in the academy, isolation, and communication with advisors. Here, it is important to keep in mind that, for Black graduate students in biblical studies, these challenges are exacerbated by instructional ethos in general; and the dynamics of language classroom in particular.

Challenge 1: Ways of Being in the Academy

For Black doctoral students, an important part of the mentoring process involves helping students manage the challenge of "*being* in the Academy." Students learn early that they must have a public face. During their doctoral programs, fellows are challenged by their differences. Fellows work to maintain a public face as they struggle with problems communicating with their advisors and persons in authority. Fellows also suffer from isolation among their colleagues. Furthermore, many fellows are challenged by the social customs and norms of academic spaces and culture. This is particularly challenging for international students and first generation graduate students of color born on American soil. For instance, academic methodologies in theological education may require a different worldview than many Black students may be comfortable with. Many of these students have been formed in and supported by conservative faith-based communities, and much of the critical *academic* study of the Bible challenges (their) long-held beliefs. While the students embrace that challenge, and even excel in their learning, this new intellectual formation makes it difficult for them to return home and reintegrate into the religious spaces that have nurtured them. Additionally, many of our students confide that they were uncomfortable initiating relationships with their colleagues and vice versa—many of their colleagues seemed uncomfortable and/or appeared unwilling to initiate relationships with them. This information suggests that the admissions strategies of graduate programs must consider the make-up of non-Black students who will be part of our students' cohorts. Those responsible for sourcing students and faculty for graduate programs cannot overlook potential racist foundations that make it difficult for some students and faculty members to share space equitably and equally with students and faculty of color. Institutions must foster intellectual incubators that are intentional about including students and faculty that are comfortable engaging difference from both sides of the historical and cultural chasm. Black doctoral students who are navigating ways of being in the academy and unhealthy relational dynamics make the second concern—isolation—even more pronounced for students and scholars of color.

Challenge 2: Isolation

The self-isolation brought on by coronavirus safety protocols exacerbated preexisting feelings of isolation for some students of color in graduate programs. In order to mitigate isolation, the Forum for Theological Exploration works to share community accountability best practices with fellows throughout their doctoral programs. The Forum works to create spaces for collaboration and check-in among students and mentoring cohorts. This leads me to the third challenge for students of color in theological and religious studies programs that the mentoring data reveals: communication with advisors.

Challenge 3: Communication with Advisors

Communication with program advisors is critical for our students. Many of our assigned mentors share that program advisors are busy and are looking for the fellow to initiate (and follow up on) routine meetings and check in sessions. This is particularly difficult for students who are already statistically by themselves in these programs—in other words, they are the minority in their academic spaces. In addition to the advisor-student power dynamics at play, to expect a minoritized student—new to the program, still establishing trusting relationships, and living in isolation (with all of its attendant vulnerabilities)—to proactively drive the advising process is almost untenable. This approach discounts the historic systemic issues that render these students Other in academic spaces in the first place. Furthermore, this approach imprints forms of micro-aggressive systems that even the most well-intentioned institutions, seeking to expand their endeavors in diversity, equity, and inclusion, often read over. Graduate departments need to think deeply and take decisive actions toward creating collegiate communities that support Black students at the levels of peer conversation partners and faculty advisory support.

To be clear—in the discussion of #BlackScholarsMatter, mentoring matters. Especially in the area of biblical studies. Furthermore, unique to students in biblical studies is the additional burden of acquiring proficiency in the ancient languages.

Experiences of Language Acquisition

While many capable emerging Black scholars shy away from the language requirements for Bible degrees for various reasons, we cannot discount the very real and unhealthy experiences of Black students, especially Black female students, in language classes. I can point to anecdotal data and testimonials of Black female students who have experienced a double-edged sword of sorts while seated around the table in Semitic and Greco-Roman language courses. Sword is the correct metaphor here because navigating language courses and competencies can be a matter of life or death for many of us in biblical studies.

One edge of the sword that Black students encounter is the presumption of incompetence in language studies. This belief in our students' incompetence manifests in instructors not inviting them to participate fully in class exercises (perhaps because they do not want to slow down the rest of the class) and, in some cases, instructors sending nonverbal signals that they have, indeed discounted the student altogether. I have heard of Black women shutting themselves down because their instructors have not taken their questions seriously.

The other edge of the sword Black students encounter is the presumption of hyper-competence. In these cases, instructors do not provide our students with the needed second look or ask cognition questions because they think these students do not need any help. For some Black women, in particular, these classroom dynamics result in seeking and paying for tutoring (or teaching) to provide the *mentoring* in language translation and interpretation they are not receiving in the classroom. Importantly, this phenomenon of presumed incompetence or hyper-competence extends beyond the language classroom for black, brown, and beige bodies, and in the discussion of #BlackScholarsMatter, this matters.

We must attend to the ways we are constructing academic spaces that build collegial communities and conversation partners for Black biblical studies students. Moreover, an important intervention that calls for more attention is the way we disrupt archaic patterns of teacher-student interactions, built on Greco-Roman models of intellectual apprenticeship, which did not have to account for the historical inequities and exclusions exacted on our contemporary society's intersectional identities of, *at minimum*, race, class, and gender.

In conclusion, I do not have all the answers, but I am convinced that a conversation around #BlackScholarsMatter must include doubling down on the commitment to attend to matters of mentoring and instructional ethos in our field.

#StayWoke:
The Next Generation of Black Biblical Scholars, the Society of Biblical Literature, and the Central Challenges of Ethical Leadership

ABRAHAM SMITH

More than fifty-three years ago, on March 31, 1968, a few days before a sole gunman and a single bullet from a high-powered rifle would take the life of the Reverend Dr. Martin Luther King Jr., the Georgia seer delivered his "Remaining Awake *through* a Revolution" sermon at the National Cathedral in Washington, DC. In the sermon, King deployed a political allegory from George Washington Irving's "Rip Van Winkle" to stir the United States from its slumbering contentedness, its benumbed, desensitized, and anesthetized response to the human rights revolutions that were taking place within it and all around it.

In the Georgia seer's own words, "one of the great liabilities of life is that all too many people find themselves living amidst a period of great social change and they fail to develop the *new attitudes* and *new mental responses* that the new situation demands" (King 1986, 269). They are asleep, without the capacity to respond appropriately to what is happening around them.

Now more than fifty-three years later, and for about seven years running, the idea of staying awake is *en vogue* again. The call to stay awake this time though is not a call to stay awake *through* revolutions. It is the call to stay awake *for ethical leadership*. It is the call to generate the ethical consciousness and literacy capacity deemed necessary to challenge what King (1967, 10) would have called *complacency*, "*cunning obstruction*" of oppression, and a *credibility gap* or the crisis of some aggrieved groups' lack of confidence to believe that their lives really matter.

For those who face setbacks because of gender disparity or patriarchy, from where will the ethical leadership emerge? For those who are often excluded because of medical models of disability, from where will the ethical leadership appear? For those who are caught in the throes of a carceral system that has produced an unprecedented mass of incarcerated bodies, a carceral system long in the making and yet short on its rehabilitative delivery, from where will the ethical leadership arrive?

To be sure, many young persons are providing some of that leadership. To urge all of us to stay awake, the hashtag #StayWoke, one of the more recognizable hashtags of the Black Lives Matter Global Network and the larger Movement for Black Lives, was developed. It appears frequently in social media, from Twitter, Tumblr, and Instagram accounts to Facebook. Furthermore, the hashtag #StayWoke appears in the title of the actor/activist Jesse Williams's documentary on the Black Lives Matter movement:"*#StayWoke: The Black Lives Matter Movement*" (Richardson and Ragland 2018, 44).

The meaning of the expression #StayWoke is straightforward. Elaine Richardson and Alice Ragland (2018, 43) define the term *woke* or *awake* (as traditionally understood) as "a political consciousness type of being awake." Thus "stay woke" means to remain vigilantly conscious or politically aware of the contradictions of US society. It means to have the consciousness and capacity to recognize the many faces of oppression and to know why it is so insidiously difficult to contend against it. It means to keep our eyes open in the fight for full equity and to recognize the embeddedness of unequal relations of power, especially in an age when one considers the reality of James Baldwin's "bloody catalogue of oppression" (Baldwin and Peck 2017, 23), made newly visible in the asphyxiation-death of George Floyd by a police officer who placed a knee on Floyd's neck for more than eight minutes and the killing of Breonna Taylor (by three Louisville Metro Police Department officers who fired twenty rounds of shots into her apartment after arriving with a no-knock search warrant in Louisville, Kentucky).

So, if one of the questions that should be asked is "what advice would you give to the next generation of Black scholars?," a question I am eager to answer because I have now taught biblical studies for some thirty-five years, my short answer would be to stay awake for ethical leadership *in* the classroom, *on* college/university/seminary campuses, and *for* communities that have been rendered as disposable and insignificant. Yet, let me answer that question more carefully, as I look at each of the aforementioned venues in the remarks that follow.

1. Staying Awake *in* the Classroom

Whether the classroom is virtual or face-to-face, the next generation will need to stay awake to unmask operations of power in such cultural productions as cartographies and canons. As for cartographies, Africa is the second largest continent, but some maps render it of little importance, if not invisible altogether. Some, as Randall Bailey (1991, 166) has stated, even de-Africanize what we now know as Africa by referring to "African territories" as the Near East.

As for canons, here, too, we must analyze operations of power. Canons of any kind—scriptural (what we call lists of authoritative books) or methodological (what might be called rituals of certification)—have cultural capital. While I am not advocating the dismissal of biblical canons altogether, I am suggesting more work is necessary to show the struggles and political contestations that produced scriptural canons. I am also in agreement with Musa Dube (2000, 50), who implores postcolonial biblical readers to pay attention to "our Other canons, written and unwritten … because imperialism proceeds by denying the validity of the narratives and values of its victims, while it imposes its own 'master narratives' on them."

I am also suggesting that we need to broaden our methodological approaches beyond traditional and sometimes tepid approaches such as historical criticism, sociocultural criticism, and literary criticism. Why not join Stephen Breck Reid (1995, 37–49), for example, who deploys Cornel West's typological grid of responses to hegemony to assess both Daniel and the political theory of W. E. B. Du Bois? Why not join Judy Fentress-Williams (2010, 80–88), who takes Hip Hop poetics—the distinction between a sample (separating an evoked musical tradition from its roots and broad thematic development) and a remix (expanding on the broad thematic development of an evoked musical tradition for the sake of relevance)—to explain the uses of the exodus tradition in the Hebrew Bible and beyond? Why not join Gay L. Byron (2002) who combines gender criticism, ethnocriticism, and rhetorical criticism to assess early Christianity's ethnopolitical othering?

When we contest cartographies and canons in our classrooms, we create spaces to decolonize minds, radicalize hearts, and equip ministerial and other professionals with the coinage and theoretical sophistication they need to appraise those texts and traditions that otherize, terrorize, and demonize human subjectivities. So, #StayWoke!

2. Staying Awake *on* College/University/Seminary Campuses

Before my now thirty-five-year professional journey began, I was blessed to have had the best of teachers who tried to prepare me not only for the classroom but for the power dynamics operating in institutions. You will not find a better set of teachers than Dorsey Blake and Leon Weinberger, who taught me at the University of Alabama; Randall Bailey, H. Wayne Merritt, Stephen Breck Reid, and David Rensberger, who taught me at the Interdenominational Theological Center; and Mary Ann Tolbert, Fernando Segovia, and Daniel Patte, who taught me at Vanderbilt University. While all of them brokered for me to be hired and promoted, to receive prestigious national grants and academic pre- and postdoctoral fellowships, some were fully privileged and educated me about legal contracts *in* institutions and *with* publishing houses; some were inside-outsiders keenly aware of the matrix of domination that worked against their own subjectivities and they taught me the value of decentering privilege by learning to listen and to reflect on the marginalization of others before responding; some honestly told me that I would suffer—euphemistically speaking—some occupational hazards.

All were trying to *awaken* me to the nature of institutions. They were right. Sometimes, they admonished, your spoken words will be minstrelized (with printed publications that almost sound like dialect despite your ability to furnish a recorded or manuscript copy of what you have said). They were right. Sometimes, your stances on an educational policy will be mischaracterized (as if you were advocating a ludicrous argument that could facilely be dismissed but you were not). My mentors were right. Sometimes, your suffering will be minimalized through the microaggression of micro-invalidation (as if your point does not matter and as if you are invisible).

Thus, in staying awake, the next generation will need to develop the literacy for demystifying white privilege. You will need to know how class—not in a vulgar, universalizing Marxist manner (à la economic determinism)—intersects with race as happened with some of the New Deal and Fair Deal social legislation policies that ostensibly were directed toward all the poor or the working class but were tailored structurally to offer affirmative action to whites because of the power of Southern Democrats. Furthermore, when you are afforded some measure of power granted to you earnestly—and not as result of cow-towing or of being the so-called racialized voice of reason that repeatedly absolves white people from having to speak at all in the climate of racial unrest—you—in your awakened state—must not then become the thing that you hate. If you are invited to join a campus group that advocates equity for women and you are a male, you do not set the agenda. You listen, learn, and take up whatever role the women assign to you within your powers. If you are invited to work with a campus group that advocates on behalf of Vietnamese refugees, you do not have the right to set the terms and directions of that group's goals and objectives. You listen, you learn, and you take up whatever role they assign for you within your powers. So, #StayWoke!

3. Staying Awake *for* Communities Deemed Disposable

Surely, for this and the next generation of Black scholars (and let me cast the net more widely to all the members of the Society of Biblical Literature), what we do as teachers is not solely a profession but also a platform to call attention to the plights of those who are underserved by physical, structural, and ideological forms of violence in our larger societies. Surely, we did not learn all of these languages, including sophisticated theories that feel like languages themselves, simply to teach in classrooms and work through the arcane and insidious labyrinths of status-quo-justifying institutional politics *and* to tally up a list of books that could establish us with distinguished chairs and that is all there is to our life's work. Surely, we will not end our professions having never been informed by any grassroots community and thus perpetuating domination through an arrogant politics of exclusion or more insidious apologies that justify exclusions without, as the late bell hooks (1990, 128) would say, "securing spaces for inclusion"!

You must decide which grass-roots communities will inform your work, but for the rest of my vocation and even beyond, at the least, I want to call attention to the plights of those deemed disposable. Thus, to stay awake, our scholarship cannot be isolated from quotidian assaults with which others perennially live.

In the age of our COVID-19 pandemic (with its death toll of 6.1 million and 474 million confirmed cases worldwide as of March 2022), one could place a spotlight on the risks to the homeless, the risks to immigrants in detention centers, or the risks to Latinx and Blacks who are disproportionately affected because of preexisting comorbidities, poor access to health care, and the density of residential or workplace spaces. If I may offer but one example to illustrate a community of concern, I will select the issue of mass incarceration. As I have stated in a recent work published for Brill press, an underdeveloped theoretical-political project in biblical studies is that of a focus on mass incarceration. According to Bryan Stevenson (2014, 15), the founder of the Equal Justice Initiative, "today ... [the United States has] the highest rate of incarceration in the world. The prison population has increased from 300,000 people in the early 1970s to 2.3 million people today. There are nearly six million people on probation or on parole. One in every fifteen people born in the United States in 2001 is expected to go to jail or prison; one in every three Black male babies born in this century is expected to be incarcerated." Furthermore, as Kelly Lytle Hernández, Khalil Gibran Muhammad, and Heather Ann Thompson (2015, 19) have noted, "Immigrant detention—that is, the process of forcibly confining immigrants during deportation proceedings—is now the largest system of human caging operated by the U.S. government."

The statistics cited are astounding and alarming. They bespeak fundamental structural problems with the US Justice system: its disproportionate percentage of prisoners compared to its population (Pfaff 2017, 1); its propensity to incapacitate its young rather than to educate them (Hinton 2016, 5); its racial disparities in policing, prosecuting, and sentencing (Mauer 2011, 87–101); its voter disenfranchisement and "legalized discrimination" (Stevenson 2014, 15; Alexander 2010, 1–2); and its tolls of social stigmatization, collateral disruption of families, and tax dollar prodigality (Kilgore 2015, 1–2).

There is certainly a wedge provided in the Christian Bible to give incarceration the time and study it deserves. Detaining centers or dank dungeons are repeatedly mentioned throughout the biblical texts. Remarkably, though, despite this textual gift of a wedge, biblical scholars on the whole, have not pressed the imprisonment narratives of the Hebrew Bible or of early Christianity to challenge the prison industrial complex of our own times. This failure is odd, though, because the United States has less than 5 percent of the world population but 20 percent of the prison population. Indeed, we have the highest incarceration rate in the world (with "one in every 100 adults" behind bars) (Leipold 2019, 1580). Thus, for the next generation of the Society of Biblical Literature's Black scholars or indeed for all its scholars, the issue of mass incarceration—and more broadly—the entire criminal justice system—is a growing edge that deserves our attention. So, please #StayWoke!

Works Cited

Alexander, Michelle. 2010. *The New Jim Crow: Mass Incarceration in the Age of Colorblindness*. New York: The New Press.

Bailey, Randall C. 1991. "Beyond Identification: The Use of Africans in Old Testament Poetry and Narratives." Pages 165–84 in *Stony the Road We Trod: African American Biblical Interpretation*. Edited by Cain Hope Felder. Minneapolis: Fortress.

Baldwin, James, and Raoul Peck. 2017. *I am Not Your Negro*. New York: Vintage.

Byron, Gay L. 2002. *Symbolic Blackness and Ethnic Difference in Early Christian Literature* London: Routledge.

Dube, Musa W. 2000. *Postcolonial Feminist Interpretation of the Bible*. Saint Louis: Chalice.

Fentress-Williams, Judy. 2010. "Exodus." Pages 80–88 in *The Africana Bible: Reading Scriptures from Africa and the African Diaspora*. Edited by Hugh Page Jr. et al. Minneapolis: Fortress.

Hernández, Kelly Lytle, Khalil Gibran Muhammad, and Heather Ann Thompson. 2015. "Introduction: Constructing the Carceral State." *Journal of American History* 102:18–24.

Hinton, Elizabeth. 2016. *From the War on Poverty to the War on Crime: The Making of Mass Incarceration in America*. Cambridge: Harvard University Press.

hooks, bell.1990. *Yearning: Race, Gender, and Cultural Politics*. Boston: South End.

Kilgore, James William. 2015. *Understanding Mass Incarceration*. New York: The Free Press.

King, Martin Luther, Jr. 1967. *Where Do We Go from Here: Chaos or Community?* New York: Harper & Row.

———. 1986. "Remaining Awake through a Great Revolution." Pages 268–78 in *A Testament of Hope: The Essential Writings and Speeches of Martin Luther King, Jr.* Edited by James Washington. San Francisco: Harpers.

Leipold, Andrew D. 2019. "Is Mass Incarceration Inevitable." *American Criminal Law Review* 56: 1579–1620.

Mauer, Marc. 2011. "Addressing Racial Disparities in Incarceration." *The Prison Journal* 91: 87–101.

Pfaff, John. 2017. *Locked In: The True Causes of Mass Incarceration—and How to Achieve Real Reform*. New York: Basic Books.

Reid, Stephen Breck. 1995. "The Theology of the Book of Daniel and the Political Theory of W. E. B. DuBois." Pages 37–49 in *The Recovery of Black Presence: An Interdisciplinary Exploration (Essays in honor of Dr. Charles B. Copher)*. Edited by Randall C. Bailey and Jacquelyn Grant. Nashville: Abingdon.

Richardson, Elaine, and Alice Ragland. 2018. "#StayWoke: The Language and Literacies of the #BlackLivesMatter Movement." *Community Literacy Journal* 12: 27–56.

Stevenson, Bryan. 2014. *Just Mercy: A Story of Justice and Redemption*. New York: Random House.

Part 3
#BlackScholarsMatter:
Accountability and Next Steps

Latinidad in Dialogue with Africana Biblical Studies: A Perspective

EFRAÍN AGOSTO

On May 25, 2020, George Floyd was brutally murdered by a police officer during an attempted arrest in Minneapolis, Minnesota. The video of the choking of Mr. Floyd by a knee on his neck went viral, the police officer was eventually tried and convicted of murder, and his fellow officers on the call were also convicted of aiding and abetting in the murder. Nationwide protests ensued during the summer of 2020 and beyond, and Black Lives Matter organizers and many others joined in this moment of reckoning for the history of racism and sanctioned anti-Black violence in the United States.

On June 1, 2020, exactly one week after the Floyd killing, the then president of the United States had the park and streets near the White House cleared of peaceful protesters with tear gas and armed police officers, some on horseback, so he, the president, could walk through the park and stand in front of a church with Bible in hand for a photo op, declaring that this country is great and its streets will be kept safe. Soon thereafter, the Council of the Society of Biblical Literature issued a public statement in response to the police killings of George Floyd and also Breonna Taylor two months before Floyd in Louisville, Kentucky, as well as the president's unwarranted walk through the park with a Bible. The Council denounced those actions, the racial injustices in the United States they demonstrated, and the weaponized use of the Bible by people in power to foment and defend white supremacy.[1] Beyond that statement, posted in early June, the Council formed a Black Scholars

---

1. As described in Efraín Agosto, Council Chair's Annual Report, SBL Annual Meeting, December 10, 2020.

Matter Task Force, organized to explore the kinds of actions, activities, and policies we should be undertaking as a Society in response to racial injustices both in the society at large and in our scholarly biblical guild. Late that summer, on August 12 and 13, the task force sponsored a virtual symposium, which was well attended, in which senior Black biblical scholars analyzed "Where Have We Been in Black Biblical Scholarship" and midcareer Black biblical scholars shared ideas on "Where Are We Going in Black Biblical Scholarship." Those presentations are the basis for this volume, in addition to other reflections on the theme of Africana Biblical Studies—past, present, and future. As chair of the Society of Biblical Literature's Council during these developments in summer and fall of 2020, I focus in this essay on Africana biblical studies from the perspective of *Latinidad*—in dialogue with Latinx perspectives on biblical studies, scholarship, and activism.[2]

I am the son of Puerto Ricans who migrated to New York City over seventy years ago in 1951. My sisters and I grew up in the Puerto Rican diaspora of the South Bronx and Williamsburg, Brooklyn, and our mother took us to a Latinx Pentecostal church at an early age. I learned to love the Bible in Sunday School class and Sunday evening preaching service. When I found out after college that I could have a profession in biblical studies, I went to theological school and then graduate school. I have been teaching New Testament studies full-time since 1995, twenty-six years in two theological schools (Hartford and New York), and this last year in an undergraduate liberal arts college, teaching more broadly in religion and Latinx studies. This essay represents an effort to continue a long-time interest and practice of Black-Latinx dialogue in biblical studies.

The Contours of an Africana-Latinx Biblical Studies Dialogue

In this essay, I will dialogue with recent works in African American biblical studies reflection and hermeneutics. I begin with Angela Parker's *If*

---

2. For the purposes of clarity, I use *Latinx* when referring to the Latina/o/x community or persons as a whole, and a gender-specific reference when talking about me or someone I know to be male (Latino), female (Latina), or transgender or nonbinary (Latinx). For a brief description of the use of these terms, including in biblical studies, see Agosto and Hidalgo (2018, 3–5).

God Still Breathes, Why Can't I? Black Lives Matter and Biblical Authority (2021). Like me, Parker comes from an evangelical background and has reflected on the struggles with those influences in her biblical studies scholarship. Thus, this first engagement will explore religious perspectives on being Black and being Latino and reading biblical texts. Some of us, both African American and Latinxs, have arrived at biblical scholarship as a profession by way, at least initially, of religious experience and questions and studies thereof. This recent published work by Parker is a helpful conversation partner with me in this regard for this essay. What commonalities and differences are there in Black and Latinx approaches to biblical studies, especially in light of religious experience, in this case in the stories and reflections of two minoritized scholars raised and trained in evangelical contexts?

A second section of this essay seeks to engage in dialogue with another recent work by an African American scholar whose interests also cohere with mine. Lisa Bowens's recent work, *African American Readings of Paul* (2020) explores over two hundred years of African Americans—women and men; preachers and teachers; enslaved, formerly enslaved, or descendants of the enslaved—reading the texts slave masters used against them or their forebears, namely, sections of the letters of Paul. Bowens shows the resistance hermeneutics of these readers, and I found her study powerful and illuminating and a conversation partner for my work on Paul as a Latino biblical scholar. Thus, this essay will exemplify Black-Latinx dialogue on Pauline studies—in brief—as I engage Bowens's important work.

Third, reading across minoritized perspectives has been explored previously, of course, most notably in the edited volume, *They Were All Together in One Place?* (Bailey, Liew, and Segoiva 2009). The introduction of that book describes the parameters of such engagement and I want to revisit that conversation for this essay, specifically to explore the question, "What can I, a Latino New Testament scholar, bring to the table of inter-ethnic (Black, Asian, Latinx) dialogue in biblical studies?" Again, the focus of the question will be on Black-Latinx dialogue in biblical studies.

With these three foci—the religious experience of doing Black and Latinx biblical scholarship; the approach to a particular aspect of biblical scholarship by a Black and a Latino Pauline scholar; and the ongoing dialogue about doing this work across various ethnic communities—I hope to contribute to the ongoing assertions of why and how Black scholars matter.

Angela Parker: Why "Religion" Matters

Parker often asks her seminary students, "What is your relationship to the Bible?" In many ways, *If God Still Breathes, Why Can't I?* asks the same question. In doing so, Parker (2021, 3–4) wishes "to hold the idea of Scripture as authority, while interrogating the doctrines of inerrancy and infallibility," which she learned in church and seminary. Yet, rightly, she now believes those doctrines are "tools of White supremacist thought." Moreover, as a womanist biblical scholar, Parker aligns inerrancy and infallibility with what she calls "White Supremacist authoritarianism," which is different from "authority." Biblical authority is not always problematic, claims Parker, because it can be creative and empowering, once we have engaged the Bible in interpretative approaches that are life-giving, affirmative and liberative. In contrast, "White supremacist authoritarianism," represented in insisting on the inerrancy and infallibility of the Bible, as if it were equal to God, does not equate to biblical authority. For example, posits Parker, the notion of "God-breathed" scripture from the text of 2 Tim 3:16–17 is not really about inerrancy at all, as many of us who went to evangelical seminaries were taught. In fact, Parker reminds us, the author of 2 Timothy was not working with a full canon in writing these words, no recognized New Testament texts at all, most likely, and maybe some authorized texts from the Hebrew Scriptures. Notions of inspiration of scriptural writings available to this author was what motivated the ascription of "God-breathed." In any case, Parker reminds us, inspired as they may have been considered, such texts were *not* also considered to be equal to God. Why, then, have so many *male* biblical interpreters, in particular, insisted on that text teaching us the doctrines of inerrancy and infallibility to the Bible as a whole (Parker 2021, 10)? Black and other minoritized bodies in biblical scholarship, Parker insists, understand the white supremacist foundations of these doctrines and the death-dealing they entail, that is, death to creativity, to diverse interpretations, and to broad questioning of the text, which, for example, Parker reminds us, is foundational to womanist biblical hermeneutics.

When Parker turns to more specifically discuss the training many of us have received as biblical scholars, she describes it as training "to act as a white Biblical scholar" and thereby stifle creative efforts to interrogate the cultural contexts of texts—then *and* now. In saying so, she includes both "Black and minoritized bodies" and our "attempt to contort [our]selves to fit within evangelicalism, usually without success" (11). Parker asserts that we need to "de-center" these interpretative limitations and avoid the "social death" they bring. At the same time, she affirms the "affection" and "trust" she has for the Bible as Scripture, but only together with "critical thinking" (11).

As a Latino biblical scholar who was trained at an evangelical seminary in the early 1980s, I learned strict historical-critical exegetical approaches to biblical studies, even in my seminary's master of divinity program. I thus resonate with the analysis Parker offers. A focus on biblical studies that incorporates an absolutist approach to truth and interpretation does harm to individual scholarly inquiry, especially by people of color such as Black and Latinx scholars, who have been too often quieted in our search for interpretative approaches that include and empower our communities. Parker continues in her book to share how asking questions of the Pauline letters from the perspective of ministry in the African American community, for example, helps see Paul from both a positive *and* negative side, rather than always in the right, which a belief in inerrancy tends to insist upon. When we ask questions of the biblical text from "lived experience," as Parker proposes, our "breathing" doesn't get "stifled" (17). In fact, she states, "for me to ask new questions of Pauline literature, specifically related to the bodies of enslaved Black women in the colonial United States and their relationship to Paul's metaphorical use of slavery language, would actually provide avenues of liberation for actual women in contemporary churches" (18). But if Paul is the absolute authority on any number of things he discusses in his letters and in the letters his followers wrote in his name (which many evangelical scholars also accept as Paul's very words), then oppression of Black and Brown bodies follows, as has been the case for centuries, including in the United States.

However, Parker rightly points out that this is not just an evangelical problem. The whole notion that biblical interpretation must avoid "personal matters" and must be as "objective" as possible, a quality expected across the field, must be challenged. And Parker does so, strongly: "Objective reality as a stance for biblical interpretation is ... one of the systematic evils of academic biblical studies" (19). Rather, the effective biblical scholar ought to engage "issues of identity" and "construct ways and means of reading biblical texts that are relevant in the halls of the academy, in the pulpits of the churches, and on the sidewalks of society where lived experience occurs" (19–20). Moreover, "relationships across identity lines" help in this endeavor, and thus, Parker, a Black womanist biblical scholar, invites other minoritized biblical scholars to join in this deconstruction of white supremacist absolutist control of the exercise of biblical interpretation.

What does a Black womanist and liberationist approach to biblical scholarship look like? Parker proposes several signposts, including the need to discern a variety of voices in the biblical texts and how they point to a liberating but not static God (28). She notes how equating God with the Bible can be called "bibliolatry" (29–31). Indeed, she asserts that the "irrational reverence of the Bible is often a form of *White* supremacist authoritarianism, because it is usually White men who have wielded the power of the Bible" (30). Further, "inherited Eurocentric traditions around the biblical text, such as doctrines of inerrancy and infallibility, actually minimize Black people's ability to exert our God-given, inspired breath— our authority" (31). We note Parker's religiosity in these assertions; to be out front with one's faith claims in dialogue with the historical, contextual, and literary aspects of the biblical texts makes for a more fulsome, authentic approach to the biblical studies. It is an approach that resonates with many of us Africana and Latinx scholars of the Bible.

Where does that leave claims for authority? Parker makes a strong case for biblical authority that is based, in part, on creating authentic community. What happens, she asks, if a community assumes "shared views about inerrancy and infallibility" but "such ideas are detrimental to the identity of some members of the community?" Invariably, Parker suggests, the latter have to "contort themselves into the mold created by the doctrines of inerrancy and infallibility," which are in effect "tools of White supremacist authoritarianism" (42). As someone who used to contort myself to try to fit into the mold of either evangelical biblical scholarship or objectifying approaches to historical biblical criticism, I appreciate Parker's insistence that authentic authority in biblical work builds community and works toward justice in our world. Both Parker and I, as well as other minoritized biblical scholars, ask, "Why else do the work?"

Parker helps us understand the broad range of persons to be included in the quest for a more inclusive effort in biblical studies. She writes, "By 'minoritized identities' I mean women, Black and minoritized bodies, Indigenous people, folk of Asian descent, etc." (47). Some might misconstrue such inclusion as identity politics. Parker, citing Martin Luther King Jr., sees it as "embracing a beloved community of common humanity" (48). Why shouldn't the enterprise of biblical studies create such a broad community of scholars, indeed more intentionally? Many of us from diverse backgrounds over the years have been told that we should only worry about teaching "the 'plain meaning' of the biblical text without raising any awareness of racial and cultural differences" (49). As Parker writes, to do the latter, in the eyes of some, would be "bringing too much of [ourselves] and 'the voices of [our] people'" to our classrooms. Rather, teaching "the plain sense of the biblical text is better for students than thinking critically about connections between oppressed people in the text and oppressed people today" (50). Such an approach—looking for some kind of universal meaning that transcends questions by marginalized communities then and now—should have no standing among any authentic biblical scholarship today and certainly not among biblical scholars of color. Speaking specifically about Africana women scholars, Parker asserts: "Black women's lived experience and Black women's reasoning must be brought to bear in the reading of the biblical text, providing an avenue for churched African American women to experience power and testimonial authority stemming from biblical authority and not the stifled breathing brought on by White supremacist authoritarianism in the present age of Black Lives Matter" (53). Whether or not scholars of color are in dialogue with religious institutions or religious faith, one context Parker explores in her book and cites here, our attention to reading texts and their impact from and to minoritized communities is essential, whether the classroom, the research project, or the wider society.

Lisa Bowens: Reception and Resistance in African American Readings of Paul

Lisa Bowens, in *African American Readings of Paul: Reception, Resistance and Transformation*, dug deep into the historical reservoir of African American writings on Paul for over three centuries. One can learn about little known interpreters of Paul, such as Jupiter Hammon, Jarena Lee, and Zilpha Elaw, from late eighteenth and nineteenth centuries, all of whom write illuminating and powerful reflections on the Paul, whose letters were used against them as enslaved or formerly enslaved persons in the US South. Bowens also includes persons with whose history I was more familiar, such as James Pennington, who pastored the historic Faith Congregational Church in Hartford in the 1840s, not far from where I live today. I was not familiar with his readings of Paul, however. The great Howard Thurman, of course, saw little use for Paul, but his mentee from when Thurman was University Chaplain at Boston University, Martin

Luther King Jr., wrote "Letter to American Christians" in the voice of Paul and "Letter from Birmingham City Jail" in the style of a Pauline prison letter. Both of these are critical readings for all Pauline scholars, across the theological, racial, and cultural spectrum. I was particularly fascinated to read about the great Black Pentecostal forebears of the Latinx Pentecostal experience I grew up with in Brooklyn. William Seymour, founder of the Azusa Street Revival Mission in Los Angeles in 1906, preached sermons, which Bowens has retrieved for us, about the Spirit language in Paul. He also wrote about the importance of Paul's Jerusalem collection as a model for giving to the poor and needy. Bowens also discusses how Charles H. Mason, founder of the Church of God in Christ, the largest Black Pentecostal denomination in the United States, read and deployed Paul effectively in his pioneering ministry. I did not know, for example, that Bishop Mason used a Pauline phrase, "the Church of God in Christ" to name his historic denomination, founded in the 1890s. I also was not aware of Bishop Mason's strong antiwar stance, specifically in the deployment of Black bodies to fight a war for freedom in Europe, when freedom was denied those very same bodies in the United States.

For this essay, I am particularly interested in what we learn from the Black hermeneuts Bowens studies for the practice of Pauline hermeneutics today, especially in conversation with a Latinx hermeneutical perspective on Paul. First, I agree with Bowens when she posits that, given the abuse of Pauline texts to enslave African Americans in the United States and then continue the abuse postbellum through long, painful periods of segregation, Jim Crow, and discrimination to this day, it is amazing that so many of the African American hermeneuts that she studied found in Paul's words a resistance hermeneutic (as summarized in Bowens 2020, 305). How a liberating Paul could be found—through interpretations, for example, of Paul's teachings on the Holy Spirit, his language of equality of all believers in Christ, and a body hermeneutic that insisted that all bodies mattered, including Black bodies—is an astounding record of reception history and interpretation.

More generally, Bowens asks, "How does putting African Americans' *reception* of Paul at the center of Pauline hermeneutics affect the study of Paul?" (292, emphasis original). In summarizing the various themes that came out of reading the African American interpreters of Paul since the 1700s through the middle part of the twentieth century, Bowens found these themes to include liberation, equality, shared experience, and the "cosmic Paul." She also found how some interpreters connected to Paul because of his conversion and spiritual experiences. Further, Bowens notes those interpreters who explored Paul's emphasis on the presence of God's Spirit did so because such presence, in their minds, is an authentic sign of human identity, dignity, and empowerment over against how slave masters and white supremacists were interpreting Paul, and Black bodies. In Paul, Black interpreters found a liberating body hermeneutic of Paul—Black bodies matter because, like all human beings, they belong to God.

As a Latino biblical scholar deeply embedded in the issues Bowens expounds, I am especially appreciative to explore her focus on reception history. In the final chapter of her book, however, she asks how does the text—in this case the Pauline text as received by African American interpreters—move from the matter of reception to the overarching question of interpretation per se? In engaging this important matter with Bowens, I would like to posit the question this way: what do we learn about Paul, as received by minoritized communities—Black and Latinx in particular—that is both a matter of how we receive the text, but also what important lessons about *hermeneutics* do we learn? For example, the question of experience—Black experience, including enslavement, segregation, and discrimination—not only influences specific receptions of the Pauline texts but how such *experiences* become lessons in interpretation and hermeneutics for all of us to learn. Indeed, Bowens puts the matter this way: "These interpreters demonstrate that experience can play a role in biblical interpretation when interpreters bring their experience to the text and at the same time allow the text to interpret their experience" (296). Following this line of thinking, I would like to suggest that all biblical interpreters should learn from these African American readers of Paul studied by Bowens and accept *experience*—the interpreter's experience—as an interpretative tool, as foundational, in fact, for all biblical interpretation. In that sense, Bowens's work is not just an accounting of a reception history, but one that issues into a hermeneutical principle, which Bowens calls "a dialectic of experience." This is a major contribution of this work—reception is interpretation is hermeneutics—one which resonates with how Latinx readers engage the biblical text, including Paul.

In the last section of her final chapter, entitled "Where do We Go from Here," Bowens asks, "which additional interpreters employ Paul in a resistance and protest hermeneutic?" (305). She goes on to recommend these dynamics as reflected in African American arts, literature, and music, as well as biblical texts beyond Paul. I would add that intersectionality with other minoritized communities—such as Latinx and Asian American, who also read Paul for liberation and empowerment—would be important as well. Moreover, this astounding time travel from eighteenth to twentieth century African American readers that Bowens has brought us through made me think about one Latin American luminary, in particular: the twentieth century Black Puerto Rican thinker, activist, and revolutionary, Pedro Albizu Campos, who fought for Puerto Rican independence through the 1920s and 1930s. He was imprisoned in the United States in the 1940s, released in 1947, and returned to Puerto Rico to organize a failed revolt in 1950 that ended in his imprisonment until shortly before his death in 1965. He was known from early in his career as the "Apostle of Puerto Rican Independence." He got that appellation, as far as I have been able to ascertain, after traveling to Latin America in the late 1920s to promote his vision, evangelizing for Puerto Rican independence from the American empire.[3] I doubt Albizu invoked the apostle Paul directly in his speeches, essays, letters, or newspaper columns, which constitute the bulk of his extant writings. There may be evocative or implied language from Paul about the "Lordship of Jesus Christ" over against the Roman imperial order, given Albizu's devoted Roman Catholicism, which he often references. Thus, the antiimperial Paul in comparison to the Afro-Latino Albizu's quest for Puerto Rican independence from the American empire, merits continuing research. In any case, this is an example of one Latino biblical scholar's response to the engagement with the historic, but lesser known, African American interpreters of Paul, as introduced to us by Bowens in her important volume.

Reading for Relationality:
They Were All Together in One Place?

After engaging two African American biblical scholars from my social location as a Latino biblical critic, I want to explore further in the final part of this essay what reading across difference looks like with Other minoritized communities in view. The 2009 volume *They Were All Together in One Place? Toward Minority Biblical Criticism* made a major effort in that direction. Edited by veteran biblical scholars Randall C. Bailey (a participant in the August 2020 #BlackScholarsMatter Symposium), Tat-siong Benny Liew (an

---

3. An initial foray into my research on Pedro Albizu Campos can be found in Agosto 2015.

organizer of that symposium), and Fernando F. Segovia, the volume brought together fourteen different scholars from African American, Latinx, and Asian American perspectives, respectively, including the three editors. I read an early manuscript of the work in preparation for a Society of Biblical Literature session in November 2008, in which I shared reflections, and here I explore further on how we might continue this type of dialogue and joint work in light of asserting that Black scholars matter in biblical studies and beyond.

The volume and the discussion that preceded and succeeded it was intended to create even greater alliances than what had been done in biblical scholarship beforehand. Many of us had participated in conferences and volumes on biblical studies within our own affinity groups, but this was an effort to ask how much further being all together in one place can we take the discipline. Much had already changed in the discipline as a result of several decades of racial ethnic work by minoritized communities in biblical studies. Why look for another place, the editors asked. It was precisely our internal diversity as minoritized persons in the profession that had us searching for more horizontal connections across so-called minority groups. How can our horizontal relations inform our "vertical relations, individually and collectively, vis-à-vis the dominant group" (Bailey, Liew, and Segovia 2009, 5)? The editors argued that a new place of horizontal relationality creates a more robust place of engagement with dominant structures. Moreover, we keep the goal of transformation (the field, our communities, society, etc.) in mind even as we come together in new ways and new places, the editors asserted. Toward that end, we need historical and theoretical frameworks with which to do our work; we need to understand that the term *minority* is more about power than numbers. The authors in the volume as a whole reminded us of the disparity that exists between the large numbers of the so-called minority communities and those who actually yield power—political, social, and economic power, including within the academy.

Thus, I appreciate the discussion at the outset of this volume around defining the term minority as actually a result of a process of minoritization by those in power. As such, therefore, minoritized persons need to understand our own and each other's cultures, as African Americans, Asian Americans, and Latinx persons, those communities specifically represented in this volume. Knowing each other better can create "springboards for new interpretations and critical interventions" (7). At the same, however, we all understood, and still understand today, that we need to preserve and develop each group's distinct cultural realties and self-understanding on its own terms.

Indeed, it was only just in 2008, a year before *They Were All Together in One Place?* came out, that the first two sessions of a US Latino/a and Latin American Biblical Interpretation consultation in the Society of Biblical Literature had inaugural meetings. Both African American and Asian American groups had been in existence for years, and, of course, US Latinx biblical scholars had been doing productive work both individually and collectively for many years. But only in the 2008 Annual Meeting of the Society of Biblical Literature was a formal program unit of our work inaugurated. This spoke to the need of further cross-fertilization internally, even as we engage crossing the color lines with other minoritized groups. The editors of *They Were All Together in One Place?* acknowledged this reality. They cautioned that "reading as looking out from a certain site or location does tend to imply a likelihood to forget and/or a difficulty in seeing one's place" (9). The natural tendency is to stay "inward," but we realized that there are "good and compelling reasons for minority scholars within the U.S." to become "partners in a common cause with other minority communities of color" (9). The violence perpetuated against Black bodies in particular in the spring and summer of 2020 rightly focused our agenda as an academic biblical studies society on why Black scholars matter. *And* collaboration and joint activism and scholarship must also be continued and built upon.

What are some reasons for joint efforts? The editors of *They Were All Together in One Place?* discussed the opportunity to engage "alternative vision and practice," to retire the notion of the winner-take-all model of academic scholarship, and the "cultural politics of conquest." Ultimately, it is about coalition building to overcome the divide and conquer strategy of US dominant society, including scholarly societies (9–10). The history of racialization in the United States, which the editors also discussed in their opening essay and which we saw in such ugly, violent ways in mid-2020, but also before and beyond, compels efforts to "confound" this history "by forming an alliance that comes close to being a new racial/ethnic group" (14). Yet, again we caution against the loss of identity for any one group, although we know hybridity is unavoidable, and no culture is sealed off from the other. Joint efforts and overlapping identities can empower all, including for the task of biblical criticism. Yet, Bailey, Liew, and Segovia also warned us that even a new construct, as discussed in their book—minority criticism—does not protect us all from "essentialization, commodification, and/or ghettoization." Indeed, minority criticism entails dialogue without necessarily reaching consensus or eliminating difference (16).

Another helpful theoretical frame for minority biblical criticism as outlined by this volume's editors entails the notion of joining partners as biblical scholars with area studies, such as African American, Asian American, and Latinx studies (30). These disciplines within such fields as historical, literary, and cultural studies are the important allies for minority biblical critics. They provide space for dialogue about, for example, how peoples of color have been treated in the United States. Such discussions in turn become hermeneutical frames for interpreting texts. Related to this is the necessary conversation with the work of biblical hermeneutics in Africa, Asia, and Latin America. This current 2022 volume insists that we must talk about Africana biblical studies to recognize the reality of the African diaspora in the work of African American biblical scholarship. In the same way, being in dialogue with Latinx-Latin American and Asian-Asian American scholarship enriches our conversation all the more to combat racism, colonization, and marginalization wherever it is found, including in the work of biblical scholarship.

How this work gets done is also a theme of *They Were All Together in One Place?*[4] We must foreground the reader's context, so as to counter a "received model of contextualization" and a notion of universal objectivity. As already noted, we must be eminently interdisciplinary and transhistorical and thereby not objectify antiquity. Such an agenda challenges how biblical critics are trained—much more interdisciplinary than we have been in the past, certainly in my formative years. Race and ethnicity must be in the foreground of biblical interpretation and not the background. And we must desacralize the text and the religious/theological frames it represents, deconstructing its absolutization in order to construct a more liberating vision, similar to what we discussed earlier in this essay in the work of Parker. The editors recognize that "the Bible is for many a canonical book of mastery, power, and domination." Minority biblical criticism involves readings that both "go along with as well as go against the 'good book'" (8). These as well as other guidelines outlined by the editors are exemplified in the various essays of the volume. One of those essays

---

4. For the ideas that follow in this paragraph, see in particular Bailey, Liew, and Segovia 2009, 25–36.

which struck a particular chord with me given my interests in reading the Roman imperial order in the context of the New Testament as a Latino was Gay Byron's (2009) essay, "Ancient Ethiopia and the New Testament: Ethnic (Con)texts and Racialized (Sub)texts." Byron demonstrates that the Roman Empire is not the only empire to be given consideration in the New Testament and that the African presence is essential. Again, my interests in reading the New Testament against the backdrop, for example, of Puerto Rican status as a colony of the United States empire, puts me into direct conversation with the work of Byron.[5]

Further, following the insistence of Bailey, Liew, and Segovia that our work as minoritized biblical scholars needs to be *interdisciplinary*, the essay by Latina theologian Mayra Rivera in the volume exemplifies just that. She understands herself to be "a theologian in dialogue with biblical scholars" and explores "the theology of racial and ethnic approaches to biblical interpretation" (Rivera 2009, 313). Rivera proposes that when we speak about the engagement of racialized and minoritized communities of color, we are in fact creating an embodied biblical hermeneutic. We are rejecting that notion that we can create "an essential meaning beneath or behind the biblical text," one that dismisses the impact of sociopolitical ideology in the biblical words (314–15). When we practice a biblical hermeneutic that foregrounds race and ethnicity, we in fact localize God rather than imagine God as an external reality, absolutely unaffected by creation, a God too worthy "to get mixed up in the in the squalor of our lives" (315), as Rivera quotes Brazilian theologian Ivonne Gebara. In this way, Rivera gives a theological context for the rhetoric of the volume on minority biblical criticism: God is an embodied God in the messiness of everyday life and so should biblical interpretation. Minority biblical criticism aids in this process and is thus eminently theological, as well as interdisciplinary and interethnic. Black scholars matter in biblical studies, all the more because of these ongoing dialogues with Latinx and Asian American scholars and a broad swath of disciplines beyond biblical studies.

---

5. For an example of my work putting the New Testament (specifically the Pauline letters) in conversation with history, religion, and politics of Puerto Rico, see Agosto 2018.

Conclusion: Religion, Resistance, and Relationality in Africana and Latinx Biblical Studies

I started this essay suggesting, with Angela Parker, that religion matters. The religious experiences and perspectives that drove many of us into biblical scholarship did not stay in the same place. We grew and developed in the field, not the least of which because we brought our communities—Black and Brown—with us. When we therefore explore the contours of the field—be it Hebrew Bible, gospel studies, or Pauline studies—we insist on opening up the texts with ancient and modern contexts and readers fully engaged and with resistance to oppressive aspects of both contexts—and their texts, including the biblical text—fully available for critique and appropriation where liberative. We affirm that Black lives matter because too much of the United States of America does not so affirm. Latinx biblical scholars join in the struggle because we do better in relation to each other.

Works Cited

Agosto, Efraín. 2015. "Confronting Empire: The Apostle Paul and Pedro Albizu Campos, The Apostle of Puerto Rican Independence." *Apuntes* 35.4:118–33.

———. 2018. "Islands, Borders and Migration: Reading Paul in Light of the Crisis in Puerto Rico." Pages 149–70 in *Latinxs, the Bible and Migration*. Edited by Efraín Agosto and Jacqueline Hidalgo Cham. Switzerland: Palgrave Macmillan.

Agosto, Efraín, and Jacqueline Hidalgo, eds. 2018. *Latinxs, the Bible and Migration*. Cham, Switzerland: Palgrave Macmillan.

Bailey, Randall C., Tat-siong Benny Liew, and Fernando Segovia, eds. 2009. *They Were All Together in One Place? Toward Minority Biblical Criticism*. SemeiaSt 57. Atlanta: Society of Biblical Literature.

Bowens, Lisa M. 2020. *African American Readings of Paul: Reception, Resistance and Transformation*. Grand Rapids: Eerdmans.

Byron, Gay. 2009. "Ancient Ethiopia and the New Testament: Ethnic (Con)texts and Racialized (Sub)texts." Pages 161–90 in *They Were All Together in One Place?* Atlanta: Society of Biblical Literature.

Parker, Angela N. 2021. *If God Still Breathes, Why Can't I? Black Lives Matter and Biblical Authority*. Grand Rapids: Eerdmans.

Rivera, Mayra. 2009. "Incarnate Words: Images of God and Reading Practices." Pages 313–29 in *They Were All Together in One Place?* Edited by Randall C. Bailey, Tat-siong Benny Liew, and Fernando Segovia. SemeiaSt 57. Atlanta: Society of Biblical Literature.

Contemplative Collegiality: Caring for the Souls of Black Biblical Scholars

GAY L. BYRON

> We bear witness not just with our intellectual work but with ourselves, our lives.
>
> —bell hooks

As the #BlackLivesMatter movement was rising to a heated pitch during the spring of 2020, I was teaching my New Testament courses online as a result of the COVID-19 pandemic. I was also pastoring a church due to an unexpected turnover in leadership. Using the same desk for the virtual delivery of lectures and sermons challenged me to remove a wall or the well-constructed boundaries that had marked my identity as a biblical scholar. This unintentional intersection of my professorial responsibilities with my priestly commitments has caused me to ask questions about the meaning of my scholarship, the purpose of my teaching, and the scope of my vocation. I have already reflected on such matters (Byron 2019), but now much more is at stake. In the face of the unrelenting swath of murders stemming from police violence and other forms of white supremacist terrorism, as well as the sudden and ongoing loss of lives from a virus that at that time was raging without an end in sight, I began to lean ever more deeply on what Howard Thurman (1963) calls "disciplines of the spirit." I now realize that the very spiritual practices that have sustained me in my personal and professional life have not been publicly disclosed in my scholarship. It was not until I was in a clergy residency program from 2020–2021 sponsored by the Shalem Institute for Spiritual Formation[1] that I finally had a context to enable me to put words around the necessity of circles of collegiality, communities of accountability, and models of support and care. Through this program I experienced "contemplative collegiality," a phrase I coined to capture what happens when colleagues dare to be vulnerable with one another and find ways to work through cultural differences, microaggressions, and other forms of subtle racism that creep into our classrooms and other spaces of teaching, learning, and worship.

What Is Contemplative Collegiality?

At the same time as I was connecting with a new set of clergy colleagues in the Shalem program, my Society of Biblical Literature colleagues were hosting a virtual symposium on #BlackLivesMatter.[2] These colleagues whom I have admired over the years shared stories of how they negotiated unfamiliar and often unwelcoming spaces in academia. They offered reflections on the lessons learned, the struggles encountered, the paths pursued to find more healthy ground, and the questions that still linger in the face of institutional roadblocks and systemic racism that keep them consumed with invisible labor. This invisible labor (primarily evidenced by an inordinate amount of committee work as a representative or spokesperson of one's ethnic group or in some cases all people of color) leads to fatigue, burnout, and poor health outcomes (Winters 2020). This may account for why, as of 2019, women of African descent in the Society of Biblical Literature account for only 3.4 percent of its approximately eight thousand members. During the symposium, my colleagues noted the importance of mentoring and the value of finding space and opportunities to share their stories and unique ways of interpreting biblical texts. They also discussed the isolation, loneliness, and lack of collegial support that sometimes hindered their progress and even caused them to walk away from the traditional path of academic advancement measured by the tenure clock.

---

1. "Going Deeper: Clergy Spiritual Life and Leadership," August 13, 2020–July 12, 2021. https://shalem.org/programs/going-deeper-clergy-spiritual-life-and-leadership/
2. "#BlackScholarsMatter: Visions and Struggles; Lessons and Hopes," August 12–13, 2020. https://www.sbl-site.org/meetings/blackscholarsmatter.aspx.

The Shalem program on Clergy Spiritual Life and Leadership gave me space and time to step away from the academic metrics that defined my understanding of accomplishment and offered a framework and a community through which I could become more intentional about self-care, Sabbath-keeping, and contemplative-mindfulness. To put it more precisely, I entered the experience pondering, *Why are my spiritual and self-care practices cut off from my scholarly life?* These new clergy colleagues offered a safe space for tearing down the internal wall that was blocking my full productivity as a biblical scholar *and* a religious leader. There was a total of eighteen participants in the program, and I was assigned to a smaller cohort of six who would meet during the first summer intensive residency and continue meeting monthly until the second summer intensive. We called ourselves the "Coast to Coast" group with participants in every time zone, from California; Wyoming; Iowa; Pennsylvania; Washington, DC; and Florida. We bonded instantly around a shared desire to deepen our respective ministries through cultivating spiritual practices such as silent retreats, deep listening, and caring support of one another across miles and through virtual meetings. We never met face-to-face during the entire program, but our care for one another was palpable. In addition to this peer support, I formed a listening group of laity from my congregation for another level of spiritual deepening and mutual support and accountability. In this regard, I invited my congregation as a whole, and this laity circle in particular, into my process of learning a new way of serving in leadership in our faith community. The outcome of all this connectivity was an ethos of personal and congregational care, trust, and discernment based on deep listening. This is contemplative collegiality.

What Does Contemplative Collegiality Look Like?

In theory, contemplative collegiality involves accountability, engagement, connection, mutual support, and deep listening—all for the purpose of creating spaciousness where there is mutual belonging, indwelling, and opportunities for discernment. But what happens when our best intentions do not materialize? When disconnections happen and old patterns and ways of doing things take over when expedient decisions need to be made? What happens when institutional structures don't match the realities of individuals called to lead or contribute to the goals of the group or organization? What happens when we realize there is still so much to learn about the ways in which we have been formed by our experiences and misinformed about the experiences of others? This is when it is useful to have another angle for reflection, another approach for decision-making, another perspective through which to respond to awkward, difficult situations with grace and compassion. This is when colleagues who have been on the journey, who have taken the bumps, who have traveled the detours, and even pulled over on the side of the road to rest and regroup can offer the gift of presence, encouragement, and accountability.

As wonderful as the first residency of the Shalem program was in offering spiritual resources, guest lectureships, and overall spaciousness for nurturing the spirit and connecting with like-minded peers, there was an overall awareness among the Black participants in the program that we were being immersed in a contemplative experience that was still overwhelmingly Eurocentric in orientation and leadership.[3] In addition there was an incident at the end of the program during which one of the leaders unwittingly shared a piece of music that harkens back to a stark image of slavery—a whipping post.[4] After a colleague brought this to his attention, our leader offered an apology to the group via email on the following day, but there was no acknowledgement of the incident in the group's final plenary session. His well-intentioned message to the group fell into the abyss of silence. We finished the session with expressions of gratitude despite the unfinished business that lingered in the air. The Black subcohort of participants met after the session and discussed the incident and, as is often the case, reached out to the director and leader to express our concerns and to ask for more education and awareness around cultural

---

3. Shalem has since that time addressed this imbalance in its readings and programs. In 2021, Shalem held a gathering of Contemplatives of Color (Black, Indigenous, and People of Color [BIPOC]) who had participated in its programs since its inception back in the 1970s. The first gathering was held virtually on September 25, 2021 for the purpose of sharing experiences and devising strategies and resources for expanding program offerings.

4. "Whipping Post" by The Allman Brothers Band. This song is about a man expressing his hurt and frustration over losing his girlfriend. "I've been run down and I've been lied to. And I don't know why, I let that mean woman make me a fool. She took all my money, wrecks my new car. Now she's with one of my good time buddies, They're drinkin' in some cross-town bar. Sometimes I feel, sometimes I feel, Like I've been tied to the whippin' post. Tied to the whippin' post, tied to the whippin' post. Good Lord, I feel like I'm dyin'."

metaphors and racialized imagery that on the surface are innocuous but can be hurtful and polarizing to those who are still reckoning with the trauma of slavery and other injustices.

In retrospect, I was inspired by my colleague's willingness to acknowledge his lack of sensitivity and his unintentional offense and even more encouraged by the fact that I could engage him around this microaggression and know that regardless of this misstep, we have a common thread of trust that enables us to speak candidly and to learn from each other without judgment, resentment, or fear. Indeed, the teachable moment was missed when the incident occurred during the first residency, but the leadership team took time to reflect on the incident and responded to the feedback from the Black cohort by taking ownership of the work *they* needed to do. One specific action resulted in a seminar during the second residency on "Learning from Stumbling" designed to provide a guided opportunity for all the participants to reflect and share any concerns or learnings related to the incident. This was facilitated by an African American woman, a former Shalem program participant, current board member, and academic administrator.

Throughout this session, I found myself disconnected from the discussion because it seemed too late--a whole year had elapsed! But this gave the non-Black participants in the group an opportunity to reflect more deeply on the incident and also to gain a glimpse of the invisible work the Black participants had been doing all along, well after we had returned to our primary ministry responsibilities. This session also created space for deep listening and personal and communal accountability. The facilitator slowed things down and created space for reflection and discernment on how best to move forward. Indeed, apologies were registered. Yet, the real work and the true learning from this stumble will be evidenced in the sustainable practices and policies the leaders of the organization will put in place so that a safe and hospitable environment is created for every participant in the program. In other words, "a contemplative organization [is] an organization whose structures and processes mirror its mission … an organization that walks its contemplative talk" (Benefiel and Lee 2019, 132). Likewise, each facilitator and presenter, in particular those who are still carrying the invisible knapsack of white privilege (McIntosh 2010), are being called to take on the responsibility of learning more about the history and culture of Black, Indigenous, and People of Color (BIPOC) communities.

Caring for the Souls of Black Biblical Scholars

So what does all of this have to do with Black biblical scholars? The notion of contemplative collegiality that has come into sharp focus for me over the past couple of years has taken place in a context of care. First and foremost, self-care, imbued with spiritual practices. Second, community care, informed by deep listening. And third, caring for the souls of those in my realm of influence. While pastoring, this involves my parishioners. As a professor, this involves my students as well as faculty and staff colleagues. And as a Black biblical scholar, this involves a recognition, with deep gratitude, of those who have come before to pave the stony road and a commitment, with deep hope, to those who are coming after to carry on the legacy of Africana biblical scholarship.

Divinity schools, seminaries, universities, and professional guilds are beginning to write policy statements and implement diversity, equity, and inclusion (DEI) initiatives to address what can no longer be hidden behind surface efforts of inclusivity. In addition, books about racism, antiracism, whiteness, white privilege, and the like have been written and continue to multiply in a market-driven publishing world that now sees the *value* of Black lives. The work of Black biblical scholars is not simply the work of scholarly production, though now more than ever monographs, edited volumes, peer-reviewed articles, critical essays, public discourses, podcasts, and other platforms for the dissemination of our scholarship are endless. But until *we* start to do the necessary work of caring for our bodies, caring for our souls, and caring for one another, those who hold the reins on institutional infrastructures will continue with business as usual. I suggest contemplative collegiality is one way of doing this care work. As the late bell hooks (1999, 122) has so poignantly observed, "We bear witness not just with our intellectual work but with ourselves, our lives." If we say that #BlackLivesMatter, then it will take more of us to model how to put this into practice.

The virtual desk that housed my Bible for sermons, the textbooks for my classes, the sick-and-shut-in list of my parishioners, and the contact information for my colleagues is the place where I realized the value of my spiritual practices and the need for contemplative collegiality. The Shalem Institute gave me an opportunity to experience collegiality in a new way through care, trust, and discernment. This essay has focused on care work for Black biblical scholars and all those who have a stake in teaching the next generation and transforming the Society of Biblical Literature into a context for fostering biblical scholarship that recognizes the multidimensional lives of Black biblical scholars.

Works Cited

Benefiel, Margaret, and Bo Karen Lee, eds. 2019. *The Soul of Higher Education: Contemplative Pedagogy, Research, and Institutional Life for the Twenty-First Century.* Charlotte, NC: Information Age Publishing.

Byron, Gay L. 2019. "My Society of Biblical Literature Journey: Service, Scholarship, and Staying Connected to the Call." Pages 157–66 in *Women and the SBL.* Edited by Nicole L. Tilford. BSNA 29. Atlanta: SBL Press.

hooks, bell. 1999. "A Life in the Spirit: Faith, Writing, and Intellectual Work." Pages 108–23 in *Remembered Rapture: The Writer at Work.* New York: Holt.

McIntosh, Peggy. 2010. "White Privilege: Uncovering the Invisible Knapsack." Pages 172–76 in *Race, Class, and Gender in the United States.* Edited by Paula S. Rothenberg. 8th ed. New York: Worth Publishers.

Thurman, Howard. 1963. *Disciplines of the Spirit.* Richmond, IN: Friends United Press.

Winters, Mary-Frances. 2020. *Black Fatigue: How Racism Erodes the Mind, Body, and Spirit.* Oakland, CA: Berrett-Koehler.

Black Bible Scholars Matter—Especially amid Perennial Crisis

Hugh R. Page Jr.

Starting Close to Home

Increasingly, I am reminded of several truisms that have been guideposts throughout my life as a scholar. The first is that small things matter—details, minor nuances, et cetera—in research, teaching, and life in general. The second is that there is more to reality than meets the eye and that one's attentiveness to matters not always readily apparent, some of which are hidden in plain sight, is prudent and necessary. The third is that we write and create most effectively when we begin with experiences that are, actually or metaphorically, closest to us. Perhaps this is proof or an extension of the adage that "charity begins at home" and recognition of the fact that the work we do as *Africana* scholars is often undertaken amid crises not of our own making: dangerous endeavors that yield few rewards.

Taking Context Seriously

As I have written and edited this essay, the COVID-19 pandemic continues to rage, despite the fatigue and social disincentives that hinder frank discussion about its ravages. Straightforward discussions about local, national, and international mitigation strategies remain highly politicized and data-informed common sense decision making appears hard to come by. We have seen the passing of several pioneering Black luminaries: Sidney Poitier, Ronnie Spector, bell hooks, Lani Guinier, to name just a few of those in that number. Within our educational institutions, faculty, staff, and students are encountering unprecedented pandemic-related stressors. They are especially acute among those from Black, Indigenous, and People of Color (BIPOC) communities, who are typically subject to various forms of institutional labor for which they are neither adequately compensated nor publicly acknowledged. Miami Dolphins head coach Brian Flores has taken legal action against the National Football League, several of its constituent teams, and his former employer, for discriminatory labor practices and other actions that violate the league's stated policies related to diversity, equity, and inclusion. He has received support from other Black coaches who have experienced similar treatment and vitriolic pushback from those he has accused and was hired by the Pittsburgh Steelers as an assistant coach. There have been bomb threats against more than a dozen Historically Black Colleges and Universities, including two (Morgan State and Coppin State Universities) in the city of my birth—Baltimore, Maryland. We are witnessing armed conflict between Russia and Ukraine, in which African immigrants have been at points denied access to safe environs outside of combat zones. Women's National Basketball Association star Brittany Griner has been detained by Russian police and remains in custody. Most recently, ten African Americans were murdered at a Tops Friendly Market on May 14 in Buffalo, New York, by Payton Gendron, an eighteen-year-old adherent of white supremacist ideology. To my horror, an article published in the 18 May 2022 edition of *Black Catholic Messenger* noted that the 180-page screed authored and published online by Gendron before his violent rampage drew on research by one of my Notre Dame faculty colleagues (Tinner-Williams 2022).

These are just a few of the elements that provide the backdrop against which I "live, move, and exist" (Acts 17:28) as a Black Bible scholar and philologist in 2022. I've described myself elsewhere as "a left-leaning, decidedly liberal Anglican priest," "Bluesman," and "poet" whose "work blends close reading with *sociopoetics* and *autoethnography*" and "seeks evocatively to blur the traditional boundaries between scholarship and art" (Page et al. 2009, xiii). I am also part of an institutional *matrix* built to shore up European colonial expansion and an American democratic experiment that has commodified Black bodies as engines to drive its growth. Acknowledgment within this academic machine, here and elsewhere, of the need for both reform and reparations, is only now beginning.

Truth-Telling and Troublemaking

Recognition of these sad facts commends embrace of the priorities for the Black scholar's vocation proposed by Vincent Harding more than four decades ago (1974), as well as consideration of how our (collective) research, teaching, administration, and service can be deployed in becoming what Bayard Rustin called "angelic troublemakers" courting what John Lewis termed "good trouble."[1] For me, the challenge is trying to figure out how to *conjure* change as an "inside outsider" or "outside insider" depending on how I am viewed within the academy or in BIPOC settings; how to *mess with* seemingly intractable structures that dehumanize and demean; how *to fix* systemic problems that are inimical to Black thriving and lead inexorably to social death; and how to create—*doctor up*, as it were—pockets of resistance, maroon communities—within and outside of primarily white universities where Black scholars and allies can thrive.[2]

Efforts of this kind seem to me more important than ever, given my own difficulty these days embracing Clyde Lovern Otis's hopeful sentiment (immortalized by Dinah Washington's voice) in the song "This Bitter Earth"—about the academic landscape for *Africana* Bible scholars in particular—perhaps not being "so bitter after all" (Washington 1997), and my increasingly frequent, typically unvoiced yet trenchant, retort for those making light of the dangerous American ethos we have to negotiate. Simply put, in the words of Blues artist Bobby Rush: "I ain't studdin' ya" (2021).

Then, Now, and When?

Some memories endure, though not all are meant to be disclosed publicly. A few should be shared, particularly if they help oneself and others make

---

1. The late John Lewis referred to "good trouble" in several of his public speeches. One particularly poignant occasion was an address given for the Barbara Lee and Elihu Harris Lecture Series, April 21, 2012, captured on video here—https://www.youtube.com/watch?v=Xdbz6q1AP44 (accessed 20 July 2022). Rustin's reference to "angelic troublemakers" is noted in one of the speeches recorded in the documentary about his life—*Brother Outsider: The Life of Bayard Rustin*, codirected by Kates and Singer (2003).

2. Here, I take inspiration from Vincent Wimbush's (2011) provocative address when he assumed the presidency of the Society of Biblical Literature and the lexicon of African-American *rootwork* in describing these transgressive endeavors.

sense of the present or figure out the next station stop on an uncertain journey. It is in this spirit that the following free verse musings on my pilgrimage to and through the academy are offered. They are random, more suited to revealing at the outset in poetry rather than prose.

FRAGMENTA

1977—A Lot Happened after Commencement

Incredulous looks
Aspirational disbelief
"*They* don't let *us* become Old Testament scholars"
"*They* say Black folk can't learn ancient languages"
"*We* have too many Episcopal *priests* already"
"Maryland hasn't ordained anybody *Black* in years"
"Have you considered being a *lawyer?*"

1984—What Planet Is This?

"Hampton? Did you mean Hampden-Sydney?"
Incredibly, maybe intentionally, bad advice on courses to take
A handwritten and incomplete *syllabus*—at Harvard?
The *Black Scale*–91% on a 100-point test = B+

1988 to 1990—OK, Survival Is Possible, Maybe

Take comprehensive exams in the hardest languages
Leave no doubt about your competency …
Handshake—"Best comprehensive exam I've *ever* read"
"Don't care what your specialty is,
Someday you'll be asked to run a Black Studies program …"
"If we hire you as a faculty member,
Can you handle labor relations with disaffected Black staff?"

1992 to 2021—Survival Maybe, But Thriving?

Job Security
Program Director
Department Chair

Associate Dean, Dean
Vice President and Associate Provost
One Semester of Sabbatical
... in Thirty Years

2022—And Now

Educational equity ...
How much progress have we made?
"No Knock" warrant in the Twin Cities and Amir Locke's death—When will it stop?
Ukraine is horrible ... doubly dangerous for those with dark skin

Then there is the BA.2
And other COVID variants...
Chris Rock, Jada Pinkett-Smith, and Will ...
Justice Brown-Jackson
And ongoing Supreme Court drama ...

And now, 10 dead in Buffalo, NY
A hate-filled terrorist assault
And a young man's screed
Citing a colleague's research ...

Coming out of Hampton University in 1977 I was, in a word, naïve. I knew precious little about the church and the academy. I envisioned a relatively straightforward middle-class life, with seminary training, graduate education, and employment at some college or university and/or church in the offing. Leaving the Black Baptist fold to join the Afro-Anglican branch of the church was, in retrospect, an act of intellectual and spiritual defiance. The same was true of my choice to be a Hebrew Bible scholar. Both were choices of a twenty-one-year-old who had no real clue about the implications of such actions or the at times painful and life-changing realizations they would elicit. I would learn, as some say, "quick, fast, and in a hurry," about the peculiarities of Black Episcopal life and the intersectional dynamics that have long shaped the academy. In retrospect, the fear, incredulity, and gatekeeping I encountered from a few *Africana* peers came, I suspect, from a place of genuine concern. I'm not nearly as sanguine about similar behaviors from the largely white faculty, academic administrators, review committees, commissions on ministry, standing committees, examining chaplains, clergy colleagues, and church officials with whom I interacted from 1977 to 1983. That I survived, relatively sane, is miraculous.

The same can be said of my time in Cambridge, Massachusetts: years spent in debt, barely skirting poverty, dodging homelessness, and managing occasional food insecurity while trying to get by as the only—and then one of three—Black students in an elite doctoral program in Near Eastern Languages and Civilizations. Among the hard lessons learned: many of my peers knew nothing of Hampton Institute, my undergraduate alma mater; evaluative scales for BIPOC folk in elite spaces can be subjective and unfair; and at times, when reliable guidance and support are lacking, you must: read between the lines, traverse *medial* spaces, rely on contested knowledge systems, trust your gut, be comfortable standing (literally and figuratively) alone, and never, ever *internalize* opinions about your value as a person or an intellectual from those who don't have your best interest at heart.

Entering the workforce—first, as a soon-to-be and then as a newly minted PhD—had its own unusual dimensions. Some did not know what to think about a Black Harvard Near Eastern Languages and Civilization graduate specializing in Hebrew Bible and having secondary proficiencies in Akkadian and Ugaritic languages. Also, there was very little institutional nuance in the diversity, equity, and inclusion efforts around faculty hiring at most of the places where I sought employment. I will not rehearse the litany of odd questions asked, inappropriate comments made, or peculiar reasons given about why certain job offers were not extended. Suffice it to say, I learned quickly that others perceived me to be a smart, self-possessed, and articulate Black Man well versed in disciplines (biblical studies, Semitic philology, ancient Near Eastern studies, Ugaritology, etc.) that made me, for some, an *ill fit* in certain kinds of professional spaces.

Now, closer to a career sunset than to that hopeful dawn some three decades ago, I wonder how I got and why I am still ... here. My recurring *mantra* these days is, "maybe it's time to tend *your* garden"; to escape further soul-draining servitude in colonized religious and academic spaces; and to cultivate what author Grey Gundaker (1998) has termed "home ground." As I assay the ravages that have accompanied fighting the good fight as a Black cleric (for more than forty years), Bible scholar (for more than three decades), and academic administrator (since 1999), I wonder about: the *impact* of my efforts; at what cost the ticket for this strange journey has come; how I might help prepare the next generation of those following me to survive the struggle; and how to manage day to day being an *Africana* Bible scholar in an academy where white supremacist thought continues to thrive and in an America where, as Ta-Nehisi Coates (2015, 103) reminds us, "it is traditional to destroy the Black Body."

I take this work seriously, all the while realizing that it comes with few rewards, little thanks, and enormous peril. Being an effective threshold *docent* at institutions not created for BIPOC scholars is anything but easy. There are hard choices and sacrifices to be made, some with career changing implications. Those that facilitate the passage of others often find themselves lagging or forgotten, their own professional advancement stalled, their dreams attenuated.

It pains me deeply to acknowledge that I've experienced dimensions of this firsthand throughout my career in both academic and ecclesial settings. Nonetheless, I've reoriented my scholarship and teaching to bring *Africana* epistemologies and lived realities into conversation with biblical and ancient Near Eastern texts and research and situated my efforts squarely within the context of twentieth- and twenty-first-century Africana Bible scholarship.[3] I've agreed to take on administrative positions and service obligations that, while rewarding in many respects, have been deemed of less value than production of large quantities of high-profile mainstream publications. I've helped launch diversity, equity, and inclusion initiatives and build programs. I've been the noisy minoritized presence in the classroom, on the front lines, and behind closed doors voicing uncomfortable truths about racism and justice to superiors and peers. At times I've been silenced, rendered hyper-visible, and erased. My body and soul bear the scars. Nonetheless, I continue these efforts because: it is the right thing to do; I'm too stubborn to quit; our lives—Black lives—absolutely depend on such efforts, however modest; and I contend that we have the capacity both to discover common ground[4] and embrace a radical love ethic that honors human dignity. I still believe we can instantiate an eschatological vision of the Beloved Community here and now. I am also conscious of my responsibility as a senior scholar, cleric, and academic administrator to create safe space for colleagues in the academy and church engaged in difficult endeavors. Toni Morrison's

---

3. On these conventions, see Smith 2017.
4. Here, I embrace the understanding of this phenomenon advanced by Howard Thurman (2000).

(2019: viii) counsel regarding writers working in dangerous situations is instructive in this regard:

> Writers who construct meaning in the face of chaos must be nurtured, protected. And it is right that such protection be initiated by other writers. And it is imperative not only to save the besieged writers but to save ourselves.

This advice is sobering and timely for those of us working in higher education and/or the church. It speaks to the need for communal nurture and self-care.

It is for these reasons that whatever the cost, amid crisis, I hold that my interventions and those of my *Africana* colleagues in biblical and cognate studies—philological, interpretive, expressive, and so on—are mediators of a power, an *àshe*,[5] that is truly transformational. Despite what anyone says, we matter.

Works Cited

Coates, Ta-Nehisi. 2015. *Between the World and Me*. New York: Spiegel & Grau.

Gundaker, Grey. 1998. "Introduction: Home Ground." Pages 3–23 in *Keep Your Head to the Sky: Interpreting African American Home Ground*. Edited by Grey Gundaker. Charlottesville: University Press of Virginia.

Harding, Vincent. 1974. "The Vocation of the Black Scholar." Pages 3–29 in *Education and the Black Struggle: Notes from the Colonized World*. Cambridge: Harvard Education Review.

Kates, Nancy D., and Barrett Singer, dirs. 2003. *Brother Outsider: The Life of Bayard Rustin*. San Francisco: California Newsreel.

Morrison, Toni. 2019. *Mouth Full of Blood: Essays, Speeches, Meditations*. London: Chatto & Windus.

Page, Hugh, et al., eds. 2009. *Africana Bible: Reading Israel's Scriptures from Africa and the African Diaspora*. Minneapolis: Fortress.

Rush, Bobby. 2021. *I Ain't Studdin' Ya: My American Blues Story*. New York: Hachette Books.

---

5. On the meaning of this term, see Thompson 1983, 7.

Smith, Mitzi, J. 2017. *Insights from African American Interpretation*. Edited by Mark Allen Powell. Insights: Reading the Bible in the Twenty-First Century. Minneapolis: Fortress.

Thompson, Robert Farris. 1983. *Flash of the Spirit: African and Afro-American Art and Philosophy*. New York: Random House.

Thurman, Howard. 2000. *The Search for Common Ground: An Inquiry into the Basis of Man's Experience of Community*. Repr. Richmond, IN: Friends United Press.

Tinner-Williams, Nate. 2022. "Catholic Professor from Notre Dame Cited in Buffalo Shooter's Manifesto." *Black Catholic Messenger*. https://tinyurl.com/SBL03112g.

Washington, Dinah. 1997. *Ultimate*. Baarn, Netherlands: Polygram Records.

Wimbush, Vincent. 2011. "Interpreters—Enslaving/Enslaved/Runagate." *JBL* 130:5–24.

We Should Be There for Them: Creating Communities of Support and Mentoring for Africana Biblical Scholars

SHARON WATSON FLUKER

This essay explores *creating communities of support* and *mentoring* for Africana biblical doctoral students and early career faculty. I argue that social capital, rich and dense networks of mutuality and reciprocity, is an indispensable asset that empowers students and faculty to survive and thrive in higher education institutions. I use *survive* to suggest that the retention of Africana scholars and other rising identities[1] is often difficult because of ongoing discrimination, and therefore, some choose to remain and fight for impactful change while others leave higher education altogether (Jones 2019). I use *thrive* to highlight that career satisfaction is attainable but only through the development of specific practices that support these scholars on their journeys (Gasman 2010). Yet survive and thrive must be understood within the limitations of the numbers game and the institutional context of religious, theological, and biblical studies. Specifically, there has been little progress with regard to the number of Africana biblical scholars within the lexicon of diversity, equity, and inclusion. In 2019, the Society of Biblical Literature, which is described as "the oldest and largest learned society devoted to the critical investigation of the Bible from a variety of academic disciplines," reported that among its members who were US citizens, 4.1 percent were of African descent and 85.6 percent were of

---

1. See Pinder-Amaker and Wadsworth 2021, 4. In n. 2 of chapter 1, the authors indicate that Dr. Melanie Tervalon suggested the term *rising identities* as an alternative to *marginalized*. Pinder-Amaker and Wadsworth view the term as more empowering, and I agree. I use it here in the introduction. In other parts of this essay, I use *underrepresented* to signal a specific time frame of my work when that term was more commonly used.

European/Caucasian descent ("2019 SBL Membership Data"). This data has changed very little over the past several years.

More recently, the importance and presence of Africana scholars has been elevated since the Black Lives Matter protests against police brutality of African Americans begun by the death of George Floyd in Minneapolis, Minneapolis, on May 25, 2020. Eerily the images of these protests remind us of the Norman Rockwell painting, *The Problem We All Live With*, published in *Look* magazine in 1964 with its depiction of a young Ruby Bridges walking between US Marshals in 1960 as she desegregated the New Orleans Public Schools. The voice of James Baldwin also resonates here as he recounts with alarm a similar incident while living in Paris of seeing the newspaper photos of Dorothy Counts, a fifteen-year-old young girl facing an angry and violent mob as she walked into Harding High School in Charlotte, North Carolina for the first time in 1957 (Glaude 2020, 29–31). The continuing resistance to the desegregation of schools across the South following the 1954 *Brown v. Board of Education* decision and bearing witness to its horror, led Baldwin to proclaim, "Some one of us should have been there with her!" (31*)*. As Rockwell's painting and Baldwin's reflection changed the conversation about race and civil rights and woke up a new generation and initiated an era of freedom fighters in the 1960s, we are also challenged by contemporary freedom struggles. BLM not only involved wide scale protests lasting several months but ignited a global response as well. The social fallout extended beyond the academy into the sequestered halls of corporations, government agencies, nonprofits, and private businesses and led to calls for broader understanding, awareness, and action leading toward social justice and equity.

Yet, the number of Africana biblical scholars *does* tell a story. They have been a part of the larger academy for decades, but their small numbers reveal the misconceptions about their status in doctoral programs and how Africana faculty struggle for survival in predominantly white theological schools, seminaries and universities. While we are learning more, we still need even more data that speak to the unique experiences and issues facing them so that they can be fully addressed. Our continued learning and awareness are critical if we hope to move beyond rhetoric about diversity and live into authentic equity and inclusion practices. Authentic equity and inclusion practices will be costly and require nothing short of dismantling and restructuring long-standing practices that erase institutional memory and policies that maintain the status quo. Reactionary window dressing and benevolent gesturing are not adequate for the formidable tasks wrought by protracted and systemic racism in our cherished fields of biblical scholarship and teaching. To look forward to a better future "will mean taking action when you hear of something that could be done to make the system more just" (Pinder-Amaker and Wadsworth 2021, 178). It will also mean working alongside and in some instances following the lead of Africana scholars.

Meanwhile …

Given this incredibly complex and arduous context, the question becomes: How do Africana graduate students and emerging faculty survive and thrive in the many multilayered structures and labyrinths of race in the academy? Below I briefly map out some of the climate challenges for Africana doctoral students and faculty. In addition, I provide a short narrative of my own doctoral journey and the need for creating communities of support and mentoring as forms of social capital using the Fund for Theological Education's[2] doctoral program in the late 1990s as a case study.

The Climate Challenges for Africana Doctoral Students and Faculty

By and large, academic institutions have acknowledged the need to end institutional racism by embracing diversity plans, policies, and programs as benefits to their long-term futures. Yet, despite many efforts across higher education, progress has been slow among faculty in tenure-track and tenure positions. (Matias Lewis and Hope 2021).

In August 2020, the Society of Biblical Literature held a virtual symposium entitled #BlackScholarsMatter with twelve Africana biblical scholars exploring some of the institutional climate issues that remain challenges.[3] Reflections by the participants were based on their own experiences and observations as doctoral students and faculty in the academy. These discussions outlined several ongoing challenges for Africana scholars including the paradox of encouraging students to pursue doctoral studies while the job market is uncertain and the ethical issues this raises; getting funding for their research when it is considered marginal or not valued; advising

---

2. The Fund for Theological Education was renamed The Forum for Theological Exploration in 2014.
3. https://www.sbl-site.org/meetings/blackscholarsmatter.aspx.

and committee overloads that can impact time available for teaching preparation and research; tenure concerns in a time of financial uncertainty; developing a research agenda that has clear impacts for the communities they serve, et cetera. *What we learned was* that career advancement and job satisfaction are impacted by the lack of an environment of support and instances of racism. *What was also clear* were the institutional failures in the accountability structures for hiring, promotion, and research funding for early career faculty. The lessons learned from this virtual symposium speak profoundly to the challenge of supportive environments and mentoring and the need to develop capacity through the acquisition of social capital among peers, faculty, and other resources in institutions and beyond.

Building Social Capital: What Does That Mean?

Within the context of democracy and civil society, Robert D. Putnam in *Bowling Alone* suggests that social capital includes dense networks of relationality and reciprocity for a civil society to exist. He goes on to say that these networks and deep connections are built on "high levels of trust and citizen participation … through a variety of mechanism(s) to produce socially desired outcomes" (Putnam 2000, 288). In other words, social capital is a critical asset, and possessing it can have clear benefits. For example, social capital can encourage collaboration efforts; produce innovation and progress in everyday interactions; increase our understanding of how we are linked as individuals and communities; support the flow of communication and information for both personal and professional gain; and bring general satisfaction to our lives (288–89).

Although Putnam's discussion of social capital is focused on the strengthening of civil society, having social capital can also be a much-needed asset for Africana biblical scholars especially in a white dominant academy. As scholars begin their careers, it becomes essential that they build support for their research and teaching and that they have communities of personal and professional support to enhance their individual lives. How does this happen when the academy, based on its history, is not necessarily welcoming, accessible, or open to Africana scholars? How can we envision a future that is transformative, acknowledging the past and yet working toward something new and bold? Access to *a community of support and mentoring* built on shared interests and values is an important way to begin to think about that future. These were the levers used to help Africana biblical scholars and others build social capital as fellowship recipients in the new doctoral fellowship program for African Americans begun at the Fund for Theological Education in the late 1990s, which I discuss below. But first, I offer my own doctoral journey as an example of the issues involved and as a case for creating a community of support and mentoring as social capital.

A Personal Guidepost: My Doctoral Journey

Mentors

Before beginning my teaching and administrative career in the 1980s, I learned as a graduate student that *having a mentor* was an important means of acquiring social capital. I entered graduate school in the late 1970s as the only African American in my small cohort of first-year students. In addition, I was a fully funded graduate student bringing a prestigious fellowship from outside the department, but that had its pluses and deltas as I would later learn.[4] When it came time to serve as a teaching assistant or compete with my peers for a position on grant funded projects in my department, I knew I had to develop and sustain professional and structured personal relationships with a few professors in order to be considered. It was simply not enough to show up for classes or greet the professors in the hallways. Moreover, coming from a small historically black liberal arts college, I understood how beneficial mentors could be in a tight knit community helping me through a myriad of issues during times of uncertainty. And in my graduate school experience, being aware of racial dynamics, the culture shock of a larger university setting, and learning to manage my time well would mean accessing a number of new strategies and practices.

After listening and observing for a few months, I expanded my graduate school success plan to include getting to know some key faculty to

---

4. Often teaching and research opportunities were automatically given to graduate students directly funded by the department. In rare instances during this time, unless teaching was part of the departmental requirements, students receiving external support had to lobby for teaching or research assignments. In my case, serving as a teaching assistant was a requirement. Research positions were more competitive.

ensure I received program guidance, support, and career advice. In a couple of instances, I chose faculty mentors who were some of my hardest professors and were *not* in my areas of interest. I set up my meetings with selected faculty and outlined our conversations in order to explore mutual expectations and goals moving forward. This proved helpful for me as I was always interested in multiple perspectives. I also wanted to build these relationships before I actually needed them. Over time, even my assigned department adviser became a mentor and was instrumental in guiding me toward my first postdoctoral fellowship and later teaching positions. My plan worked well, and I took away many lessons on *identifying* mentors through a bit of trial and error and *using* them effectively as I progressed in my professional career.

Accessing External Resources and Communities of Support

My external fellowship at that time did not come with additional resources or support outside of funding. By that I mean there was no mentoring offered or a community of support among other fellowship recipients locally or nationally—our names were simply listed in a directory. My tuition and basic living expenses were covered by the fellowship, which was designed specifically to identify promising African American students for doctoral study across several disciplines. While my community of support was limited on campus, I sought personal relationships off campus at a local church and built long time relationships that have lasted to this day. However, this church community was unable to understand my day-to-day routines or feelings of campus isolation. As I remember that directory of fellowship recipients from my external fellowship, I wondered at that time what it would be like to meet some of those other fellows. What experiences were they having in their departments? How were they preparing for comprehensive exams? How were they thinking about their first job interviews? There were many questions.

    I would later understand the value of a community of support when I managed my first doctoral fellowship as an administrator at a major private university. The Dorothy Danforth Compton Fellowship was a multi-year fellowship designed to support underrepresented groups in the academy across a variety of arts and science disciplines at ten targeted universities. Each institution had a fellowship coordinator who was the contact for all fellowship students on its particular campus. The fellowship included meetings and receptions for recipients across the university's departments during the academic year and a biennial conference inclusive of all fellowship recipients attending the ten schools.[5] From this administrative experience, I also acquired lessons on program development and design in building a supportive environment for doctoral students from underrepresented groups in the academy.

Building A Supportive Community and the Power of Mentoring

The Fund for Theological Education's African American Doctoral Program as a Case Study

My administrative positions for well over twenty years have included working with fellowship programs designed to provide greater access to students from groups that have been traditionally underrepresented in higher education settings. In the late 1990s, I accepted a position as a program director at The Fund for Theological Education. Begun in 1954, the organization had a long history of providing funding for students from underrepresented groups to pursue doctoral study to diversify theological school faculties and funding for quality candidates for ministry. In addition, there were established commitments from its leadership advocating for faculty diversity through its growing networks. Leaders at that time such as John D. Rockefeller Jr., Nathan Pusey, Robert Rankin, Benjamin E. Mays, C. Shelby Rooks, and others from across ministry, education, and foundation sectors elevated the dialogue on diversity to the forefront of higher education and it has remained there for well over fifty years. Experiencing a rebirth in the late 1990s with new innovative ministry and doctoral programs, funding from Lilly Endowment and other foundations, and new leadership, the Fund for Theological Education expanded its work. The organization would continue to experiment with programs, challenge the status quo in theological education, and build on its learning (Strom 2004, 5–40).

---

5. The Dorothy Danforth Compton Minority Fellowship was established in 1981 by the Danforth Foundation. The fellowship supported traditionally underrepresented students in higher education to pursue the PhD across disciplines among ten institutions to help diversify university faculties. The ten institutions included University of Chicago, Columbia, Cornell, Howard, Stanford, University of Texas (Austin), University of California (LA), Vanderbilt, Washington (Seattle), and Yale.

My work focused on designing a new fellowship program that would continue the important work of the Fund for Theological Education in supporting African American students in doctoral programs in biblical studies, theology, and religion. This opportunity was unique because I could be creative in imagining new components of the program. My own educational and early career experiences had taught me that while receiving funding was a top priority for students entering doctoral programs—*mentoring* and creating *an environment of support* would be critical in long-term student success and important as they sought to build social capital.

The overall *goal* of this fellowship was to provide funding to support promising African American doctoral students in biblical studies, theology, and religion. Entering doctoral students received funding for the first two years of course work but could also later apply for dissertation year support. At this time, it was believed that, by providing this external funding, students would feel less burdened with having to take out loans or work outside the graduate program, which sometimes prolonged their progress. Aside from funding, there were other questions to consider as the program was designed: Could an external fellowship program help mitigate the impacts of the racial dynamics some students were experiencing in their departments? What other resources beyond funding could the fellowship provide? How might we use African American faculty and others concerned with faculty diversity more intentionally? As a support, could the doctoral fellowship help students complete their degrees? Could the program build collaborations with institutions and doctoral departments to build allies for the program? These questions and others helped to further design the fellowship program.

From the beginning, I had a two-pronged approach after ensuring students were receiving their funding on time with few bureaucratic hurdles: (1) develop a set of *shared experiences* that were bonding and (2) encourage *a mentoring network* of faculty and peers that could assist students and early career faculty in navigating the academy.

Creating Shared Experiences and an Environment of Support

Shared experiences are the hallmarks of community building and the basis of friendships that can last a lifetime. I began with designing an *annual conference* with the doctoral fellows and African American faculty serving as presenters and mentors throughout a weekend. The conference always had a theme highlighting a research area or broad educational landscape issue important in theological education with sections also devoted to doctoral student life and career issues. This framework set the stage for rich dialogue around the teaching and research contributions that African American students and faculty could make to change and transform the academy and impact the communities they represented.

For decades, Africana biblical scholars had been excluded as the producers of knowledge and critical research in the field while also having their realities sometimes distorted by white scholars in scholarly journals, in classrooms, and in professional organizations. Resistance to this omission and defining their own realities were already taking place among other Africana biblical scholars, and the belief was that a new generation of scholars would continue the work.[6] As a community of fellows, these biblical students and others were affirmed in their identities while also exploring possibilities for change through their own work. Each year, new doctoral students were attending the conference building trust, sharing experiences, and developing faculty and peer mentoring relationships and *creating dense networks of mutuality and reciprocity.*

There were other shared experiences with the fellows in varied professional contexts. For example, they received stipends to attend the Annual Meetings of the American Academy of Religion and the Society of Biblical Literature where they could reconnect with one another and attend panels, lectures, and conference receptions; some attended other discipline-area conferences where they presented papers or had unique research needs that required additional funding; and dissertation year fellows participated in an annual writing workshop with editors specifically chosen who could encourage and mentor them in the writing process. What did these experiences do for the fellows and for the larger academy? Fellows became acquainted with one another and sharpened their teaching and research interests in community making them feel less isolated. For some, they were the only Africana graduate students in their department. What's more, fellows were able to serve as peer mentors to one another establishing accountability structures and cheering each other on in their research, writing, and job searches. This doctoral community also became

---

6. The nascent periods of Africana biblical scholarship, struggled within the limited paradigm and restricting harness of the historical-critical method over three decades. Several Africana biblical scholars during this time included Charles Copher, Randall C. Bailey, Gay Byron, Dwight Callahan, Michael J. Brown, Cain Hope Felder, Clarice J. Martin, Renita J. Weems, Vincent L. Wimbush, among others.

visible in the academy not only among the individual institutions they represented but in the larger academy as their numbers grew. This became evident during the annual receptions begun in the late 1990s at the Annual Meetings of the American Academy of Religion and the Society of Biblical Literature where they were presented as a community. Fellows were meeting foundation executives, presidents and deans, faculty, and other administrators from a variety of institutions, and these new relationships would pay off in a number of ways. Most notably, this visibility was important in the diversity numbers game as theological schools, seminaries, and universities sought to identify persons of color for advertised teaching or administrative positions at their institutions.

The Power of Mentoring

In exploring the delivery of doctoral education across most disciplines in the academy, mentoring relationships have long been accepted as a practice between more senior scholars and graduate students as part of an apprenticeship model. This mentoring relationship can sometimes begin at the very start as new doctoral students are accepted into programs based on the shared research interests between faculty members and incoming students. It is more likely that over time in a program, a student might choose a faculty mentor and together that relationship grows built on shared trust, values, interests, and respect. We have learned over time that this one-on-one mentoring relationship can be viewed as limiting since one mentor typically cannot meet all the needs of a student.

As we have gathered more research on the mentoring relationships and practices, students have been empowered to build structured personal relationships that support their individual journey with *multiple mentors* (Cosgove 2021, 50–52). A *mentoring network* can help students explore broader issues about their lives beyond the doctoral program. In addition, it is not unusual for undergraduate and graduate programs to have both formal and informal mentoring programs among other tools and strategies to assist students in building social capital.

We have known for some time that for Africana biblical students and early career faculty, it can sometimes be difficult to find mentors with whom they share common interests or cultural backgrounds. We have realized these students and faculty often feel isolated since they are not the beneficiaries of a department's informal support and nurturing typically reserved for white males. (Cosgove 2021, 46). Willie James Jennings (2020,

24–33) in *After Whiteness: An Education in Belonging*, describes the advantages of this nurturing up close in an interview committee's final decision to select a white male over another compelling black woman candidate. As a result, Africana doctoral students are sometimes not as familiar with informal rules of the doctoral journey and lack adequate career advice or preparation. The lack of mentors can be a stumbling block especially at the beginning of a career when many key decisions are made affecting life and profession. As a result, many students have sought other strategies in finding mentors including external fellowship programs and identifying Africana faculty at other institutions.

In developing a mentoring practice for the The Fund for Theological Education doctoral fellows, an informal mentoring model was employed during these early years of the new fellowship. All of the shared experiences and programs included a group of selected Africana faculty and others from a variety of area disciplines to serve as mentors. This allowed the fellows to develop organic relationships with faculty. Each conference or program, for example, had a different configuration of Africana faculty as presenters and lecturers. Exposure to a variety of faculty seemed particularly important since, in some cases, the institutions the students were attending had no Africana faculty. In sharing meals, after panel presentations or lectures, and student group discussions, faculty were encouraged to be available to students for conversations and mentoring opportunities. The students had agency to determine who they wanted to talk with and develop ongoing mentoring relationships over time. This seemed the best strategy given the finite face-to-face time available and the focused questions students often had for specific faculty. It was not unusual for students to request appointment times with a faculty member ahead of a conference.

In addition to faculty mentoring, peer mentoring was a part of the community building process. All those questions I had asked myself in my own doctoral program when I did not have a community, I could hear students asking each other when they gathered at the Fund for Theological Education conferences and programs. Students who had been in their programs longer freely shared with newer doctoral students about their experiences and solutions to common issues. Again, the peer mentoring model was an informal one. Students were encouraged to build these relationships among themselves. Many students have lasting friendships today in the profession that began during these early days as doctoral fellows.

Toward a Different Future

In summary, this discussion contends that by building a community of support and developing a mentoring practice, Africana scholars accrue social capital that can help them survive and thrive in the academy by retaining it in higher education and providing career satisfaction. As social capital, these practices specifically help mitigate some of the impacts of race, gender, sexual orientation, and other forms of discrimination for Africana graduate students and faculty as we seek to imagine a more diverse and sustainable professional culture.

Returning to Rockwell's painting and Baldwin's reflection during these current times reminds us of the continued resistance to change and the timeless pursuit toward faculty diversity in the academy. To paraphrase Baldwin's words here, "*We Should Be There For Them!*" Without a doubt, the summer protests of 2020, the police killings of unarmed African Americans, and the ongoing health pandemic brought issues of injustice and inequities to the forefront not only in the United States but globally. The paths before us in the academy, the nation, and indeed the globe call upon us to reimagine our future and the futures of emerging scholars and faculty who will inherit that future. The goal is for Africana biblical scholars to live into their full humanity. The challenge of mentoring and creating strong and sustainable environments of learning that are diverse, equitable, and inclusive *is our calling* and our contribution to that new future.

> You cannot stop the call of history—freedom, justice for all humankind.
> —John Lewis (1940–2020), Civil Rights activist, member of the United States Congress

Works Cited

Cosgrove, Charles H., ed. 2021. *Voices of The Mentored: Scholars of Color Speak*. Atlanta: The Forum for Theological Exploration.

Gasman, Marybeth. 2010. *Ten Ways To Retain Faculty of Color*. Diverse. June 21. https://tinyurl.com/SBL03112i.

Glaude, Eddie S. 2020. *Begin Again: James Baldwin's America and Its Urgent Lessons for Our Own*. New York: Crown.

Jennings, Willie James. 2020. *After Whiteness: An Education in Belonging*. Grand Rapids: Eerdmans.

Jones, LaMont. 2019. "Endless Exodus: Faculty of Color Leave the Academy in Search of Fulfillment." Diverse. July 30. https://tinyurl.com/SBL03112h.

Matias, J. Nathan, Neil Lewis Jr., and Elan Hope. 2021. "Universities Say They Want More Diverse Faculties: So Why Is the Academy Still So White?" FiveThirtyEight. September 7. https://tinyurl.com/SBL03112j.

Pinder-Amaker, Stephanie, and Lauren Wadsworth. 2021. *Did That Just Happen?! Beyond Diversity—Creating Sustainable and Inclusive Organizations*. Boston: Beacon.

Putnam, Robert D. 2000. *Bowling Alone*. New York: Simon & Schuster.

Society of Biblical Literature. "2019 SBL Membership Data." https://www.sbl-site.org/assets/pdfs/sblMemberProfile2019.pdf.

Strom, Jonathan. 2004. *A Half-Century of Strengthening Christian Ministry: The Fund for Theological Education*. Atlanta: The Fund for Theological Education.

Come Join Us, Sweetheart!

MAI-ANH LE TRAN

> May I write words more naked than flesh,
> stronger than bone, more resilient than
> sinew, sensitive than nerve.
>
> —Sappho[1]

I was a Blue Bandanna on that day. It was Monday, October 13, 2014, an organized Moral Monday in St. Louis, Missouri, which concluded a long Weekend of Resistance in a series of Ferguson October actions that was part of the Ferguson Uprising following the shooting death of the African American teenager Michael Brown.

On that weekend, mindful of the fact that every movement needs multiple parts and roles, not all of which need to be visible to be impactful (or, more honestly speaking, not all of which I had enough courage to undertake), I volunteered to serve as a marshal, or "peacekeeper." Since I had gone to one (just one) training session and had served in earlier events that weekend, for that Moral Monday march the marshal leader sorted me into the elite team of roughly ten to twelve volunteers, assigned to so-called high-risk buffering work. We were each given a blue bandanna to wear in some visible way, and our task was twofold: block traffic for a crowd that was estimated to be several hundred so that they could march from a local United Methodist church to the Ferguson Police Department; and, upon arrival at the police station, create a buffer zone between a group of clergy seeking arrest and the rest of the marchers who had no such intention. I had absolutely no business being with the seasoned peacekeepers. They were twenty-something activists, cool and swift. Next to them, I was a stodgy

---

1. As cited by the late author and artist Theresa Hak Kyung Cha in her avant-garde novel *Dictee*.

academic, inexperienced with community organizing work, let alone movement leadership, with barely enough wit to exercise active followership.

As I would later describe through written work (Tran 2017b), the church was packed that morning. There was praying, singing, nervous idling commingled with contemplative waiting. Organizers huddled to review sketches of marching routes and formations. We were instructed to take bold markers and write the phone number for bail support onto our arms—a phone number etched on our arms in case of arrest. I had never so much as scribbled notes on my hand. The marshal leader repeated: "Remember, no matter which formation the march ends up taking, you need to stand between the clergy who are risking arrest, and the rest of the people behind them." Pumped with both fear and purpose, I had more questions than real-time action would allow, and since everyone looked like they knew exactly what they were doing, I followed along. It began to rain. We Blue Bandannas got into our first position: a straight line cutting across the street outside of the church. Behind us was a barricade of media crews and their equipment, lenses fixed upon the door of that church from which marchers would emerge. We waited a good while in the drizzling rain....

Suddenly, it began. The church door swung open, and rows of arms-locked bodies began spilling out into the street in rhythmic fashion. Out of their mouths was that familiar spiritual so piercing its amplitudes could have parted the rain, "Ain't gonna let nobody turn me 'round ... turn me 'round ... turn me 'round...."

I had participated in protest marches prior to this. Only a few, but enough to remember the power of their kinesthetic energy. For all of them, however, I had only been but a particle within a multitude and had always done my best to maneuver away from cameras to avoid any attention or solicitation of some eloquent rationale for my semi-public act. On that Monday, however, for the first time in my life, I was standing smack in the middle of the street, facing an assembly of bodies determined to pray with stomping feet ... and they were headed straight at me, with no indication of relenting.

"What do we do?!" I heard a whisper. The Blue Bandannas were flummoxed as the crowd continued to quicken its pace toward us, and the singing grew louder. Before I could hear instructions to break formation and "get out of the way," the wall of arms-locked bodies swept right over me ... and in the midst of the loud singing, a faint voice beckoned toward my direction, "Come join us, sweetheart!"

Those words have haunted me to this day. I have written about this incident and drawn lessons on the public pedagogies of bodies exercising public witness against unjust social systems (Tran 2017a; 2017b). I have also waxed with some indignation with friends on the existential marginality of an Asian female body being called "sweetheart"—a form of gendered negation in the trenches, if you will. Yet, I have not sufficiently acknowledged what power those words had on me in that moment. The caller—and I would bet it was some prominent faith leader from among the front rows—must have known. Whatever assumptions I had cautiously constructed about solidarity, allyship, and public action for the reclamation of Black dignity and Black lives were being chipped away piece by piece on that day—by the ink against my yellow-tone immigrant flesh, by the rain that washed off the thin veneer of theatricality, by the human wave that made me cower and my body bent over. Don't be a bystander, the seer must have meant. Join the movement as if your very life depended on it.

In the hours that followed, I caught glimpses of what it is like to be swept up by "mimetic ecstasy" (Tran 2017b, 17), a regenerative power of positive mimesis, when I found myself enjoining a body of people who learned through proximal mirroring how to extend oneself for another. Locked arms made impenetrable human chains. Each time a grip broke loose due to over-exertion or over-extension, another would grab hold, the gap restored, and the collective body was protracted. If the inertia of disimagination (28) lures us into a state of moral apathy, being swept over and then swept up by the multitude of that day reenchanted me to new existence possibilities for this world. Black lives don't just matter in rhetorical abstractions. *Black lives always matter in the flesh.* Standing in that social space-time, drenched in unrelenting rain, all of my resident-alien-turned-naturalized-citizen self knew that I needed new bones, sinews, and nerves for that new invitation toward interdependent enfleshment.

They don't teach you that in graduate school. Nor did my teaching up to that point as then eleven-year "veteran" theological educator aspired toward such telos.

Of Bones, Sinews and Nerves

I am a scholar, educator, and administrator of Vietnamese descent, whose personal journey towards racial conscientization was catalyzed by several powerful teachers of Black, diasporic, Africana descent, whom I secretly looked to as mentor figures through peripheral learning. I first learned of the work of literary giant, cultural worker, and social activist bell hooks and the foundations of emancipatory, transgressive teaching from practical theologian Evelyn L. Parker. I remember a class session in which Evelyn (who, for the longest time, remained my "Dr. Parker") had her class listen to a selection from an album of the Black American singer, songwriter, rapper Lauryn Hill, titled "The Miseducation of Lauryn Hill." Evelyn asked us to get up from our seats and dance to the lyricism of Hill's neo soul beat. I stood still, my Asian female body only knew then the performance of paralysis, having never danced publicly in my life. Evelyn flashed a knowing smile; her body kept its steady rhythm. How true ring the words of Korean American literary genius Theresa Cha (2009, 3): "From the back of her neck she releases her shoulders free. She swallows once more. (Once more. One more time would do.) In preparation. It augments. To such a pitch. Endless drone, refueling itself. Autonomous. Self-generating." It might have just been a twitch, but my stiffened body was on its way toward self-regeneration.

The aesthetic enchantment of one Black educator tinkered with my critical affect as much as it expanded my capacity for critical thinking. As Baltimore bead artist Joyce Scott said, art can enrapture you with its beauty and then smack you upside the head and wake you up (Craft in America 2022). It was far more than scholarly exposure—a tack often deployed in graduate theological study to either expand or subvert disciplinary canons. Rather, it was an invitation to existential entanglement that generated synapses for more lasting sinews and nerves of connection. As a graduate student, I was no stranger to selectively curated Black literature and Black theology, having *had* to study them from/with white teachers whose own racialized melancholia (Cheng 2001) prevented them from ever making space for me as an Asian foreigner-within and my version of the world within the Black and White continuum. But somehow, in learning to release my shoulders free alongside a freedom-seeking practical theologian who excavated the soul stories of subjugated peoples, while mesmerized by how a thinker and dreamer like bell hooks could sustain enduring dialogue on engaged pedagogy with the Vietnamese Buddhist teacher Thích Nhất Hạnh, and flailing about amid a public liturgy of protest—these became the "boundary events" (Trinh 2011) that made porous and permeable my horizon of understanding and human capability for life-long reciprocal entwinement with those who are Other to me due to colonial differential racialization. It is what helped to explain my own "self-discovery" and "self-recovery" (hooks 1999, 5) when marking time with faith leaders and movement organizers on the streets of Ferguson,

Missouri, on that Moral Monday in 2014. I learned only later that there with me in Ferguson were the spirits of revolutionaries like Yuri Nakahara Kochiyama, whose home was a place of hospitality and radical social dreaming for cross-racial and pan-ethnic civil rights activists. It is what allows me to be sustained in an embrace with a young millennial activist, who broke into sobs as she murmured, "I'm tired...." Tired that hate still wins, violence prevails, and systemic injustice continues to be shrouded by impunity. It is what allows me to look in the eyes of a white student and ask them to imagine what difference it would make for their existence-possibilities if they were to surrender themselves to the forming and transforming power of a Black professor. Not just learn the knowledge that they impart but be refashioned under the life force of their wisdom. It is what allows me to receive the criticisms of Black colleagues who wish that my voice of resistance wasn't so muted, as I, in turn, insist that they recognize my silence as a form of speech and my conspicuous invisibility within the racialized continuum of Black and White.

Enchanted[2]

Increasingly, scholars have looked to third spaces—a safe distance from where they must labor for economic and professional security—to overcome the prevailing absence of scholarship from the margins by minoritized scholars in mainstream institutional curricula. The dearth is not incidental but rather organized and designed. As has been pointed out, selective voices and embodiments may be lauded, even canonized, but their body of work (and their bodies at work) seldom materialize at the level of meticulous, expansive, exhaustive study within mainstream scholarship. Who goes out of their way to call out for us and the scholarship that is mediated by our bodily, sense-filled meaning-making? It is too easily treated as ornamental additive (I have heard it referred to as "perspectival") or relegated to the status of revered relic, admired from afar. A sprinkle here or there—proof-texted, out of context, praised for existence on the slant, yet vulnerable to being thrust against that white background for interrogation and disintegration. The poet Claudia Rankine (2014, 25) reminds us of Zora Neal Hurston's prescient words, "I feel most colored when I am thrown against a sharp white background."

---

2. A nod to the notion of ecstatic enchantment as developed by Philip Wexler (1996).

I don't just want to take the opportunity here to reinforce the argument that biblical scholarship grounded in the Black, diasporic, Africana experience *matters*, just as we shouldn't have to, but know that we must, necessarily argue anyway that Black lives matter. Instead, through bits of autoethnographic memory, I ponder how such bodies of scholarship *teach* us, enrapture us, and smack us upside the head. A couple of ways for consideration, as gleaned from the phronesis of writer and teacher bell hooks.

First, the body of scholarship grounded in the Black diasporic Africana experience teaches from the wellspring of counter-hegemonic insistence and resistance. With due acknowledgement of gender differentials, we note the self-generative power of Black female authorship, as each authorial voice as teaching body is a medium for revelatory learning. As bell hooks (1999, xiii) posited, when Black women write, "there is always someone [or some force] standing ready to silence the natural impulse to create as it arises ... and so to write [is to] resist." And the resistance is not solitary, for it is powered by the existential heft and spiritual reservoirs of ancestors who suffered on these shores (xvi) and of their descendants who continue to bleed on the streets. It must have taken the combination of muscle, social, historical, and generational memories of their racialized and gendered bodies for the Black millennial activists to have claimed the power to become their own "diseuse" (Cha 2001, 3), narrators who voice the suffering of their ancestors as they insisted on collective ethical responsibility for the vulnerable bodies of their generation. To know, to teach, to testify, to write, to profess and protest, to (re)direct others' understandings as if our essential aliveness depends on it, to create, to churn, to draw out, to ignite knowledge from such depths: it is scholarship that is bound to astound us with its beauty as it stuns us with its pain.

Second, biblical scholarship grounded in the Black diasporic Africana experience traces an itinerary of inter-millennial retrieval, recovery, reclamation, and regeneration—a process necessarily arduous for the scholar, yet a path toward healing, a ritual of sanctification, in the sense described by hooks (1999, 22). There is insistence on individual and communal well-being and wholeness as the spiritual grounding for scholarly grit. There is also insistence on rapturous pleasure as part and parcel of embodied knowing. These are the elements of bone, sinew, and nerve that allow us to be lifted beyond ourselves even as we dig deep into darkness, as hooks explicated. Our mind and spirit are "alchemically altered" upon encountering it (xvi).

None of this suggests warm-fuzzy celebration, superficial solidarity, or guilt-ridden idolization of bodies of scholarship and scholarly bodies that know how to face into the depth of human suffering and brokenness and demand correctives of liberation and hermeneutics of love. Black diasporic Africana scholarship (and specifically Black biblical scholarship) matters because it is constitutive of the collective conversation and sanctification of colonial, racialized regimes of knowing and knowledge. Thus, it was with ecstatic enchantment that I first cited Musa W. Dube for intersectional postcolonial feminist readings of biblical texts, had my mind blown by the self-described gadfly Vincent L. Wimbush, wished I had become a biblical scholar to coconspire with Mitzi J. Smith to expose sacralized pedagogies of oppression, and found solace in the realization that icons such as Renita J. Weems are blazes that mark destination and direction—possibilities and destinies—for more than just Black bodies and Black scholarship. The work of these scholars alchemically alters those who engage it. Touched by their magic, I in turn regained the appetite for the theological space and scriptural imaginary of my peoples, and I am reenchanted to the material concreteness of works by the likes of Hebrew Bible scholar Gale Yee, Taiwanese theologian C. S. Song, and biblical hermeneut and Sri Lankan gadfly R. S. Sugirtharajah.

Within the study of theology and religion, Black diasporic Africana biblical scholarship matters not only because it adds to historical and contemporary canons of knowledge. If that were the only reason, then one could say, "but that's not my genre," or "what about my context—does it not matter, too?" I have witnessed faculties fractured by this either/or anxiety. As though they shan't shoulder the same sky, goes a saying in Vietnamese. More dangerously, there is the subtle insinuation that "it's not my context; therefore I don't need to know it" (or, the seemingly more open-minded, "it's not my context; how could I possibly know it"). Black diasporic Africana biblical scholarship—as with other bodies of minoritized scholarship—does not invite knowing in the form of mastery, identification, assimilation, or cooptation. Rather, it is an invitation into boundary events that probe the depth of human psyches, histories, spiritualities, and scriptural imaginaries. And it invites a home-coming—a journey toward at-homeness with the bones, sinews, and nerves that constitute the respective location of each interlocutor, each a situated, social being, "[dreamer] of possible utopias, capable of being angry because of the capacity to love" (Freire 1998, 45).

Reveries

Context matters. Places and their signifiers teach as a living curriculum. Cultural stories and muscle memories choreograph embodiments. The events of that Ferguson October and the scholarship produced by Black scholars about and out of that movement have reset the discourses for many of our academic disciplines and theological curricula. What doesn't get talked about much is that part of becoming woke are the night sweats, when one realizes that one has awakened to the nightmare of one's making. Perhaps academics might take a lesson or two from the streets—the scholarship of gritty corporeal practices by young movement leaders who recited with mimetic ecstasy the words of those who came before them, that seemingly contradictory insistence upon a "duty to fight for our freedom" (Assata Shakur), which is realizable only through a nonviolent, "strong, demanding love" (Martin Luther King Jr).[3]

Works Cited

Cha, Theresa Hak Kyung. 2001. *Dictee*. Berkeley: University of California Press.

Cheng, Anne Anlin. 2001. *The Melancholy of Race*. Oxford: Oxford University Press.

Craft in America. n.d. "Messages: Joyce J. Scott Segment." https://www.craftinamerica.org/short/joyce-j-scott-segment.

Folayan, Sabaah, and Damon Davis. 2017. *Whose Streets?* http://www.whosestreetsfilm.com/

Freire, Paulo. 1998. *Pedagogy of Freedom: Ethics, Democracy, and Civic Courage*. Lanham, MD: Rowman & Littlefield.

hooks, bell. 1999. *Remembered Rapture: The Writer at Work*. New York: Holt.

King, Martin Luther, Jr. 2001. *A Call to Conscience: The Landmark Speeches of Dr. Martin Luther King, Jr.* Edited Clayborne Carson and Kris Shepard. New York: Grand Central Publishing.

Rankine, Claudia. 2014. *Citizen: An American Lyric*. Minneapolis: Greywolf.

---

3. See Folayan and Davis 2017; King 2001, 192.

Tran, Mai-Anh Le. 2017a. "'I Shall Not Bow My Head': Ghostly Lessons for Wise Leading." Pages 89–98 in *Leading Wisdom: Asian and Asian North American Women Leaders*. Edited by Su Yon Pak and Jung Ha Kim. Louisville: Westminster John Knox.

———. 2017b. *Reset the Heart: Unlearning Violence, Relearning Hope*. Nashville: Abingdon.

Trinh, Minh-ha T. 2011. *Elsewhere, Within Here: Immigration, Refugeeism and the Boundary Event*. London: Routledge.

Wexler, Philip. 1996. *Holy Sparks: Social Theory, Education, and Religion*. New York: St. Martin's.

A Call to Solidarity with Black Scholars

RAJ NADELLA

In the days and weeks following the death of George Floyd, there was much outrage in the public square about the brutal murder of unarmed African Americans such as Floyd, Breonna Taylor, Trayvon Martin, Atatiana Jefferson, Tamir Rice, Sandra Bland, and Eric Garner just in the last few years. The outrage and the subsequent national discourse focused on the extreme violence to which African Americans are subjected on a regular basis, primarily at the hands of police officers. The national discourse helpfully exposed the oppressive political and economic structures that deny a vast majority of African Americans access to resources and stifle their ability to pursue their dreams and flourish.

Many in the academy, including in the field of biblical studies, rightly turned to social media and other avenues during that time to condemn antiblack violence, advocate for substantial changes in law enforcement practices that perpetuate such violence, and critique political and economic structures that are oppressive towards African Americans. Such conversations and activism in the guild were timely and helpful responses that accentuated the outrage in the public square about antiblack violence and reinforced calls for corrective measures that would affirm the dignity of black lives.

To build upon Adele Reinhartz's remarks at the symposium, just as the various structures in the society often discriminate against African Americans and undermine their ability to flourish, some of the structures and practices in the field of biblical studies render black scholars invisible by minimizing their contributions and peripheralizing their scholarly perspectives and make it difficult for them to thrive. In a guild that is predominantly Eurocentric in its membership and methodologies, there have been few conversations about the role of black scholars, their hopes and aspirations, and the challenges they face in pursuing their goals. Even as there was much outrage about the antiblack violence on the streets, there has been insufficient attention to the persistent marginalization of black scholars in the guild.

Conversations about antiblack violence on the streets are essential in the field of biblical studies and should continue, but they should serve as catalysts for honest and constructive conversations about the marginalization of black scholars in the guild. Otherwise, the former will end up deflecting attention from and undermine the possibility of necessary reflection on the latter. The #BlackScholarsMatter Symposium was organized with the goal of calling attention to the problematic structures and practices in the guild that make it difficult for black scholars to be respected and accepted as equal voices. It was convened so that black scholars could honestly and openly articulate their hopes, aspirations, struggles,and challenges and suggest measures that are needed to address those challenges. This essay celebrates the transformative contributions of black biblical scholars, critiques their continued marginality in the guild, and calls for solidarity from nonblack scholars aimed at affecting lasting change.

Black Biblical Scholars and Their Pioneering Research

Early on in my time as a grad student, a postcolonial scholar who has been a mentor encouraged me to be intentional about pursuing the kind of biblical scholarship that explicitly engages my social location and reflects my lived experiences. Pursuing scholarship that builds upon and addresses one's social location was not a new idea, but at a time when I was still largely drawn to traditional approaches to texts, a nudge from this mentor strengthened my resolve to dig deeper into postcolonial hermeneutics, one that closely aligns with my social location as a former subject of the British Empire. Around the same time, and as a result of that conversation with my mentor, I was also drawn to *Stony the Road We Trod: African American Biblical Interpretation* (Felder 1991b), which inspired me to embrace newer approaches to reading biblical texts and provided me intellectual tools to ask fresh, hard questions of texts and derive life-giving meanings from them.

bell hooks, who has observed that much of white society has a proclivity to deny the existence of racism and impedes meaningful conversations about racial privilege, notes that "black folks/people of color who talk too much about race are often represented by the racist mindset as 'playing the race card' (note how this very expression trivializes discussions of racism, implying that it's all just a game), or simply as insane" (hooks 2003, 26–28). hooks also critiques how white scholars who discuss race are well received and depicted as superior or civilized beings (27). Her work highlights how segments of white society prefer a trivialized, watered down and comfortable discussion about race, one that is hosted by fellow whites and likely does little to disrupt the status quo.

At a time when the field of biblical studies was not accustomed to, or comfortable with, hearing scholars of color explicate biblical texts through the lens of race, Cain Hope Felder's essay, "Race, Racism, and the Biblical Narratives," in *Stony the Road We Trod: African American Biblical Interpretation* did precisely that. It forcefully highlighted the role of race as a social determinant not only in biblical texts but also in how we read texts, the questions we ask of them, and the meanings we derive from them (Felder 1991a, 127–45). While neither Felder nor other contributors in the volume directly engage my social location as an Asian American scholar, they nevertheless helped me to realize how my journey as a minoritized scholar and attendant life experiences can illuminate texts in fresh ways. In foregrounding issues such as race and ethnicity that were hitherto largely minimized in biblical scholarship and facilitating honest engagement with those issues, the contributors opened up rich avenues for exploring biblical texts and were instrumental in my growth as a biblical scholar. Perhaps equally importantly, by engaging the issues of race, ethnicity, class and gender in similar measure and to similar extents, Renita Weems's (1991, 130–38) essay "Reading Her Way through the Struggle: African American Women and the Bible" in the same volume emphasized the need for intersectionality, posited it as a fruitful framework for reading texts, and modeled a sophisticated way of doing it. Years later, reading *True to Our Native Land: An African American New Testament Commentary* (Blount et al. 2007) had the same transformative impact on my scholarship and was a positively disruptive force with regard to methodologies. It powerfully highlighted not only the role of one's life experiences in interpreting texts but also the reader's agency in making meaning of them.

My own experience of benefiting from the pathbreaking scholarship of African American scholars is reflective of the larger ways their work impacted the interpretive trajectory for many in the guild and moved the field in fresh directions. Black scholars have been centering African American voices that had been silenced, but, at the same time, their work has challenged dominant modes of thinking and spaces and made room for other voices that had been excluded. Just as the US civil rights movement spearheaded by African Americans resulted in new rights for other marginalized groups such as immigrants, the pioneering work of black biblical scholars made it possible for other minoritized voices to be heard. In the last few decades, their scholarship has broadened the horizons of biblical scholarship in irreversible ways and served as a positive disruptor in the field of biblical studies that R. S. Sugirtharajah (2002, 2) aptly characterizes as a "calm and sedate world." Despite their many contributions, black scholarly perspectives are still treated as marginal, peripheral, or biased in comparison to the normative Eurocentric perspectives. The academy makes it tough for black voices to be heard and respected as equals by limiting them to program sections that are exclusively, or primarily, designated as such.

Black Scholars and Their Leadership in the Guild

Black scholars have played a pivotal role in the formation and strengthening of committees that seek to promote the work of minoritized scholars. Their leadership in many areas of the Society of Biblical Literature—program sections that focus on African American biblical hermeneutics, various governing bodies, and committees—as well as several related organizations that focus on mentoring and pedagogy, continues to play a key role in the recruitment and professional growth of minoritized scholars. I am especially grateful for the contributions of Randall Bailey and Vincent Wimbush, who were instrumental in the formation of the Society's Committee on Underrepresented Racial and Ethnic Minorities in the Profession (CUREMP) and continued to play a key role in its strengthening over the years. Their work included encouraging more students to pursue advanced studies in Bible and shaping countless graduate students in formal and informal ways and providing support networks that would prove essential to their success.

With their advocacy work and mentoring, black scholars such as Bailey, Wimbush, Weems, and Gay Byron helped expand the presence of diverse perspectives at the table. Black scholars have also been adept at forming alliances with Asian American, Latinx, indigenous, and global scholars in order to push the guild to take note of challenges facing minoritized scholars as a whole. Their ability to build alliances and think strategically has given enhanced voice in the guild to those who had hitherto lacked it. They also formed similar partnerships in order to explore innovative and collaborative scholarship that featured scholarly voices from disparate social locations and yielded fruitful and hitherto unseen insights on texts.[1]

Continued Marginality of Black Scholars

Despite their significant contributions, black scholars receive insufficient recognition of their work, and their perspectives are often made invisible at the table. Within this backdrop, it was disconcerting but not surprising to hear Cheryl Anderson share her experience about being minimized and intimidated by a white male colleague at a session at an Annual Meeting of the Society of Biblical Literature seventeen years ago (see her essay in this volume). Such incidents of deep disrespect that Anderson described so powerfully are directed at minoritized biblical scholars with some frequency, but black scholars undoubtedly bear the brunt of it. Her experience reflects the simultaneous processes of inclusion and marginalization that the white academy employs towards minoritized, especially black scholars. On the one hand, they are occasionally invited to participate in traditional sections of the Society of Biblical Literature, but, on the other hand, they are told that their voices and methodologies are less valuable in comparison to those of their white peers.

The discrimination against black scholars in the guild does not happen nearly on the same level or to the same extent as the violence of various forms that African Americans experience in the society at large. As biblical scholars committed to justice, we should certainly be devoting much of our attention to addressing antiblack violence on the streets, but if we only respond to the most outrageous forms of antiblack violence out there, we run the risk of setting a high bar for what qualifies as racism. Consequently, any form of violence or discrimination in the guild that does not meet that high bar (i.e., is not as outrageous) will not receive the kind of attention it deserves. It is vitally important that members of the guild pay attention to lives on the streets but then invariably turn their attention to structures and practices within that disadvantage black scholars and initiate corrective measures.

---

1. Two examples that come to mind are Bailey 2009; Smith and Choi 2022.

A Call to Solidarity

As I heard those powerful presentations during the symposium, I was especially struck by Shively T. J. Smith's talk that called upon allies and colleagues to stand in solidarity with African American scholars and to do so in broad daylight. The task of addressing the challenges and obstacles faced by black scholars should not be solely, or even primarily, their responsibility. As nonblack scholars committed to supporting them, we have a moral obligation to stand in solidarity with them in their struggles for a proper place at the table and accentuate their voices without coopting their concerns or making them invisible in the process. We have a duty to leverage whatever privilege we might have in order to effect change in various contexts and advance their interests.

Smith's insightful presentation reminded me of the many ways black scholars themselves have been modeling advocacy for other minoritized scholars. I am familiar with numerous stories of the advocacy work of black scholars in the context of the guild and in institutional settings. As an immigrant scholar who has had to overcome several obstacles in my academic journey, I myself benefited immensely from the support and advocacy of black scholars at various points and am deeply grateful for it. To be clear, I received mentoring and advocacy from scholars of various racial and ethnic backgrounds, but my experience has been that, when black scholars advocated for me and others, they did so from a position of relative powerlessness and at times even vulnerability. I hope that the allies and friends of African American scholars will follow the powerful model they set and advocate for them likewise, even at a potential risk to their standing.

Concrete Steps Needed to Ensure Change

A colleague in the guild who learned about plans for this volume recently wondered aloud whether the current guild-wide focus on black scholars will continue even two or three years from now. He asked that question quite innocuously, but the question highlights the familiar danger that conversations about issues such racism are forgotten fairly quickly, or perhaps conveniently, in the absence of any major news-making events like the brutal murder of Floyd. Mechanisms need to be instituted to make sure that the current focus on the concerns raised by black scholars stays fresh in our memories beyond the symposium and the volume leading to concrete changes in the long run. The guild will be enriched immensely when black scholars are able to thrive and make significant contributions to biblical studies rather than treated as peripheral voices.

Often, conversations about racism in the guild become substitutes for change rather than catalysts for transformative change. Commitment to justice can never be an abstract idea but should always manifest itself in concrete, everyday situations. It is helpful to discuss in abstract terms our hopes for change, but one must invariably ask the question of what specific steps are being taken at the guild level to ensure that our commitment to justice will translate into concrete, measurable outcomes. Toward that end, the Society of Biblical Literature should initiate policies and structures aimed at recruiting black students from the United States and other parts of the world and on mentoring them. It should take steps to create conditions and an ecosystem that will enable black students and scholars to flourish and sit at the table as conversation partners. For that to happen, we will need to have more black biblical scholars in leadership positions in the guild, more black voices featured in premier SBL Press publications, and more of them presenting not just in African American or minoritized sections but also in sections that are traditionally seen as the domain of Eurocentric scholars. If we can envision a time in the future when black scholars are receiving premier Society awards as often as their white peers, we will then be able to say with integrity that the guild is taking black scholarship seriously.

Changes should also occur at the local and institutional level in order for it to have lasting effect. As allies and friends, each of us should leverage the privilege and power we have in our specific, institutional contexts and facilitate the transformation we hope to see at the guild level. Towards that end, attention should be given to the various components of our work as scholars and teachers—how we approach our scholarship, the methodologies we engage, the sources we cite, the design of our curriculum and the textbooks we use in our syllabi—in order to ensure that black voices are heard, respected, and celebrated as voices with authority that have something to teach and transform us.

Conclusion

As a scholarly community, the Society of Bible Literature will be better off and enriched when it takes black scholarship seriously and centers it as an essential component in its textual explorations. If the field is to continue thriving and exploring new and meaningful horizons in scholarship, black scholarship should be engaged as authoritative and central rather than as a supplement that can be consumed only when a specific situation or a moment in history calls for it. I hope that the symposium and the collected essays will spur members of the guild to realize the immense and transformative contributions of black biblical scholarship and continue to learn from its history, commitments, and innovative approaches to reading texts long after this volume has been published.

Works Cited

Bailey, Randall C., Tat-Siong Benny Liew, and Fernando F. Segovia, eds. 2009. *They Were All Together in One Place? Toward Minority Biblical Criticism*. SemeiaSt 57. Atlanta: Society of Biblical Literature.

Blount, Brian K., Cain Hope Felder, Clarice Martin, and Emerson B. Powery, eds. 2007. *True to Our Native Land: An African American New Testament Commentary*. Minneapolis: Fortress.

Felder, Cain Hope. 1991a. "Race, Racism, and the Biblical Narratives." Pages 127–45 in *Stony the Road We Trod: African American Biblical Interpretation*. Edited by Cain Hope Felder. Minneapolis: Fortress.

———, ed. 1991b. *Stony the Road We Trod: African American Biblical Interpretation*. Minneapolis: Fortress.

hooks, bell. 2003. *Teaching Community: Pedagogy of Hope*. New York: Routledge.

Smith, Mitzi J., and Jin Young Choi, eds. 2022. *Minoritized Women Reading Race and Ethnicity: Intersectional Approaches to Constructed Identity and Early Christian Texts*. Minneapolis: Fortress.

Sugirtharajah, R. S. 2002. *Postcolonial Criticism and Biblical Interpretation*. New York: Oxford University Press.

Weems, Renita J. 1991. "Reading Her Way through the Struggle: African American Women and the Bible." Pages 130–38 in *Stony the Road We Trod: African American Biblical Interpretation*. Edited by Cain Hope Felder. Minneapolis: Fortress.

A Duty to Act:
Personal Reflections on #BlackScholarsMatter

Adele Reinhartz

I am honored to be among those invited to contribute their own reflections on how and why Black scholars matter in biblical studies and, as requested by the editors, to share my own efforts in creating an ethos of welcome for Africana biblical scholars in the context of institutions within which I am active.

I view the creation of such an ethos as an ethical imperative. Now, there is no shortage of urgent issues, both within the guild of biblical scholars and in the world more broadly, that make ethical demands upon us all. Climate change, the COVID-19 pandemic, human rights abuses, and sex trafficking are just a few items on a long list. All of these, in principle, impose a duty to act: to take the steps within our power to prevent harm to others. In practice, while we might care about many different issues, we can act on only a few of them.

The choice of where to put our energies will often be motivated by personal factors. Sometimes we can identify those factors, as when they pertain directly to our own identities and life experiences. In other cases, however, we may feel drawn to an issue that, on the surface at least, does not seem personal. So it is with my preoccupation with Africana biblical scholars and scholarship. If pressed, I could probably articulate some of the reasons that this issue resonates so deeply with me. But I prefer to reflect not on why I care but on what I can do, that is, my duty to act.

My comments will focus on the two institutions that are currently the most important in my academic and professional life: the Society of Biblical Literature and the University of Ottawa.

Biblical Scholarship and the Society of Biblical Literature

I have been a member of the Society of Biblical Literature since completing my doctorate in 1983, and since 1993 I have been active in a broad range of volunteer roles, from a member of a program unit steering committee to president. Most important for me were my six years on Council (2009–2015), the seven years I spent as the general editor of the *Journal of Biblical Literature* (1 January 2012–31 December 2018), and the two years as vice-president and president of the Society (2019–2020).

In the early years, my focus was twofold: to help improve the visibility and role of women in the society and to carve out space for those who stepped outside the usual norms—what I saw as the ruts—that defined the normative demographic and normative methods in the field. My personal challenge was to overcome and set aside my naïve assumption that being Jewish and having a strong background in Jewish studies—points I viewed as an asset to my scholarship—would also be viewed as assets by my fellow New Testament scholars. (Much has changed and improved, but in the circles of Johannine scholarship and in other subfields it remains an uphill battle. At least now I am no longer oblivious to it.)

I attribute my desire for increasing involvement to several factors, including changes in the Society of Biblical Literature; the passage of time, during which I found my niche among like-minded colleagues—now friends—within the society and its leadership; and my own developing confidence that I had something to contribute both to the field and to the organization.

During this same period, since 2010, I began spending extended periods of time in the United States, taking advantage of research leaves and other opportunities during sabbaticals to meet new colleagues and acquaint myself with different academic environments. These periods coincided with pivotal moments in recent American history, such as the debate over the Affordable Care Act in 2010, the presidential campaigns and elections of 2012 and 2016, and the founding and development of the Black Lives Matter movement from 2013 onward. These periods of time opened my eyes to the complexities of race relations in the United States, which I had hitherto observed from the (somewhat) safe(er) geographical and social distance on the Canadian side of the 49th parallel.

These experiences brought home an important truth that I knew but had not examined deeply prior to that point. This truth is that the hierarchies of gender and religion—the privilege historically enjoyed by Christian men within our guild—are embedded within a hierarchical system manifested perhaps most powerfully in both overt and subtle forms of anti-Black racism. This system, referred to in shorthand as white supremacy, promotes an ideology that privileges white, Christian, straight men, and, though a creature of colonialist Europe, it remains formative in American society (and far beyond the United States), and in the modes of biblical scholarship that are prioritized within the field as practiced within the Society of Biblical Literature and in many parts of the world.

The workings and impacts of white supremacist ideologies, and the ways in which it continues to structure life and scholarship, are often invisible to those who benefit from them. Indeed, most biblical scholars, Africana scholars among them, absorbed its norms unwittingly during our graduate education. As Angela Parker (2021, 13) has written, graduate training in biblical studies aims to mold all students into white male biblical scholars. In the words of Ekaputra Tupamahu (2020, 2), "biblical scholarship training is a whitewashing machine."

Equity, Diversity, and Inclusion (EDI)

My observation is that organizations, including the Society of Biblical Literature and the Ontario university system in which I have spent my career, are striving to incorporate Africana and scholars of other marginalized groups through processes of equity, diversity, and inclusion. Indeed, the acronyms EDI or DEI, have become buzzwords in academia, as in other sectors of the corporate world.[1]

My personal experiences from the 1970s onwards as the token woman on numerous committees suggests that inclusion, while exhausting for the targets of these efforts, is a worthy endeavor and can lead to change. The mere presence of women, people of color, and others who do not conform to the white male norm can normalize diversity and provide opportunities for diverse views based on diverse experiences and sensibilities. Inclusion cannot, however, be truly effective on its own.[2] The presence of white Eurocentrist assumptions in our field is both a product of and reinforced by the systemic nature of white supremacy in American and other soci-

---

1. For a corporate take on EDI, see, for example, Ly n.d. and Bolger n.d. The latter entry appears on General Assembly's website, a company specializing in skills development for the business sector.

2. This is as true in the corporate world as it is in academia. See Morris 2020.

eties shaped by European history and culture. For this reason, inclusion and other measures such as statements of support and good will are not enough. Taking stock of the scope and the longstanding history of anti-Black racism can lead to a sense of personal helplessness. So, what can a white Canadian like myself do?

My approach to counteracting such feelings of helplessness is to remind myself of a lesson I learned during my years as an academic administrator. Even the most vigorous efforts to effect institutional change can flounder when the change requires a reorientation of certain basic, often unacknowledged and unexamined, values or stances. Frustration, among other factors, led me to leave administration and return to the professoriate, where I shifted focus. Even if we are in a position to effect institutional change, each of us, as individuals, does have a sphere of activity and influence—among friends, in our neighborhoods, and, for scholars, within the classroom, our scholarship, and our guild. I believe it is our duty to act within those spheres, and that is what I have tried to do with regard to Africana biblical scholars, within the Society of Biblical Literature and in my home department.

Beyond EDI

As a biblical scholar active in the Society of Biblical Literature, my efforts to act have taken me in three directions. First, I have tried to learn more about the big picture, including the origins of our field, the role of Eurocentric ideologies, the history of Africana peoples in the Americas, the role of the Bible—oppressive and sustaining—in the lives of enslaved peoples, in the debates around abolition, during the Civil War, and its aftermath. Second, I have been reading deeply in Africana biblical interpretation, with a special emphasis on womanist scholarship. Both sets of readings—in the broader historical and social contexts and in Africana biblical scholarship per se—have prompted me to think about what would need to change about our field and in my own scholarship and teaching in order to make room for Africana scholars and scholarship. And third, I have become mindful of opportunities where I could be effective in helping bring out change, even minor changes, that might create an ethos of welcome for Africana scholars.[3]

---

3. This is not to minimize the ongoing work needed on other fronts, such as gender, sexuality, religion, and ability. But we cannot all work on all fronts all the time,

My volunteer roles within the society provided several such opportunities. As the general editor of the *Journal of Biblical Literature*, I was able to shape the editorial board by including more Africana, Asian, and women scholars. In diversifying the board, I hoped not only to encourage diversity for its own sake but also to effect greater openness to article submissions from the full range of our membership and from diverse methodological perspectives and to ensure that such submissions would be treated fairly throughout the rigorous double-blind peer review process that is the hallmark of the journal.

I would say frankly that the jury is still out on how effective these measures are in conveying the message that contributions from Africana and other scholars working outside the traditional methodological norms are welcome in the journal. The impression of the *Journal of Biblical Literature* as a journal that tends to reject articles that are not hard-core historical-critical analyses has proven difficult to eradicate. Both as a former general editor and now as a regular reader, I honestly believe that the journal has been changing in this regard, though the process is slow and by no means complete. Recent issues, for example, have included several articles explicitly from nonwhite perspectives.[4] This is not enough, but it is a start. As a peer-reviewed journal, the *Journal of Biblical Literature* is dependent on submissions; the hesitancy of scholars working outside traditional areas to submit articles limits the ability of the journal to move forward in this direction.

Perhaps the most important move during my time as editor, however, was the publication of a forum on "Black Lives Matter for Critical Biblical Scholarship" in 2017. I had instituted the occasional forum as a way to encourage more dialogue with the Society's membership by inviting submissions that would then be peer reviewed but not through the usual double-blind process. The forum was prompted by what I saw as an urgent and long overdue need to address matters of race directly in the journal. To that end, I invited several people, most but not all of whom are Africana biblical scholars, to reflect on the theme of Black scholars matter in biblical studies. The result was a series of short contributions by Wil Gafney, Nyasha Junior, Kenneth Ngwa, Richard Newton, Bernadette Brooten, and

---

and for me at this moment, the focus is on Africana scholars and scholarship. It is my conviction, and my hope, that the work being done to transform our field in any one of these areas will work to the benefit of all.

4. See Junior 2020; Kynes 2021; Park 2021.

Tat-siong Benny Liew that has now been read by many within and outside of the Society of Biblical Literature (Reinhartz 2017).

My stint as the Society's vice-president and president also provided opportunities for action. During this period the Council created the Black Scholars Matter Task Force, which aimed both to stimulate and also to track activities related to the Society to promote mentorship of Black biblical scholars and students and other forms of participation. These include webinars, Black history member spotlights, twitter campaigns, and engagement with Theta Alpha Kappa chapters at historically Black colleges. The Society of Biblical Literature also now has an Africana Scholarship landing page.[5]

The main public role of the Society's president is to deliver the presidential address at the Annual Meeting. Sadly (from my perspective at least), the COVID-19 pandemic prevented me from delivering the address in person. Nevertheless, I was glad for the opportunity to address issues that are different from and larger than the ones I usually speak and write about. The murders of George Floyd and many others, combined with the reorientation of life required by the pandemic, increased the sense of urgency around the inequities exposed by the Black Lives Matter movement. Although I briefly entertained other possible topics, it seemed to me that this moment in our history called upon me to use the forum provided by the presidential address to explore ways that our field could and should change in order to welcome Africana scholars and scholarship.

Researching and writing the address provided a focus for the reading I had already been doing about Africana biblical scholarship. It was not only challenging but also rather daunting, scary even, to move outside the comfort of my own areas of expertise in such a public way. (Perhaps the virtual format made it easier to step out on that limb, as I did not have to face an audience in person.) Both preparing and delivering the talk convinced me even more of my main point: "The hermeneutics of chutzpah exercised by African American scholars benefits other marginalized people as well as those who have traditionally situated themselves at the core of our guild by helping us all to perceive the workings of whiteness, and to engage more honestly with the deep structures of our intellectual enterprise" (Reinhartz 2021). I leave it to others to assess whether and to what extent these actions, alongside those of many other people within

---

5. https://www.sbl-site.org/educational/AfricanaScholarship.aspx.

and outside the Society of Biblical Literature, have borne or will bear fruit. Perhaps only time will tell.

The University of Ottawa

Turning to my experiences at the University of Ottawa, I begin with a caveat: my comments do not pertain specifically to Africana biblical scholars but to Africana religion scholars more broadly. The reason for this slight shift in focus is that my teaching niche here has over the years become religious studies writ large, rather than biblical studies per se. Indeed, I have not taught a biblical studies course in many years. Rather, my usual courses include theory and method in the study of religion, as well as religion and culture, principally cinema. While I do currently have doctoral students working in the area of biblical studies, my other students work on diverse, primarily modern, topics. All this is to say that at my home university I am only occasionally involved in the education and formation of biblical scholars. My comments on Africana scholars at this university therefore pertain to religious studies rather than biblical studies scholars as such.[6]

The University of Ottawa differs from American colleges and universities as well as from most other Canadian institutions of higher education in that it is a very large (43,000 students), bilingual (French and English), public research university whose Franco-Ontarian roots are profound and a major part of its identity. The international emphasis at the university is primarily on *la francophonie*, which means that many—though by no means all—of our Africana students come from French-speaking locales in Canada as well as from former French colonies in the Caribbean and Africa. Their family and national heritages too have been marked by enslavement, but their histories and identities differ markedly from those of most African Americans.

---

6. And another caveat: here in Canada, the front-burner issue concerns indigeneity, the tragedy of the residential school system, in which so many children died and were buried in unmarked graves, and ongoing discrimination against people from indigenous and Inuit communities and backgrounds. For background on the discoveries of these graves, see Mosby and Millions 2020. Canada observed its first National Day of Truth and Reconciliation on September 30, 2021, but much work remains to be done. See Government of Canada n.d. To the small extent that I have engaged in activism on campus, it has been in support of our Institute of Indigenous Research and Studies.

The university's identity as a bilingual and multicultural institution of higher learning has created a tremendously diverse population. On the whole, the atmosphere is supportive, constructive, and respectful. Nevertheless, there have been a small number of high-profile racist incidents in the past few years: 2019 saw two incidents in which security staff racially profiled Black students; 2020 saw a highly divisive incident in which a part-time professor used a racial slur in a class session on the topic of how racial and other slurs are sometimes appropriated and reinterpreted positively by the target groups themselves. Many in the university community, myself included, believed that this professor could easily have addressed the topic without actually using the slurs in question. By using the term, the professor undermined her own effectiveness, since in pronouncing the slur she immediately turned everyone's attention away from the subject matter to the offense created by her own speech act. Others argued that, according to the principles of academic freedom, she was entitled to use the term and that its use was appropriate in the circumstances.[7] My view, shared by many, was that as a professor she had a duty of care, an ethical requirement to refrain from using language that would be hurtful even to one of her students. The issue sparked a huge debate not only on campus but also in the media in Ontario and Quebec, with the premier of Quebec himself taking a stand on the issue (Fenn 2020; Shingler 2020).

In response to these events and to the Black Lives Matter movement in Canada,[8] the university announced several initiatives. These included the hiring of a Special Advisor for Anti-racism and Inclusive Excellence, who was charged with implementing several initiatives, such as providing mentorship, scholarship, and dedicated mental health support for racialized students; increased hiring of professors of Black, indigenous, and racialized

---

7. On November 5, 2021, the university released a report that attempted to address tensions generated by this and other incidents (Bastarche 2021). The report upheld the value of academic freedom and argued that the use of the full "n" word in a pedagogical context where no harm was intended should be allowed. At the same time, the report did not address an important matter: Even if the use of the "n" word is technically permissible, is it humane, wise, and pedagogically productive? Does it help or hinder the stated university commitment to equity, diversity, and inclusion? Does it promote the well-being of racialized students? It is clear that the university report has not settled the matter once and for all.

8. The Black Lives Matter movement has had a major impact in Canada, empowering Black Canadians to speak up about their own experiences of anti-Black racism in schools and in other contexts.

professors; enriching curricula with more culturally diverse and inclusive practices (methodologies) and knowledge; developing and implementing antiracism and antioppression training; and creating a research support program for racialized researchers, so that a more equitable, diverse, and inclusive research community is established.

Some of these are in progress, others seem to be stalled. The Action Committee on Anti-Racism and Inclusion, announced by the university's president, does not seem to have materialized, at least not yet. Diversity surveys have been conducted as well as mandatory training sessions for senior administrators. Perhaps these measures will lay the foundation for change at the university—one can hope, but they offer little opportunity for rank-and-file professors to become involved.

Whereas the Society of Biblical Literature provided opportunities, at the journal and on Council, to work with others in service of the collective, at the University of Ottawa I exercise my duty to act primarily in the context of my graduate course on theory and method in the study of religion. My actions are twofold: to ensure that each student feels valued and respected and to foster a critical assessment of the origins and ongoing practices of the discipline.

One major benefit of my reading program on Africana biblical interpretation was that it equipped me to see more clearly and to articulate the history and ongoing dynamics of the Eurocentric ideologies that shaped not only biblical studies but also the field of religious studies. These readings emboldened and enabled me to reconfigure the traditional theory and method course, shifting the focus from the "founding fathers" (Weber, Durkheim, Eliade, to name a few), to the ways in which racism and colonialism shaped the origins of the discipline (Maldonado-Torres 2014; Newton 2020). We place particular emphasis on how explorers, colonizers, and settlers used European Christians and Christianity as the gold standard in order to label the peoples and practices they encountered as "savage" and "primitive" (Smith 1998; Cox 2007). I encourage students to be attentive to the remnants of these ideologies that remain in the scholarship pertinent to their specific areas of interest and in their own work as well. We explore ways of doing things differently, by critiquing the world religions model whose vestiges can still be detected in our undergraduate program and inviting guests from diverse backgrounds, including Africana and indigenous scholars, to talk about their work.

Still, we teachers learn as much from our students as they learn from us, if not more. In particular, my Africana students, most of whom are international students from Africa, have taught me the importance of recognizing their differences, not only from their white colleagues, but also from one another, and, especially, from their Black Canadian-born or American-born peers. Some have shared with their classmates and myself their sense that Blackness figures into the self-definitions of Africana Canadians far more prominently than it does for Africans. One student told me that he had given little thought to being Black until he came to study in Canada. In his country of Uganda, it is the whites and Asians who stand out. He and others have described how the particularity of their own backgrounds, identities, and experiences is often subsumed into a dominant African American narrative in ways that feel foreign to them. This reinforces my own sense that even at the Society of Biblical Literature, where most Black members are African American, we do well to remember that, while Black biblical scholars may share some experiences—especially if they live in white-majority contexts—they also have diverse histories and identities that should not be elided into a single configuration.

By definition, a duty to act involves behaving in ways that prevent harm to others. But when it comes to preventing harm, or, better, to creating an ethos of welcome for Africana biblical and religious studies scholars and scholarship, the field as a whole is enriched. Indeed, our guild and our academic institutions will thrive only when Africana scholars and scholarship are truly, fully, welcome. The #BlackScholarsMatter Symposium, the publication of the presentations delivered on that occasion, and the many other measures that are being taken individually and institutionally are steps towards this most worthy goal.

Works Cited

Bastarache, Michel, et al. 2021. "Report of the Committee on Academic Freedom." University of Ottawa. November 5. https://www.uottawa.ca/en/committee-academic-freedom.

Bolger, Meg. n.d. "What's the Difference between Diversity, Inclusion, and Equity?" General Assembly. https://tinyurl.com/SBL03112n.

Cox, James L. 2007. *From Primitive to Indigenous: The Academic Study of Indigenous Religions*. London: Routledge.

Fenn, Kirsten. 2020. "Students Call for Systemic Change in Wake of N-Word Controversy at University of Ottawa." CBC. October 23. https://tinyurl.com/SBL03112s.

Government of Canada. n.d. "National Day for Truth and Reconciliation." https://tinyurl.com/SBL03112r.

Junior, Nyasha. 2020. "The Mark of Cain and White Violence." *JBL* 139:661–73.

Ly, Sydney. n.d. "The True Value of Bringing Diversity, Equity, and Inclusion into Your Workplace." 15five. https://tinyurl.com/SBL03112m.

Kynes, Will. 2021. "Wrestle On, Jacob: Antebellum Spirituals and the Defiant Faith of the Hebrew Bible." *JBL* 140:291–307.

Maldonado-Torres, Nelson. 2014. "Race, Religion, and Ethics in the Modern/Colonial World: Race, Religion, and Ethics in the Modern/Colonial World." *Journal of Religious Ethics* 42:691–711.

Morris, Carmen. 2020. "Anti-racisim: Why Your DEI Agenda Will Never Be a Success without It." *Forbes*. December 15. https://tinyurl.com/SBL03112q.

Mosby, Ian, and Erin Millions. 2021. "Canada's Residential Schools Were a Horror." *Scientific American*. August 1. https://tinyurl.com/SBL03112p.

Newton, Richard. 2020. "Racial Profiling? Theorizing Essentialism, Whiteness, and Scripture in the Study of Religion." *Religion Compass* (July): e12369.

Park, Wongi. 2021. "Multiracial Biblical Studies." *JBL* 140:435–59.

Parker, Angela N. 2021. *If God Still Breathes, Why Can't I? Black Lives Matter and Biblical Authority*. Grand Rapids: Eerdmans.

Reinhartz, Adele, ed. 2017. "The JBL Forum, an Occasional Exchange: Black Lives Matter for Critical Biblical Scholarship." *JBL* 136:203–36.

———. 2021. "The Hermeneutics of Chutzpah: A Disquisition on the Value/s of 'Critical Investigation of the Bible.'" *JBL* 140:8–30.

Shingler, Benjamin. 2020. "Quebec Premier Warns of 'Censorship Police' after Ottawa Professor Suspected for Saying N-Word." CBC. October 2020. https://tinyurl.com/SBL03112t.

Smith, Jonathan Z. 1998. "Religion, Religions, Religious." Pages 269–84 in *Critical Terms for Religious Studies*. Edited by Mark C. Taylor. Chicago: University of Chicago Press.

Tupamahu, Ekaputra. 2020. "The Stubborn Invisibility of Whiteness in Biblical Scholarship." Political Theology Network. 12 November. https://tinyurl.com/SBL03112k.

Afterword

John F. Kutsko

The half-life of Not Getting the Point is forever.
—Loudon Wainwright, "The Strange Case of Strangelove"

The editors of this volume asked me to cast a vision for the Society of Biblical Literature's role and the role of its members in advancing diversity, equity, and inclusion in biblical studies, specific to the history of experiences that became painfully manifest during the Black Lives Matter movement and that raised them to a new level of urgency. I will first reflect on the challenges that lay at hand and then offer aspirations that lay ahead.

The quote at the beginning of this afterword is what comes to mind, reflecting on this collection of essays, regarding the Society's future. It is from Loudon Wainwright's (1964) review of the movie *Dr. Strangelove*. Wainwright was commenting on the poor reviews of the movie, reviews he rightly saw as missing the mark. His criticism was a warning, because for certain things of grave consequence, forever is forever. That is the point at which we find ourselves.

While the Black Lives Matter political and social movement began in 2013 following the death of Trayvon Martin, the movement grew nationally following the deaths of Michael Brown and Eric Garner and reached a tipping point—even though the point was tipped so many times before—with the killings of Breonna Taylor, Ahmaud Arbery, and George Floyd. This decade of death, only the most recent tip of the iceberg of centuries of violence and oppression, launched a long-overdue national reckoning in every part of society: social, cultural, political, and academic.

In the interdisciplinary field of biblical studies, we also want to rid ourselves of any strains or vestiges of Eurocentrism, colonialism, and white supremacy. While undertaking this effort, it is valuable for us to recognize that in the larger context, the wide-ranging history of interpretation and the origins of philology demonstrate that biblical studies has not always been nor need it continue to be monolithic. While we recognize the nineteenth- and twentieth-century's self-satisfaction with knowledge, who has it, who acquires it through social and cultural capital, and who dispenses it (or reproduces it), modern biblical studies did not begin in the late nineteenth century.[1] Philology's origins (which are largely the origins of biblical studies) are before and beyond so-called Western civilization (Turner 2014, 1–2). Philology (and its partners, textual and literary criticism) has not been and is not now limited to the West or simply a product of Orientalism.[2] Even Edward Said made this case in his 2004 essay "The Return to Philology." He counted himself a philologist and made a passionate case for philology, not least because, when done well, it is not only *not* cultural appropriation and colonial but quite the opposite. It can display deep respect by a reader who is both humanitarian and humanist:

> Humanism is about reading, it is about perspective, and, in our work as humanists, it is about transitions from one realm, one area of human experience to another. It is about the practice of identities other than those given by the flag or the national war of the moment. (Said 2004, 80)[3]

All scholars critically engage their sources and apply their methods with a reflective recognition of the sociology of knowledge. It may be too easy, then, to start at a particularly dark historical period of practice. I make this point because it gives me hope, not dismay, for the future of biblical studies. In short, while interpretations matter, the interpreters matter more—what they do with methods and their self-conscious use of them, how we support those bringing the interpretation of the Bible to the fight against injustice and prejudice in our communities and in the academy itself, and how we all take up that fight as members of the guild.

---

1. See, e.g., Reventlow 2009–2010; Greenslade et al. 1963–1970; Sæbø 1996–2015.

2. See, e.g., Pollock et al. 2015. The same observations can be made for pre-Linnaean botanical, biological, and chemical taxonomy.

3. See also Davis 2007 and Young 2010.

The Bible in American Life

While it became global, the Black Lives Matter movement's origins, most significant moments, and most important impacts have been in the United States. The authors of this volume express painful and personal experiences, which is not just about biblical studies but about not getting the point, which is forever. Because of this context, it is here that I want to focus my thoughts about biblical studies and its future. Starting here does not mean staying here. Focusing on this context will also help us develop the models and the means to address these concerns more broadly and more internationally, a point to which I will return.

Survey after survey have been conducted on the Bible's role in American culture. Periodic reports have been produced by Barna, and beginning in 2011 the American Bible Society commissioned Barna to conduct an annual survey of the state of the Bible in the United States.[4] Also beginning in 2011, Indiana University-Purdue University at Indianapolis undertook a three-year study of the Bible's place in the life of a representative sample of Americans. The "Bible in American Life" report was published online in 2014 (reprinted as Goff, Farnsley, and Thuessen 2017). My verdict regarding the state of the Bible in American life is that the Bible is alive but not well (Kutsko 2017).

Consider this from the "Bible in American Life" report: "Nearly eight in ten Americans regard the Bible as either the literal word of God or as inspired by God," and "less than half of those who read the Bible in the past year sought help in understanding it" (Goff, Farnsley, and Thuessen 2017, 2)

Other observations from the survey also seem prima facie surprising. Of those surveyed, African Americans reported the highest levels of Bible engagement. Seventy percent of all Black respondents said they read the Bible outside of public worship services, compared to 44 percent for whites and 46 percent for Hispanics. Bible memorization is highest among Black respondents: 69 percent, compared to 51 percent among conservative white Protestants and 31 percent among white moderate/liberal Protestants.

The Bible is even more important for African Americans than for conservative white Protestants (not to mention moderate and liberal ones).

---

4. https://www.barna.com/case-studies/american-bible-society/.

Depending on where one stands as a biblical scholar, it is either a deep frustration or a pedagogical opportunity that many parts of the public tether themselves to traditions that have literal expressions, themes, and narratives used throughout history to oppress, including in support of patriarchy, misogyny, racism, homophobia, slavery, and xenophobia. The canons of the Bible contain both soaring heights of the human spirit and humanity's basest motivations and therefore inspire both good and evil. The effort to focus on the heights not the depths is mediated by either systematic interpretation or selective reading, neither without their merits and continued practice.

Frederick Douglass is a case in point in the African American experience. In an appendix to his memoir, Douglass addresses this problem and his personal resolution of it:

> I find, since reading over the foregoing Narrative, that I have, in several instances, spoken in such a tone and manner, respecting religion, as may possibly lead those unacquainted with my religious views to suppose me an opponent of all religion. To remove the liability of such misapprehension, I deem it proper to append the following brief explanation. What I have said respecting and against religion, I mean strictly to apply to the *slaveholding religion* of this land, and with no possible reference to Christianity proper; for, between the Christianity of this land, and the Christianity of Christ, I recognize the widest possible difference—so wide, that to receive the one as good, pure, and holy, is of necessity to reject the other as bad, corrupt, and wicked. To be the friend of the one, is of necessity to be the enemy of the other. I love the pure, peaceable, and impartial Christianity of Christ: I therefore hate the corrupt, slaveholding, women-whipping, cradle-plundering, partial and hypocritical Christianity of this land. Indeed, I can see no reason, but the most deceitful one, for calling the religion of this land Christianity. I look upon it as the climax of all misnomers, the boldest of all frauds, and the grossest of all libels. Never was there a clearer case of "stealing the livery of the court of heaven to serve the devil in." (1845, 118–19)

A similar resolution was expressed 170 years later by President Barack Obama, the forty-fourth president of the United States and its first African American president, when he spoke at the 2015 National Prayer Day Breakfast:

> So how do we, as people of faith, reconcile these realities—the profound good, the strength, the tenacity, the compassion and love that can flow from all our faiths, operating alongside those who seek to hijack religion

for their own murderous ends? ... In our home country, slavery and Jim Crow all too often was justified in the name of Christ. (Obama 2015)

These are not naïve responses. They are born of an understanding of the power of interpretation, of the power of the interpreter, and of who owns what text. Contemporary African American religious scholars, such as Esau McCauley (2020), ask the same question as Douglass and Obama, yet see in biblical interpretation "an exercise in hope." He describes this form of reading as Black ecclesiastical interpretation. McCauley recognizes, too, that "Black slaves, for the most part, first encountered Christianity in America as an attempt to control and content them with their fate in this world while hoping for a better future in the next" (168). Yet there were also the narratives of liberation and freedom out of and from slavery, and the Bible's use as a primary text (because it was the only text available) became the syllabus for literacy, and literacy became a means for interpretation. As McCauley says, "If the early African American witness matters, then it is important to note that these churches did not locate the problem with the Scriptures themselves, but rather with the interpretation of these texts" (174).

This may be an apologetic response, but it is also a practical response to speak back, to (re)claim, and to reason with the unreasonable. Richard Newton (2017, 225) recently asks and answers this same question: "Still, why would African Americans follow a text that says, 'slaves obey your earthly masters' (Col 3:21)?... Because of the African American Bible, we know that this same faith gave black people a vocabulary for talking back to America."

We can also appreciate these motivations as a part of the Bible's living contextual readings, and similar to midrashic, rabbinic, patristic, and medieval interpretation, they represent a larger percentage of the history of interpretation than those practiced in the nineteenth- and twentieth-century academy.[5] I also appreciate the concerns about the location of these enterprises in the academy. While Philip Davies (2004) affirmed that the Bible belongs to everyone, he noted a sharp distinction even in the academy between biblical studies and scripture studies. In a panel discussion at the 2010 International Meeting of the Society of Biblical Literature in Tartu, Estonia, Davies reiterated that point: "I saw—and still

---

5. See, e.g., Jacobs 2008; Simonetti 2001; and de Lubac 1998–2009.

see—two kinds of academic discourse about the going on among us, each (as I believe) with its own legitimacy and its own place." To be sure, others would argue that biblical scholarship is so historically and completely influenced by religious discourse that it really has no place, strictly speaking, as a discipline in the secular academy. It is easy for this argument to extend logically to a patronizing view of those who read the Bible outside the academy.

To be sure, many of the aspirations for the text and its value in the community are interested and contextual readings, and the public, not the text, may be the genuine object of academic study. Newton (2017, 226) notes that "the African American Bible is not just 'texts' but the social forces with which Americans must reckon—regardless of one's relationship to the color line." While some might disparage such readings as theological—as distinct from so-called academic and secular—they are humanistic in the broadest sense of the word. These readings are also demonstrably public, and the efforts of the academy in speaking to (not with) the public have not been marked by respect, let alone success.

The role of interpretation and the interpretive community are the most powerful forces we have in education and efforts toward justice, equity, and inclusion. Interpretation imparts meaning, makes meaning, and can even redeem a text's value. Reading with the public is an opportunity to support communities suffering from white supremacist interpretations and to challenge those communities perpetrating them.

The Harvest Is Plentiful, but the Laborers Are Few …

What is the path forward that can move beyond the control of dominant forms of scholarship and dominant models for the formation of scholars? How will this path forward make a difference in scholars' lives and the lives of the public in order to foster diversity, equity, inclusion, and social justice?

If we start with the numbers, we will appreciate the difficult task ahead. For almost a decade, the Society of Biblical Literature has reported membership demographics. The most recent report contained data collected in January 2019 that reflect 2018 demographics, but it is typical of previous reports ("2019 SBL Membership Data"). Members were born in 134 countries (two-thirds of the countries in the world), though the majority (62 percent) were born in the United States. In the member profile questionnaire, at the urging of members, the Society limited questions about race/ethnicity to only members whose country of birth was the United States. As a US issue, then, the Society has significant challenges: 4.12 percent African descent; 3.39 percent Asian descent; 3.73 percent Latin American descent; 2.87 percent Native American, Alaska Native, or First Nation descent; and 0.23 percent Native Hawaiian or Oceanian descent. While the Society's membership has increased over the last decade in the Global South (roughly four hundred members reside in the sixty-three countries that are part of the International Cooperation Initiative[6]), members from those regions are still a minority.

Moreover, as with most learned societies and academic associations, the Society of Biblical Literature serves members as they enter, continue in, and complete graduate work. Learned societies have historically provided opportunities for professional growth through research, conference participation, and networking. While the Society of Biblical Literature may encourage and provide resources for members to make the case for prospective graduate students, the organization has no leverage over graduate school admission processes and practices. This is a source of frustration.

Several years into the Society's membership profile reports, it seemed reasonable to assume that graduate admissions were reflecting concerns for more diversity in their acceptance practices. However, a comparison of data over the decade revealed no increase in diversity among the Society's graduate student category or what could be identified as early career scholars. Coupled with the fact that time-to-completion for a PhD remains between seven to nine years, even if graduate schools admitted more diverse cohorts, no immediate change in faculty would occur for almost a decade. With the approaching undergraduate enrollment cliff caused by a drop in birth rates, an abrupt drop precipitated by COVID-19, the decline of interest in majoring in the humanities, and the reduction of graduate school admissions in response to an historically weak faculty job market, the situation for racial/ethnic diversity in the field of biblical studies is bleak.

Everything that follows should be read with these numbers in mind, because if the solutions do not involve a new form of solidarity and mutual support, I fear little will be accomplished. This afterword is written

---

6. An initiative designed to "facilitate meaningful, international, and multidirection scholarly collaboration" around the globe. See https://www.sbl-site.org/InternationalCoopInitiative.aspx.

especially to those whose experiences are not reflected in this volume to support those whose experiences are.

… Send Out Laborers into the Harvest

What can be done? How do we respond? I'll offer five hopes and ideas, followed by an overarching and final thought that is my grandest hope.

First, our getting out of the academy, into the public, and among congregations matters and will make a difference not just for how the public reads, interprets, and makes meaning, but it will help scholars reflect on how they do it and why it matters. The majority of the first half of this essay focused on that opportunity. We all know that the Bible is different in American life and culture than other texts read by the public or studied in the academy. No one worships the gods in the Iliad or reads Shakespeare in order to conduct one's life. The Society of Biblical Literature needs more members like many represented in this volume doing the work of social justice in congregations.

If there is a theme to this afterword and my most urgent call for how we can make the most impact supporting African American scholars, Africana hermeneutics, and minoritized criticism, while combating white supremacy and violence against racial/ethnic minorities, it is this. If biblical scholars are not more prominent at the congregational level throughout the United States, offering counternarratives to hate-readings, then we will continue to see more inconceivable events strike (such as the one that occurred while drafting this afterword): an eighteen-year-old male, indoctrinated into white supremacy, murdered ten African Americans in a grocery store in Buffalo, New York (14 May 2022).

Help make the Bible relevant because it already is—for good and for bad. Teaching with a focus on diversity and in ways that decenter white supremacy is an opportunity that liberal and progressive scholars ceded to those intent on maintaining white supremacy and political power. Our not being active within the public has a grave impact, as we witnessed in Charleston, South Carolina, when a twenty-one-year-old white supremacist male murdered nine African Americans during a Bible study at Emanuel African Methodist Episcopal Church (17 June 2015).

In the collection of essays *After Cloven Tongues of Fire: Protestant Liberalism in Modern American History*, David Hollinger reminds us of the contribution that mainline Protestantism made in American life.

Ecumenical Protestantism, he tells us, "sought to build equitable human communities" and "enabled Americans born into deeply Protestant environments to entertain sympathetically a vast range of ideas ... that they might not have otherwise felt so comfortable engaging" (Hollinger 2013, xi). It rose with a type of mainline, liberal Judaism, too, and it embraced science, evolution, historical criticism of the Bible, humanism, pluralism, civil rights, women's rights, social service, and social justice. It is the result of two processes, he says. One Hollinger calls "demographic diversification," which "involves intimate contact with people of different backgrounds who display contrasting opinions ... and thereby stimulate doubt that the ways of one's own tribe are indeed authorized by divine authority and viable, if not imperative, for other tribes, too" (6). This process allows a person to "treat inherited doctrines as sufficiently flexible to enable one to abide by them while coexisting 'pluralistically,' or even cooperating, with people who do not accept those doctrines" (6). The second factor was science, which allowed the historical-critical approach to challenge literal and superficial readings of the Bible. Hollinger shows how and why mainline Protestantism moved out of this interpretive role in congregations, which led to the most conservative forms of evangelicalism becoming mainstream. This ceding of the interpretive role and responsibility by mainline progressive Protestants (including scholars) had direct and serious consequences. Hollinger's forthcoming book, *Christianity's American Fate: How Religion Became More Conservative and Society More Secular*, argues that it resulted in an evangelicalism that was comfortable with patriarchy and white supremacy and became America's dominant Christian cultural force (Hollinger forthcoming).

This also means biblical scholars and the Society of Biblical Literature need to embrace the role of the Bible in theological education and support those that teach in these contexts. They are on the front line, teaching future clergy, imams, priests, and rabbis as well as religious educators (Catholic, Jewish, Muslim, and Protestant) who will have an exponentially wider impact in the public and among congregations than any scholar will have in the classroom. The Society has long had a self-defeating ambivalence toward theological education, which has not served the efforts to distribute its readings and interpretations that serve diversity, equity, inclusion, and social justice.

Inspiring the public with a vision for diversity and justice also may lead more underrepresented racial and ethnic minorities to enroll in biblical and religious studies courses in undergraduate institutions and even graduate school. That is a student's decision, of course, but give students a reason to consider it when they see that the field represents them, looks like them, and inspires them to make a difference.

Second, our colleagues need those willing to do the work with them and to reflect these concerns in their own teaching, research, and writing. This volume calls for allies from genuine and committed colleagues. For this, reread the essays by Cheryl B. Anderson and Shively T. J. Smith. What does this mean for the white members of the Society of Biblical Literature? If you want to be an ally, if you want to be a relevant teacher, bring the minoritized readings, methods, approaches, and issues into the classroom that engage students of color. Those approaches will engage all students, not just students of color, and as with educating clergy it will have exponential results. To borrow the words of Rasia S. Sugirtharajah (2003), our research needs to "get the mixture right." A critical scholar is self-critical. We all repeat words like those of Walter Lippmann (1922, 81):

> For the most part we do not first see, and then define, we define first and then see. In the great blooming, buzzing confusion of the outer world we pick out what our culture has already defined for us, and we tend to perceive that which we have picked out in the form stereotyped for us by our culture.

Our teaching and scholarship should reflect and model our self-critique. Our reviews of scholarship in our writing and the syllabi in our classrooms should do what we ask others to do. They should be capacious, curious, and inclusive. They should open up our minds and our students' minds to new methods and readings. We should be lifelong learners, too, which is a goal of a humanistic education that we seek to impart in our students.

Third, related to ally-ship and solidarity in scholarship and teaching is the role they play in professional development for graduate students and early career scholars. In this volume, Vanessa Lovelace writes about paying it forward. Kimberly Russaw and Sharon Watson Fluker focus their essays on mentorship, and Randall C. Bailey is a testimony to its impact. Raj Nadella calls for solidarity *with* Black scholars. That mentoring is both urgent and impactful is well known. Over half the essays in this volume address mentorship and mutual support.

Fourth, those that speak directly to and in support of diversity and inclusion in the field of biblical studies should become leaders in the field of biblical studies—at their institutions and in the Society of Biblical

Literature. As with all these issues, the sheer lack of numbers requires a progressive service tax. We cannot ask our BIPOC colleagues to carry the ball alone. They need a larger team, and we need to come off the bench to play. All of us who care about decentering traditional, monolithic, and unidirectional scholarship, expanding the canon of methods and approaches, and deploying our work to challenge inequity should join the team.

The Society of Biblical Literature has had a governance policy for committees and its Council that assumes each member of a committee represents all members of the organization. Practically speaking, no committee can have a representative from all underrepresented identities and demographics (race/ethnicity, religion, national origin, age, sex, sexual orientation, gender identity, gender expression, disability, institutional affiliation, career stage, socioeconomic circumstance, etc.). It may be an aspiration to seek genuine and active mutual support and representation, but it is born of necessity. Everyone representing each other's ambitions as a scholar and educator is a value that should motivate every member of every committee and editorial board.

Fifth, and most radical, is an aspiration to decenter the Society of Biblical Literature itself as an organization. The Society's roots are deeply entwined with European scholarship and the professionalization of disciplines across North America and Europe. Similar to many academic disciplines and the learned societies that represent them, the Society is fundamentally a Northern Hemisphere and Western phenomenon. The nature of organizations that represent biblical and theological studies in other parts of the world are not monolithic. Together, they represent a wider breadth of diversity: racial, ethnic, socioeconomic, and intellectual. What would biblical studies in twenty years look like if the Society were not the largest learned society for biblical studies, but one of many equals, or one that fostered the formation of independent regional associations, especially those in places the North colonized? Imagine a network with the Society of Asian Biblical Studies, the Oceania Biblical Studies Association, the Nigerian Association for Biblical Studies, and the Asociación Bíblica Argentina, to name only a few. What would such a network produce if it were driven by mutual interest and reflected long-marginalized intellectual, cultural, theological, and socioeconomic concerns? The entire field would better engage postcolonial theory, minoritized approaches, global reception, and subaltern readings by the combined number of its participants. While this is a moment that calls the Society of Biblical Literature, as an organization, to address white supremacy in the lives of

Black and Africana scholars and scholarship, it is, mutatis mutandis, a global problem.

The American Library Association has recently focused on decolonizing libraries (Crilly and Everitt 2021). What does that mean? It means to question how and why one book is catalogued here or there. Why one book is acquired and another is not. Shelving and cataloguing are codes for social and cultural priority and privilege. Libraries are canons, and they include and exclude like canons.

Consider this librarian's observation: "Western views of the world are privileged in Dewey with all numbers 200 to 289 focusing on Christianity. Non-western religions are not even mentioned until 294" (White 2017, 5).[7] Does biblical studies do this with its treatment of contextual readings, lived traditions, and reception history, all in sharp distinction to the subjects (texts and people) we study in the history of interpretation? The Society of Biblical Literature and biblical scholars might ask this: why shouldn't a field that studies religious traditions that are set in contexts of slavery and imperialism actively study receptive and contextual readings that challenge modern forms of slavery and imperialism? Challenging these ugly echoes should be natural for biblical scholars—intellectually and out of sheer self-interest to be relevant and to engage those most interested in and impacted by the subject. The Society's mission statement should be to "foster decolonization in biblical scholarship."[8] Decentering the Society and expanding global collaborations would finally integrate an interdisciplinary field that studies textual history, philology, the history of interpretation, and the history of reception.

All of these aspirations require the Society of Biblical Literature and its members to be active with and for each other.

The title of Gil Scott-Heron's 1971 performance piece, "The Revolution Will Not Be Televised," became a catchphrase for decades of social protests and political demonstrations. It was one of his most acclaimed works—a rally cry for racial and social justice—and in 2005 it was added to the National Registry.

Scott-Heron became frustrated with how often the title was misunderstood to mean literally that the revolution would not be shown live on

---

7. On the consequential judgment call involving the classification of books as either "religion" or "myth," see Fox 2019.

8. Compare the current mission statement at https://www.sbl-site.org/aboutus/mission.aspx.

television. Speaking to the filmmaker Skip Blumberg for the Public Broadcast System series "The 90s," Scott-Heron (2010) said that wasn't the point. He said, "The first change that takes place is in your mind." That is where the revolution starts, and we can't be bystanders.

That is my aspiration for the future of the Society of Biblical Literature and its members. The first change has to take place in all of our minds. We've been on the wrong page, and when we are on the right page, we may be one note behind, one beat off. The revolution will not be televised in order for us to watch. It will happen because of us, with us, and live. There are no spectators, and we can't be passive participants of change. If we are not part of the revolution, then the half-life of not getting the Point will be forever.

Works Cited

Crilly, Jess, and Regina Everitt, eds. 2021. *Narrative Expansions: Interpreting Decolonisation in Academic Libraries.* London: Facet.

Davies, Philip R. 2004. *Whose Bible Is It Anyway?* 2nd ed. Edinburgh: T&T Clark.

Davis, Lennard J. 2007. "Edward Said's Battle for Humanism." *The Minnesota Review* 68:125–35.

Douglass, Frederick. 1845. *Narrative of the Life of Frederick Douglass, an American Slave.* Boston: Anti-Slavery Office.

Fox, Violet. 2019. "What's the Distinction between Myth and Religion in Dewey? An Explainer." 025.431: The Dewey Blog. 15 December. https://tinyurl.com/SBL03112z.

Goff, Philip, Arthur E. Farnsley II, and Peter J. Thuesen, eds. 2017. *The Bible in American Life.* Oxford: Oxford University Press.

Greenslade, S. L., G. H. W. Lampe, P. R. Ackroyd, and C. F. Evans, eds. 1963–1970. *Cambridge History of the Bible.* 3 vol. Cambridge: Cambridge University Press.

Heron-Scott, Gilbert. 1971. "The Revolution Will Not Be Televised." http://historyisaweapon.com/defcon1/herontelevised.html.

———. 2010. "The Revolution Will Not Be Televised." Interview. https://www.youtube.com/watch?v=kZvWt29OG0s.

Hollinger, David A. 2013. *After Cloven Tongues of Fire: Protestant Liberalism in Modern American History.* Princeton: Princeton University Press.

———. Forthcoming. *Christianity's American Fate: How Religion Became More Conservative and Society More Secular*. Princeton: Princeton University Press.

Jacobs, Irving. 2008. *Tradition and Interpretation in Rabbinic Judaism*. Cambridge: Cambridge University Press.

Kutsko, John F. 2017. "The Curious Case of the Christian Bible and the U.S. Constitution: Challenges for Educators Teaching the Bible in a Multi-religious Context." Pages 240–48 and 398–402 in *The Bible in American Life*. Edited by Philip Goff, Arthur E. Farnsley II, and Peter J. Thuesen. Oxford: Oxford University Press.

Lippmann, Walter. 1922. *Public Opinion*. New York: Macmillan.

Lubac, Henri de. 1998–2009. *Medieval Exegesis: The Four Senses of Scripture*. 3 vols. Translated by Mark Seban. Grand Rapids: Eerdmans.

McCauley, Esau. 2020. *Reading While Black: African American Biblical Interpretation as an Exercise in Hope*. Downers Grove, IL: InterVarsity Press.

Newton, Richard. 2017. "The African American Bible: Bound in a Christian Nation." *JBL* 136:221–26.

Obama, Barak. 2015. "Remarks by the President at the National Prayer Breakfast." Washington, DC. February 5. https://tinyurl.com/SBL03112u.

Pollock, Sheldon, Benjamin A. Elman, and Ku-ming Kevin Change, eds. 2015. *World Philology*. Cambridge: Harvard University Press.

Reventlow, Henning Graf. 2009–2010. *History of Biblical Interpretation*. Translated by Leo G. Perdue and James O. Duke. RBS 50, 61–63. 4 vols. Atlanta: Society of Biblical Literature.

Sæbø, Magne, ed. 1996–2015. *Hebrew Bible, Old Testament: The History of Its Interpretation*. 5 vols. Göttingen: Vandenhoeck & Ruprecht.

Said, Edward W. 2004. *Humanism and Democratic Criticism*. New York: Columbia University Press.

Society of Biblical Literature. "2019 SBL Membership Data." https://www.sbl-site.org/assets/pdfs/sblMemberProfile2019.pdf.

Simonetti, Manlio. 2001. *Biblical Interpretation in the Early Church: An Historical Introduction to Patristic Exegesis*. Translated by John Hughes. Edinburgh: T&T Clark.

Sugirtharajah, R. S. 2003. *Postcolonial Reconfigurations: An Alternative Way of Reading the Bible and Doing Theology*. St. Louis: Chalice Press.

Turner, James. 2014. *Philology: The Forgotten Origins of the Modern Humanities*. Princeton: Princeton University Press.

Wainwright, Loudon, Jr. 1964. "The Strange Case of Strangelove." *Life* 56.11:15.
White, Hollie. 2017. "Decolonizing the Way Libraries Organize." http://library.ifla.org/id/eprint/2221.
Young, Robert J. C. 2010. "The Legacies of Edward W. Said in Comparative Literature." *Comparative Critical Studies* 7.2–3:357–66.

Contributors

Efraín Agosto is Visiting Professor of Latinx Studies and Religion at Williams College in Williamstown, Massachusetts. During the 2021–2022 academic year, Efraín served as the Croghan Bicentennial Visiting Professor in Biblical and Early Christian Studies at Williams. Previously, he had been Professor of New Testament Studies at New York Theological Seminary (2011–2021) and before that Professor of New Testament at Hartford Seminary (1995–2011). Agosto, a Puerto Rican born and raised in New York City, has degrees from Columbia University (BA, 1977), Gordon-Conwell Seminary (MDiv, 1982), and Boston University (PhD in New Testament and Christian Origins, 1996). Among his published books and essays are the monograph *Servant Leadership: Jesus and Paul* (Chalice, 2005) and the coedited volume, with Jacqueline Hidalgo, *Latinxs, the Bible and Migration* (Palgrave Macmillan, 2018).

Cheryl B. Anderson is Professor of Old Testament at Garrett-Evangelical Theological Seminary in Evanston, Illinois. Earlier in her career, she practiced law in Washington, DC for nearly ten years. Her publications include numerous articles and two books: *Women, Ideology, and Violence: Critical Theory and the Construction of Gender in the Book of the Covenant and the Deuteronomic Law* (T&T Clark, 2004) and *Ancient Laws and Contemporary Controversies: The Need for Inclusive Biblical Interpretation* (Oxford University Press, 2009). Her current research interests involve contextual and womanist readings of Scripture in the age of HIV and AIDS.

Randall C. Bailey is Distinguished Professor of Hebrew Bible, Emeritus of Interdenominational Theological Center in Atlanta, GA, where he taught for thirty-five years. He has served as visiting professor at theological schools in South Africa and Brazil. He has cochaired the African American Biblical Hermeneutic section of Society of Biblical Literature. Bailey has been a community activist and his approach to biblical interpretation is a combination of methods exploring what social systems are being described in the text, how they are utilized to support/oppress which groups, and how this helps liberate readers. Bailey is the author of one book, editor of two books, coeditor of four books.

Gay L. Byron is Professor of New Testament and Early Christianity at Howard University School of Divinity in Washington, DC. Her scholarship focuses on the origins of Christianity in ancient Ethiopia. She is the author of *Symbolic Blackness and Ethnic Difference in Early Christian Literature* (Routledge, 2002) and coeditor (with Vanessa Lovelace) of *Womanist Interpretations of the Bible: Expanding the Discourse* (SBL Press, 2016). During 2021–2022, she was a Visiting Faculty Fellow in the Franklin Humanities Institute at Duke University. Her current book project centers Aksumite and Nubian empires for New Testament and early Christian studies. She is also an ordained minister of the Word and Sacrament (Teaching Elder) in the Presbyterian Church (USA).

Ronald Charles is Associate Professor in the Department for the Study of Religion at the University of Toronto. Charles is the author of *Paul and the Politics of Diaspora* (Fortress, 2014), *Traductions Bibliques Créoles et Préjugés Linguistiques* (L'Harmattan, 2015), and *The Silencing of Slaves in Early Jewish and Christian Writings* (Routledge, 2020). His research and teaching interests are the interdisciplinary study of ancient Christian literature, Mediterranean identity and race in antiquity, slaves in the Greek and Roman world, classical reception, method and theory in the academic study of religion.

Stephanie Buckhanon Crowder is a noted scholar, versatile speaker, and prolific author. She is the first woman and first black person to serve as Vice President of Academic Affairs/Academic Dean at Chicago Theological Seminary. She is also the first black woman promoted to Full Professor at Chicago Theological Seminary. Crowder earned a BS degree summa cum laude in Speech Pathology/Audiology from Howard University; MDiv from United Theological Seminary, and MA and PhD degrees in New Testament from Vanderbilt University. Her work includes *When Momma Speaks: The Bible and Motherhood From a Womanist Perspective* (Westminster John Knox, 2016).

CONTRIBUTORS

Steed Vernyl Davidson is Professor of Hebrew Bible, Vice President for Academic Affairs and Dean of the Faculty at McCormick Theological Seminary, Chicago IL and Extraordinary Visiting Professor, Department of Old and New Testament, Faculty of Theology, Stellenbosch University, South Africa.

Sharon Watson Fluker has held several higher education administrative positions. Most recently, she served in three different roles as strategic adviser, associate director of fellowships, and program manager at the Center for Public Leadership at Harvard Kennedy School. Other positions include senior adviser to Salzburg Global Seminar's Mellon Fellows Community Initiative; Vice President of Doctoral Programs and Administration at the Fund for Theological Education; Dean for Sophomores at the University of Rochester, among others. She earned a BA (political science) from Spelman College and MA and PhD degrees (political science) from Northwestern University.

John F. Kutsko is Executive Director of the Society of Biblical Literature and affiliated faculty at the Candler School of Theology, Emory University. He earned a PhD in Near Eastern Languages and Civilizations from Harvard University and an MA in Near Eastern Studies at the University of Michigan. Kutsko is published in *The Bible in Political Debate* (T&T Clark, 2016) and *The Bible in American Life* (Oxford University Press, 2017). He is the author of *Between Heaven and Earth: Divine Presence and Absence in the Book of Ezekiel* (Penn State University Press, 2000) and coeditor of *The King James Version at 400* (Society of Biblical Literature, 2013).

Vanessa Lovelace is Associate Dean and Associate Professor of Old Testament/Hebrew Bible at Lancaster Theological Seminary. Her publications include *Womanist Interpretations of the Bible: Expanding the Discourse* (SBL Press, 2016), coedited with Gay L. Byron, and articles in *The Hebrew Bible: Feminist and Intersectional Perspectives* (Fortress, 2018), *The Oxford Handbook of the Minor Prophets* (Oxford University Press, 2021), and *The Oxford Encyclopedia of Bible and Gender Studies* (Oxford University Press, 2015). She serves on the editorial boards of *Biblical Theology Bulletin* and Bible Odyssey. Lovelace earned her PhD in Hebrew Bible from Chicago Theological Seminary, MDiv from McCormick Theological Seminary, Chicago, Illinois, and BA in Radio and Television from San Francisco State University.

Madipoane Masenya (Ngwan'a Mphahlele) is Professor of Old Testament Studies in the Department of Biblical and Ancient Studies, seconded as the acting Executive Director: Office of the Principal and Vice-Chancellor, at the University of South Africa, Pretoria. She has published numerous scientific articles and chapters in specialist books in the area of the Hebrew Bible and gender, especially in African contexts. She served as one of the associate editors of *The Africana Bible: Reading Israel's Scriptures from Africa and the African Diaspora* (Fortress, 2019). Her book, *How Worthy Is the Woman of Worth? Rereading Proverbs 31:10–31* was published by Lang (2004). She has coedited with K. N. Ngwa, a volume titled, *Navigating African Biblical Hermeneutics: Trends and Themes from our Pots and Our Calabashes* (Cambridge Scholars, 2018).

Raj Nadella is the Samuel A. Cartledge Associate Professor of New Testament at Columbia Theological Seminary. His research interests include postcolonial biblical interpretation, migration and New Testament perspectives on economic justice. He is the author of *Dialogue Not Dogma: Many Voices in the Gospel of Luke* (T&T Clark, 2011) and coeditor of *Christianity and the Law of Migration* (Routledge, 2021). He is also the coauthor of *Postcolonialism and the Bible* (forthcoming in 2022). He has written for publications such as the Huffington Post, Christian Century, and Working Preacher.

Hugh R. Page Jr. is Professor of Theology and Africana Studies at the University of Notre Dame, where he also serves as Vice President for Institutional Transformation and Advisor to the President. He holds a PhD in Near Eastern Languages and Civilizations from Harvard University. His research interests include early Hebrew poetry; Africana biblical interpretation; the role of mysticism and esotericism in Anglican and Africana spiritualities; and the blues aesthetic as theological and interpretive paradigm. He is author of *Israel's Poetry of Resistance: Africana Perspectives on Early Hebrew Verse* (Fortress, 2013).

Adele Reinhartz is Professor in the Department of Classics and Religious Studies at the University of Ottawa, in Canada. She is the author of numerous articles and articles, including *Cast Out of the Covenant: Jews and Anti-Judaism in the Gospel of John* (Fortress, 2017); *Befriending the Beloved Disciple: A Jewish Reading of the Gospel of John* (Continuum, 2001), *Jesus of Hollywood* (Oxford University Press, 2007), and *Bible and Cinema: An*

Introduction (Routledge, 2013), now in its second edition. Reinhartz was the General Editor of the *Journal of Biblical Literature* from 2012–2018 and served as the president of the Society of Biblical Literature in 2020.

Kimberly D. Russaw is Associate Professor of Old Testament at Pittsburgh Theological Seminary in Pittsburgh, PA. She is the author of *Daughters in the Hebrew Bible*, *Revisiting Rahab: Another Look at the Woman of Jericho* (Wesley's Foundery, 2021), "Wisdom in the Garden: The Woman of Genesis 3 and Alice Walker's Sofia," and "Undaunted: Reading Miriam for the Sisters They Tried to Erase." Named one of "Six Black Women at the Center of Gravity in Theological Education" by NBCNews.com, Russaw holds membership in the Society of Biblical Literature, the American Academy of Religion, and the Society for the Study of Black Religion.

Abraham Smith is an ordained National Baptist Church USA, Inc., minister and Professor of New Testament at Perkins School of Theology, Southern Methodist University, in Dallas, Texas. His recent publications include: "Incarceration on Trial: The Imprisonment of Paul and Silas in Acts 16" (*JBL* 2021); *Black/Africana Studies and Black/Africana Biblical Studies* (Brill, 2020); and *Mark: An Introduction and Study Guide (Shaping the Life and Legacy of Jesus)* (Bloomsbury, 2017).

Shively T. J. Smith is Assistant Professor of New Testament at Boston University. She has written a monograph, *Strangers to Family: Diaspora and 1 Peter's Invention of God's Household* (Baylor, 2016) and a forthcoming volume on 2 Peter and African American women (SBL Press). Her multiple essays include "Witnessing Jesus Hang: Reading Mary Magdalene's View of Crucifixion through Ida B. Wells's Chronicles of Lynching" in the thirtieth anniversary edition of *Stony the Road We Trod* (Fortress, 2021). Her scholarship also focuses on the translation and exegesis of the General Letters and Howard Washington Thurman.

Mai-Anh Le Tran is Vice President for Academic Affairs and Academic Dean at Garrett-Evangelical Theological Seminary, Evanston, Illinois. With research and teaching in religious education and practical theology, her writings include contributions to *Ways of Being, Ways of Reading: Asian American Biblical Interpretation* (Chalice, 2006); *T&T Clark Handbook of Asian American Biblical Hermeneutics* (T&T Clark 2019); *Teaching for a Culturally Diverse and Racially Just World* (Cascade 2014); and *Asian and*

Asian American Women in Theology and Religion: Embodying Knowledge (Palgrave Macmillan, 2020). She is the author of *Reset the Heart: Unlearning Violence, Relearning Hope* (Abingdon, 2017).

Renita J. Weems, PhD, currently serves as visiting professor of Old Testament studies at The Interdenominational Theological Center in Atlanta. She is the first African American woman to earn a doctorate in Old Testament studies (Princeton Theological Seminary) and an ordained elder in the African Methodist Episcopal Church. Weems is one of the founding scholarly voices in womanist biblical interpretation. She is a former professor at Vanderbilt University Divinity School.

Vincent L. Wimbush is an internationally recognized scholar of religion, with nearly forty years of professional experience. He is author/editor of several books, including *White Men's Magic* (Oxford University Press, 2014), *Scripturalectics* (Oxford University Press, 2017), *MisReading America: Scriptures and Difference* (Oxford University Press, 2013), *Theorizing Scriptures* (Rutgers University Press, 2008), *Refractions of the Scriptural* (Routledge, 2016), *African Americans and the Bible* (Yale University Press, 2006), and scores of articles and essays. His most recently published book is *Black Flesh Matters: Essays in Runagate Interpretation* (Fortress, 2022). He is founding director of The Institute for Signifying Scriptures, a forum for transdisciplinary research and programming. In 2010 he served as the first Black president of the Society of Biblical Literature.

www.ingramcontent.com/pod-product-compliance
Lightning Source LLC
Chambersburg PA
CBHW021352300426
44114CB00012B/1196